# THE REAL TAGGARTS

# THE REAL TAGGARTS

*Glasgow's Post-War Crimebusters*

ANDREW G. RALSTON

BLACK & WHITE PUBLISHING

First published 2017
by Black & White Publishing Ltd
Nautical House, 104 Commercial Street
Edinburgh EH6 6NF

1 3 5 7 9 10 8 6 4 2          17 18 19 20

ISBN: 978 1 78530 134 6

The author and publishers are grateful to STV Productions Limited
for granting permission to use the *Taggart* brand name in the title of this book.
STV Productions Limited has had no part in the preparation of this book
and takes no responsibility for the contents thereof. The views and opinions
expressed herein do not necessarily reflect those of STV Productions Limited.

A CIP catalogue record for this book is available from the British Library.

Typeset by Iolaire, Newtonmore
Printed and bound by MBM Print, East Kilbride

MIX
Paper from
responsible sources
FSC® C117931

I see a strong police force as being absolutely essential to an ordered life.

*— Elphinstone Dalglish, Deputy Chief Constable, Glasgow Police, and later Strathclyde Police*

# Acknowledgements

I would like to record my thanks to a number of people who helped in the production of this book. These include:

My wife Hazel and daughter Miranda, for their support and encouragement; the staff of the Mitchell Library, Glasgow and the National Records Office, Edinburgh; Neale McQuistin, May Mitchell and Allan Lindsay, who shared their memories of Chief Superintendent Bob Kerr; Jim Goodall and Dr Alison Kennedy, who provided valuable insights into the life and career of their father, Chief Superintendent Tom Goodall; former Inspector Alistair Morrison and former Chief Superintendent James Young, for their many entertaining stories about police life; Patricia Miller, who read and commented on the book in draft form; the late former Superintendent Joe Beattie, whose seemingly inexhaustible fund of anecdotes first kindled my interest in crime and policing in post-war Glasgow and ultimately led to the idea of this book; Alex Norton (who played DCI Burke in STV's *Taggart* series) for contributing the foreword; former Inspector Alastair Dinsmor, MBE, Curator of the Glasgow Police Museum in Bell Street, Merchant City, who generously shared his encyclopaedic knowledge of the history of Glasgow's police force, provided access to his collection of archive materials and supplied numerous photographs. Without his help, this book would never have got off the ground at all.

# Contents

# *Foreword*

Mention *Taggart* to almost anyone the length and breadth of the country and the chances are they'll put on a growly Glasgow accent and say, 'There's been a murrrder!' – despite the fact that no one ever actually said it at any time throughout the series' twenty-seven year run!

After the death in 1994 of *Taggart*'s eponymous leading man, Mark McManus, the producers were faced with the difficult choices of either scrapping the series, casting a different actor in the title role, or having a new character as the DCI. After choosing to carry on with Taggart's sidekick, DI Jardine, as the newly promoted head of the murder squad, they then had to decide whether to rename it along the lines of 'Taggart's Beat', or 'Taggart's Team' – but such was the measure of Mark's brilliant performance, they decided to honour his memory by retaining the show's original title, and so, apart from having the distinction of being the longest running detective series in British Television history, *Taggart* was also unique as being the only TV series named after a character who was no longer in the cast…

When, in 2001, I began filming on the streets of Glasgow as Matt Burke, the series' new DCI, I was often approached by passers-by who would hail me with, 'You're the new Taggart, aren't ye?', as if somehow the name was the actual rank – in fact the name Taggart has become so synonymous with the position that I think the top brass of Police Scotland should seriously consider making it official and using it in place of the title of Detective Chief Inspector!

Over the nine years I worked on the series, I had the opportunity to meet quite a few of the 'real' Taggarts, and seldom missed an opportunity to quiz them about their lives. More often than not, I found their stories much more fascinating than the fictional world of the 'telly tecs', where murders are cleverly plotted by devious and cunning killers and solved in record time by a small band of dogged and determined sleuths. One example I'd like to share with you of the yawning gulf between detective fact and fiction, was the time Blythe Duff, John Michie, Colin McCredie and I were filming a murder scene on location up a back street in Glasgow's city centre. We were having a debate with the director about whether we would be allowed to simply walk all over the crime scene without overshoes on, in case we contaminated any forensic evidence. Since Blythe was married to a real life detective inspector, we persuaded her to call him on her mobile and ask his opinion on the correct procedure. The conversation went something like this:

> Hi darling, it's Blythe. We're just having a discussion about whether we would be wearing overshoes when we're examining a body at a crime scene, and… oh, I see. Thanks, and sorry to have bothered you.

The side of the conversation we didn't hear was Blythe's husband saying he couldn't really speak right now, as he was standing in a car scrapyard, just a few feet away from a decapitated corpse, and had to get on with trying to locate its missing head – and no, he wasn't wearing blue plastic bootees…

If you're a fan of detective fiction, I'm sure you'll find Andrew Ralston's tales of real life detectives and their unique work as gripping and compelling as I do. Truth, as the old cliché has it, is often stranger than fiction, and after reading the reminiscences of some of the real Taggarts, I think you'll find yourself viewing your favourite TV cop show through a fresh pair of eyes, and agreeing with me that you really couldn't make it up…

**Alex Norton**

# Introduction

In 1959, a newspaper ran an article about the role played by a senior Glasgow detective in catching the serial killer Peter Manuel. It concluded with this prophetic observation: 'Manuel's name and his ghastly career in homicide will never be forgotten in Scotland. But who will remember Alex Brown?' Quite simply, these words sum up what this book is all about.

Over the last twenty years or so a steady flow of reading material has emerged on the endlessly fascinating subject of crime in Glasgow. Former criminals and police officers alike have put their reminiscences on paper, while investigative journalists have mined the rich seam of Glasgow's violent past. As a result, there is no shortage of books about the most dramatic murders and robberies and those who carried them out.

Yet, for all that has been written about the crooks, the crimes and the court cases, comparatively little attention has been given to the detectives themselves. This book is an attempt to redress the balance. It is the first to provide an overview of crime in post-war Glasgow through the careers of those in charge of the CID. In so doing, it endeavours to put faces to names and traces their progression through the ranks – which, in some cases, was surprisingly slow. What emerges is a consistent picture of personal sacrifice and total dedication to the job.

It is, of course, true that the notion of the brilliant detective solving murders single-handedly by a process of logical deduction belongs more to the world of Arthur Conan Doyle or Agatha Christie than to reality. In real life, crimes are solved by patient accumulation of evidence, painstaking forensic examination and, above all, teamwork. As the 1950s CID Chief Robert Colquhoun once said, 'Being a policeman is more a matter of slogging inquiries, underworld contacts, patience and a darned good memory.' Even so, there are still occasions where an individual's discovery of a vital piece of evidence, or some inspired guesswork, provides the key that unlocks the mystery.

The book covers a period of approximately twenty-five years from 1945 onwards. It begins with Glasgow in the grip of one crime wave – when the transition from war to peacetime created many opportunities for lawbreakers – and ends with another, the late 1960s, when violent crime reached unprecedented levels.

However, the aim is not to provide a complete history of crime in the city during these decades but to focus on the five Chief Superintendents who were in charge of the CID between 1946 and 1969 – William Ewing, Gilbert McIlwrick, Robert Colquhoun, Robert Kerr and Tom Goodall – and to examine some of the crimes that took place on their watch. Separate chapters are also devoted to two outstanding deputy chiefs, Alex Brown and Joe Beattie. There were, of course, many other remarkable individuals in the CID but it is only possible to deal with a limited number in the space of one volume. Major enquiries would be handled by a team comprising several senior figures and in some instances a separate chapter is devoted to a more detailed examination of particularly interesting cases where new source material has come to light.

There were certainly plenty of dramatic incidents in the Glasgow area in this period, like the Ibrox bank raid in 1955, the mass killings carried out by Peter Manuel between 1956 and 1958 and the so-called Bible John murders over a decade later. All of these have been written about elsewhere and are therefore not the main focus of this book. When they are mentioned in these pages, it is in order to examine the role played by the detectives involved rather than to retell the whole story in depth. Many other cases not covered in existing publications are also examined, especially ones that provide an insight into how individual detectives handled investigations in their own characteristic ways.

These events took place against a background of profound change in Glasgow. A programme of slum clearance and the building of new housing schemes completely altered the character and layout of the post-war city, and also created new challenges for the police force. At times the authorities struggled to stem the seemingly unstoppable tide of criminality. Eventually the structure of policing in the city was completely reorganised and in 1975 the Glasgow force – whose origins go back to 1800 and predate even Sir Robert Peel's Metropolitan force in London – became part of the much larger Strathclyde Police, covering the local government region of the west of Scotland.

In the past, the progress of police investigations would be avidly followed by the public in their morning and evening newspapers – something that's difficult for a generation with instant access to news online to understand. An army of crime reporters for the *Glasgow Herald, Daily Record, Evening Times, Evening Citizen* and *Scottish Daily Express* recorded the activities of detectives on a daily basis and the top CID men were household names. Even when they had nothing tangible to tell their readers, the journalists were able to evoke an atmosphere of tension and anticipation in a masterly way. Reading the descriptions of midnight manhunts, it is not difficult to visualise a stream of black Wolseleys and Humbers filled with shadowy figures in hats and raincoats racing through the rain-swept streets of 1950s Glasgow. Such reports preserve for posterity the details of each murder hunt as it unfolded, and they are perhaps even more thrilling to read now, with the benefit of hindsight. Permission has also been obtained to quote from various criminal case files that shed new light on several murder cases. In addition, retired police officers have shared many anecdotes that cannot be found in written sources.

Over thirty years ago, Scottish Television launched *Taggart*, a series which turned out to be so popular that, after 109 episodes, it achieved the status of the UK's longest-lasting TV police drama. Broadcast across the globe to places as far apart as Japan and Afghanistan, the show conveyed an image of Glasgow as a gritty city policed by DCI Taggart (and later by DCI Matt Burke) and his team of tough, no-nonsense law-enforcers.

The hope is that this book will give an insight into what the 'real' Taggarts were like and, in doing so, ensure that these remarkable figures from the past will not be entirely forgotten.

# 1

## A Shadowy Cesspool of Crime

### Glasgow's Post-War Crime Wave

The *Daily Record* summed it up perfectly: 'Glasgow went daft with joy last night'.

On 7 May 1945, the BBC announced that the war in Europe was over. Moments later, crowds began to appear on the streets of Glasgow, bonfires were lit, effigies of Hitler burnt and 'midnight frolics ensued' as 'high-spirited young people … gave expression to their feelings'. The next day – VE Day – saw huge celebrations in George Square with floodlit open-air dancing. A seething mass of people meant that every flower bed and every blade of grass was trampled into the ground, but Chief Constable Malcolm McCulloch praised the crowds for being 'most orderly' and added that 'drunkenness was almost negligible'. On the following Sunday, 3,000 servicemen marched past the Cenotaph in George Square at a Victory parade and churches were crowded for Thanksgiving services.

That, at least, is the 'official' version…

Policemen on duty saw things rather differently. The behaviour of an element of the celebrating crowds quickly got out of hand – empty properties were forced open and windows frames ripped out to add fuel to the bonfires. In Townhead, an angry crowd pushed two police constables into the fire. 'On the third night', says Douglas Grant in *The Thin Blue Line*, his history of the Glasgow police force, 'stern measures were taken, particularly in George Square, where many arrests were made to end what had become sheer hooliganism on the part of many.' The cleansing department collected nearly three tons of empty bottles afterwards. Presumably they had not all contained lemonade.

Then, on the same day that the respectable citizens of Glasgow were at church giving thanks, a man was arrested for the murder of Charles Kelly, a fifty-year-old labourer with a family of three, who had been found dead in Govan.

The war may have been over but it was clear that one thing about the city had not changed, and that was the prevalence of crime.

Lawlessness had, in fact, flourished in Glasgow during the war. Blackout conditions led to an increase in thefts and violence, turning the city into what 1950s CID Chief Robert Colquhoun later called 'a shadowy cesspool of crime'. Servicemen on leave, newly paid and determined to have a good time, were favourite targets. Far from diminishing when peace returned, crime in the city merely took a different form. Looking back on 1945, the Chief Constable reported that:

> There is ample evidence of the crime wave which swept the country during the latter half of the year. Reaction to the hardship and restrictions of war has led to a general slackening of self-discipline which, among certain classes, has found expression in a growing disregard for law and order.

The increase in drunkenness and illegal gambling, for example, was attributed to 'the return from the services of a great many young men who, after several years of disciplined existence, found themselves with a liberal supply of money and a period of idleness in which to spend it.'

While shortages and rationing continued, the black market prospered. Peacetime did not lead to free availability of produce – in fact, some commodities were now in even shorter supply. 'Food cuts soon' reported the *Glasgow Herald* on 18 May, flagging up a coming reduction in the meat ration in view of world shortages. The situation was made still worse by frequent dock strikes, which held up the distribution of food. Many law-abiding citizens reckoned they had put up with wartime restrictions long enough and were now entitled to acquire the goods they wanted, even if that meant paying a bit more and not asking questions about where these goods came from. Such people, said the Chief Constable, 'would be appalled at any suggestion of complicity in resetting stolen property'.

But there were plenty of others in the city who had no such scruples. Among those returning from the forces were an estimated 10,000 deserters who, lacking proper identity papers and ration books, would attempt to survive by preying on others and stealing food, clothes or anything else they could sell on the black market. Housebreakings and burglaries of business premises were on the rise, partly explained by opportunists taking advantage of the reduced street lighting caused by the need to conserve power supplies. Altogether, nearly 18,000 break-ins were reported in the Glasgow area during 1945 and police statistics from the period show that housebreaking and other thefts accounted for something like 85% of all recorded crime.

One type of criminal who flourished in the post-war years when shops and offices often kept cash takings on their premises was the safe blower, popularly known as a 'peter man'. By 1951, it was estimated that there were around 300 safe blowers active in the city compared to a third of that number before the war. As with other crimes, the increase was attributed to the presence of deserters, some of whom would steal explosives from coal mines. Newspapers of the time are full of reports of these crimes, sometimes carried out in a rather amateurish manner. There were, for example, the thieves who broke into Cuthbertson's music shop in Sauchiehall Street by climbing up a disused lift shaft onto the roof where they smashed a glass pane and dropped down twelve feet inside. Following the usual methods, they gathered up soft furnishings like carpets and cushions to muffle the blast and opened a small safe. This netted them £30, but they did not realise there was another safe nearby which contained a much larger sum. Publishing that useful piece of information in the newspapers made it more or less inevitable that another group of thieves would raid the same premises shortly afterwards. They blew open the larger safe and helped themselves to more than £100, but at least the crooks had some sense of morality – they left a Red Cross collection box untouched.

In another league altogether was the most talented of Glasgow's 'peter men', Johnny Ramensky from the Gorbals, whose incredible life story has been told by Robert Jeffrey in *Gentle Johnny Ramensky: The World's Most Extraordinary Safe Blower* (2010). One detective said that Ramensky might as well have signed his name on the wall above each safe he blew, so distinctive were his methods. Johnny spent more than two-thirds of his adult life behind bars and became something of a folk hero for his extraordinary exploits during the war when his skills were employed on sabotage missions and raids on safes containing Nazi documentation. In the course of one day's work, he is said to have opened the safes of as many as fourteen different foreign embassies, allegedly going beyond his remit and helping himself to some of the contents while he was at it. There's even a folk song about him called *The Ballad of Johnny Ramensky:*

> Now Johnny was a gentle lad,
> there was only one thing wrong:
> He had an itch to strike it rich
> and trouble came along.
> He did a wee bit job or two,
> he blew them open wide
> But they caught him and they tried him
> and they bunged him right inside.

Old habits die hard and with the return of peacetime he resumed his criminal activities. But he was slowly losing his touch. In 1964, he failed to blow open a safe in Woolworth's in Paisley but succeeded in blowing out all the windows. In 1970, he was badly injured when he fell off a roof in Stirling. He died in Perth Prison in 1972.

★ ★ ★

Ramensky was known as 'Gentle Johnny' because he refused to resort to violence but that was the exception rather than the rule. Glasgow was awash with guns and other weapons brought back from the war as souvenirs and for a spell the city was plagued with a new type of crime: the armed hold-up.

Petty crooks soon found that pointing a revolver in someone's face and demanding money was an easy way of making a living. In separate incidents in the normally tranquil areas of Milngavie and Langside during October 1945, men sat waiting in stolen cars until a suitable victim came along and leapt out to demand money or valuables. On another occasion, two men kept a watch on a tobacconist's shop in Hope Street and, when there were no customers inside, rushed in brandishing a revolver and knife and demanded the contents of the till. Just before Christmas, a twenty-year-old man who had been discharged from the Merchant Navy after four years' service was found guilty at the Sheriff Court of possessing two revolvers without a certificate, of robbing a man and woman in Howard Street by pointing a firearm at them and of breaking into business premises in Washington Street with two accomplices. Almost as if they were acting out what they'd seen in American comics or gangster movies, the trio covered the lower parts of their faces with handkerchiefs and pointed guns at a woman employee, forcing her to open a safe and hand over the contents.

Some of these crimes were no doubt little more than acts of bravado carried out by irresponsible young men freed from the confines of military life. In other cases, the perpetrators were driven by sheer desperation. In September 1945, three young Polish servicemen carried out a series of raids in different parts of the city. They held up a pedestrian in Dennistoun with their revolvers, forcing him to hand over £19. Then they burgled a house in Castle Street and stole clothing but their luck ran out when, during a break-in at another house in the Finnieston area, they assaulted three police officers and threatened them with a gun.

Details of the Poles' histories came to light during their trial at the High Court in Edinburgh. They came from good families but found themselves conscripted into the German and Russian armies when Poland was invaded. Their advocate offered a powerful defence: 'Fresh from school, all three had been thrown into violence and war. In this country they deserted when the war finished and found themselves without family, friends, money and clothing. These crimes had not been committed by men of long criminal experience but by youths in dire circumstances.' Nevertheless, they received sentences ranging from eighteen months to three years for their misdemeanours.

The fear generated by the spate of armed hold-ups could sometimes produce a disproportionate response. A report in the *Glasgow Herald* in January 1946 described how on Christmas Day a twelve-year-old boy pointed a toy pistol at a doctor and said 'I'll blow your brains out'. It sounds like a prank that hardly merited reporting in the press, never mind pursuing through the courts. The medic didn't want to take the matter any further but the boy found himself before a magistrate who decided it was in the public interest to punish him and imposed a fine of £5 with the alternative of 28 days' detention.

★ ★ ★

If post-war conditions produced new types of crime in the city like armed hold-ups, they also saw a resurgence of old ones. Familiar territorial rivalries were rekindled and gang warfare broke out in the streets – what one seasoned cop described as the 'plain, simple old-fashioned Glasgow stuff of the knife-in-the-chest variety'.

The blackout, which had led to an increase in street robberies, had, paradoxically, diminished the amount of casual violence as youths were less inclined to gather in groups in darkened streets. With the return of street lighting, albeit on a restricted basis because of the need to conserve fuel, hooligans started ganging together again in the evenings, with predictable results. A particularly unpleasant incident of this type occurred in October 1945. Nineteen-year-old John Brady was discharged from the Navy and had only been back at his family home in Carrick Street in Anderston for five days when he was caught up in local gang activities – with fatal consequences. He was returning from a dance hall when his mother told him that a horde of youths from a gang called the Crosbies, armed with sticks, knives and a gun, had rampaged through the area chasing a member of the rival Dougie Boys. Such flagrant invasion of Dougie Boy territory could not be tolerated and he set off in pursuit with some of his mates. The two groups confronted each other in Washington Street but when the Dougie Boys saw the strength of the opposition they decided to make a hasty retreat. Unfortunately, Brady slipped and fell while his companions ran ahead. He was immediately set upon by his pursuers, stabbed sixteen times and left to bleed to death.

It didn't take the CID long to round up a number of suspects and, by December, four men aged between seventeen and twenty-eight appeared in the High Court. One received three years' penal servitude for assault and breach of the peace, but the jury found the other three guilty of murder and they were sentenced to death. At the last moment, two had their sentences commuted to penal servitude for life leaving one man, twenty-one-year-old John Lyon, to gain the dubious distinction of being the first prisoner ever to be executed at Barlinnie Prison (on 8 February 1946) and the first to be hanged in Glasgow since 1928. The judgement has caused controversy over the decades and, to this day, different opinions continue to be expressed on the extent of guilt to be attributed to each of these four men.

Another typical example of what the men on the beat referred to as a 'ned' was the twenty-year-old called up for active service who escaped and returned to Glasgow to reprise his role as 'self-confessed leader of the Chain Gang'. By November 1945 he had been sent to prison for one year for a series of violent acts including striking a woman in the face and attacking two Canadian soldiers with a knuckleduster and bayonet.

The incident is a reminder of the cosmopolitan nature of the city at the time when so many ex-servicemen from various countries were passing through. As well as that, the Clyde was still the busiest river in Britain – though it's hard to imagine today – and in January 1946 as many as 115 vessels were under construction in shipyards between Glasgow and Greenock. Sailors of all nationalities could be seen coming and going in busy dock areas and some inevitably became mixed up in the seedier side of city life.

On Christmas Eve 1945, a number of Polish sailors on leave from a destroyer at Gourock were arrested after a fight in Glasgow Central Station. Significantly, one said in court that the situation had been inflamed by members of the public shouting remarks about Poles in general and 'he felt that very keenly, considering he had been fighting for five years'. One of the group was fined £5 and the other four £1 each.

Chinese sailors had an even more difficult time. It's reckoned that some 5,000 were employed on British shipping at the start of the war, a figure that doubled after Japan occupied Hong Kong in 1942. These seamen were mostly found in Liverpool and Glasgow and their resentment at being paid at a far lower rate than indigenous crew members led to much industrial unrest. That was the background to an incident that occurred in the Govan area in June 1946. Although the headline 'Man dies from stab wound' was, sadly, familiar enough in Glasgow papers, in this instance the circumstances were unusual as twenty-one-year-old Norman McPherson died in the Victoria Infirmary after an altercation with three Chinese sailors near a Seamen's Hostel in Govan Road.

In September, two of them, Wong Lung and Oh Wing-tong, appeared at the High Court charged with murder and gave evidence through an interpreter. It emerged during the trial that there had been what the defence counsel called an 'accumulated campaign' against Chinese sailors in the area. Lord Cooper, Lord Justice-Clerk, explained that the victim and a friend had been drinking too much and had picked a quarrel with the seamen but the evidence suggested McPherson was killed by only one man and identifying the killer was the point at issue. Reflecting the attitudes of the day, he said that 'In Western eyes one Chinaman looked very much like another' – though for the sake of balance he did at least add that 'I suppose that to the eyes of a Chinaman one Scotsman looks very much like another.' The jury decided that Oh Wing-tong had struck the fatal blow and, taking into account the element of provocation and racial abuse to which he had been subjected, found him guilty of culpable homicide rather than murder. He was sentenced to ten years' penal servitude.

It would be a long time before more enlightened racial attitudes would prevail, but even in the late forties, Govan did have a sufficiently large Chinese community to warrant the opening of Scotland's first Chinese restaurant.

While the rest of the population was busy fighting for King and country, an element of Glasgow's underclass continued to fight on the streets, oblivious to events in the wider world. The notorious Patrick Carraher had appeared in court on a murder charge before the war in 1938 for knifing a soldier who happened to get caught up in a street argument; six years later, he was back in the dock for doing much the same thing. Known to those who frequented the pubs of the Gorbals as 'Carry', he had a long history of convictions for burglary and assault but no witnesses at his 1938 trial could positively state that they had seen him commit the deed and as a result he was convicted only of culpable homicide. Rejected as unfit for military service on his release, Carraher was soon back in prison for a further assault. Out on the streets again in November 1945, he heard his brother-in-law was involved in a fight in a Townhead pub and made his way there to join in. En route, he ran into a former Seaforth Highlander who had served at Dunkirk, and on the assumption that he must have been the one who had attacked his brother-in-law, stabbed him to death with a chisel.

This time, there was no evidence of any provocation so that, as the judge said at the trial, 'the element of reducing the character of the crime from murder to culpable homicide was out of the picture.' Dr Angus MacNiven, physician superintendent at the Glasgow Royal Mental Hospital at Gartnavel – whose expertise was frequently called on in murder trials of this kind – described Carraher as a man with a great lack of moral sense who spoke of the events of the night in question as if they were a 'frolic' rather than anything serious. He could distinguish between right and wrong but seemed unable to appreciate fully the consequences of his actions. 'Such people,' explained MacNiven, 'could not stand frustration. They behaved like children and if they wanted something they must have it, by hook or by crook.'

The jury only took twenty minutes to reach a unanimous verdict of guilty and the one time 'Fiend of the Gorbals' was executed on 6 April 1946.

★ ★ ★

Maintaining law and order on the mean streets of Glasgow has never been an easy job, but the scale of the challenge after 1945 stretched police resources to the limit – and beyond.

The main problem was lack of manpower. At the start of the war the police force was classed as a reserved occupation but officers had been called up for military service at a later stage. The way it worked was that the last to join up were the last to be demobilised. To make up for the shortfall, special constables had been recruited but now that the war was over, they were standing down. At the end of October a civic reception was held to thank them for their contribution, attended by 1,000 out of the 4,000 men who had helped out in this way over the previous six years. Chief Constable Malcolm McCulloch pointed out that 190 full-time officers had still to be demobilised and he was of the opinion that their release should have been a matter of priority.

The obvious solution was to recruit more officers but that was easier said than done. A six-day working week, inconvenient shift patterns, a minimum height restriction of 5 feet 10 inches, strict discipline and low pay hardly amounted to the kind of package that would produce a queue of eager young recruits outside the Glasgow Police Training School in Oxford Street. Even those who did join up frequently left as soon as they found a better paid job. Of sixty-three men who resigned from the force during 1947, no fewer than thirty-six were recruits with less than two years' service. Then there was the question of housing. Single men may have been willing to accept the communal living arrangements of police accommodation but young married men were unable to find suitable homes for their wives and families or pay the high rents asked for furnished flats. 'Under present circumstances the Police simply cannot successfully compete in the labour market for the type of men required,' concluded McCulloch. The only remedy lay in an improvement in pay and conditions.

His force might have been seriously under strength, but the Chief Constable was under intense pressure to take measures to 'smash the crime wave that is sweeping the West of Scotland', as the *Scottish Daily Express* put it. His personal reputation was at stake, too, for Malcolm McCulloch must have been very conscious that he was following in the footsteps of the legendary Percy Sillitoe, the man credited with tackling the razor gangs of the 1930s. Sillitoe had been knighted for his efforts before he moved on to Kent in 1943 and was subsequently appointed Director-General of MI5 in 1946.

The post of Chief Constable in Glasgow went to David Warnock but McCulloch, who was Assistant Chief Constable, unexpectedly found himself taking over the top job in 1943 when Warnock died suddenly after holding the position for only a few months. McCulloch had once been a deckhand on the yacht of Sir Thomas Lipton of Lipton Tea fame. Legend has it that when he decided to join the Glasgow police force, the new recruit was asked what he had previously worked at and, on the basis of his nautical experience, found himself assigned to the Marine Division in Partick which policed the dockside area of the River Clyde, where he would have encountered rather less glamorous vessels than fast ocean-going yachts.

As a short-term move to combat the post-war crime wave, McCulloch announced that he was placing his men on compulsory overtime and doubling patrols during peak periods of crime at night. This only served to antagonise his already hard-pressed officers, who were not satisfied with an extra payment of just two shillings [10p] per hour. By 8 January 1946 he had placed a ban on police holding a mass meeting to protest.

Another high profile measure was the combined police and army operation carried out just before New Year 1946 in an all-out effort to round up deserters and gunmen. Assistant Chief Constable Walter Docherty was in charge when – to use the pressmen's favourite expression – police 'swooped' on dance halls, billiard saloons and other places of entertainment in a synchronised operation. At the famous Barrowland dance hall, the music stopped and a police inspector addressed the dancers from the microphone. Exits were sealed, tables placed in the middle of the dance floor and male dancers asked to queue up and present their identification cards. Joe Loss and his Orchestra had just taken the stand at the Glasgow Playhouse but even he had to step down and let the police take over.

Chief Constable McCulloch further suggested that the government should take some steps to deal with the question of guns. Many law-abiding servicemen had brought back weapons as souvenirs or trophies with no intention of using them. The more intense the search to root these out, the more the innocent possessors took fright and passed them on to someone else, until they eventually ended up in the hands of criminals. McCulloch accordingly recommended a national amnesty for weapons handed in by a certain date and also that port authorities should thoroughly search those coming into the country and confiscate any weapons found. These steps had a certain amount of success and by March 1946, Glasgow police reported that they had so far received 406 firearms as well as shells, knives, incendiary bombs and even a machine gun.

Just to keep up the pressure, Glasgow's crime problems were raised in Parliament by John McGovern, Labour MP for Shettleston who had been one of the leaders of the hunger marches from Glasgow to London during the Great Depression of the 1930s. At Scottish Questions he asked George Buchanan, Under-Secretary of State of Scotland, what was being done about the question of 'terror gangs' in Glasgow. The reply was that police were employing 'motor patrols equipped with wireless' to deal more quickly with trouble on the streets, and that a new police recruitment campaign was planned.

The embattled Chief Constable had an opportunity to justify his performance in a *Glasgow Herald* interview after Christmas when he sought to reassure the public that 'the number of arrests made were keeping pace with the rise in the numbers of offences'. As far as the new scourge of armed hold-ups was concerned, the police had a success rate of more than 80% in catching the culprits and a new sheriff had been appointed to tackle the growing volume of work in the courts. But he also urged the public to play their part by securing their property and by informing the police of anything suspicious. In 1945, the 'Dial 999' service had only been around for a few years and does not seem to have been very well publicised – in the month of October, there had been no more than twenty-five callers.

'Give us the tip and leave it to the police,' was McCulloch's plea to the people of Glasgow: he confidently claimed that the force had at its command forty cars equipped with wireless apparatus and that by dialling 999, one of these would be at the scene in minutes.

How exactly they were going to manage that in a city of 1.1 million people when (as McCulloch admitted elsewhere) the shortage of manpower meant that not all of these cars were in use is another matter...

# 2

## *500 Pairs of Eyes*

*Post-War Policing: the Men and the Methods*

'Is Glasgow slipping back to the old era of gangsterdom, when the cosh and the razor made a midnight walk an adventure? Are the police in any way to blame and, if so, how?'

These searching questions were raised by Brendan Kemmet of the *Scottish Daily Express* in 1950. The Chief Constable's old adversary, Labour MP John McGovern, had again raised the issue of Glasgow's crime rate in Parliament. This time he asked the Scottish Secretary to set up an inquiry into how the city's police force was run.

At dusk each night, the streets of Glasgow and the safety of its citizens were in the hands of the men on the beat. The spotlight was now on how well equipped they were to carry out this awesome responsibility.

Under Chief Constable Percy Sillitoe in the 1930s, the Glasgow police force had been reorganised into eight divisions. Central or 'A' Division had its headquarters close to Glasgow Green in Turnbull Street. The Marine (B) Division office was located at the corner of Anderson Street in Partick not far from the docks and shipyards on the River Clyde. The Eastern (C) Division, covering East End areas like Shettleston and Dennistoun, was based in Tobago Street while Southern (D) Division operated from Craigie Street near Queen's

Park. The Northern (E) Division in Maitland Street covered the Cowcaddens district, which in the nineteenth century had been the most densely populated urban area in the whole of Western Europe. Maryhill (F) Division was based near the Maryhill Barracks where Hitler's second in command, Rudolf Hess, was once detained. Govan (G) Division had its headquarters in Albert Street, now named Orkney Street. In addition to these, the headquarters and administrative offices of the City of Glasgow police (known as H Division), from which the Traffic Department and the Criminal Investigation Department operated, were in St Andrews Street near Glasgow Green.

Today, none of these buildings are in use as police stations. The Maitland Street HQ are long since demolished and, although the Eastern and Central premises still stand, they are in poor condition. On the other hand, the Partick station has been adapted for other purposes, the Southern Division offices in Craigie Street and the St Andrews Street headquarters have been converted into flats, while the successfully renovated Maryhill Burgh Halls and adjacent police station now house a café and auditorium which can be hired for weddings. The Govan office has been redeveloped as an Enterprise Centre and the former lock-up cells are now used as offices for small businesses.

Back in the forties, police constables would muster in these imposing buildings at the start of their shifts before setting out on foot on their patrols. Chief Constable McCulloch affirmed in 1945 that 'regular patrolling by policemen in uniform is the most important single factor in crime prevention' and, though the concept has long been superseded by other approaches, many people to this day – including politicians at election time – will still tell you that it's the only solution to crime and social problems. The streets in each division were separated into beats, ranging in number from twenty-seven in the case of Maryhill to forty-six in the Marine.

Before he took to the streets, the new recruit would undergo a period of instruction at the Police Training School in Oxford Street in the Gorbals. This usually lasted for three months but the urgent need to increase manpower after the war meant that for a time the lessons were compressed into an eight-week course covering basic procedures and the law, combined with intensive physical exercise. After training, recruits would have an induction process before being 'let loose' on their own. For several weeks they would go on a different beat each night in the company of a more experienced officer and because they flitted from one place to another these recent recruits were known as 'flying men'.

The resources at their disposal were limited to a whistle and truncheon, and communication was via the police box. Yet another of Percy Sillitoe's innovations, these blue structures were strategically placed over the city – in 1947, there were about 350 of them – and they contained a telephone and various essentials like a first aid box or fire extinguisher. A light on the roof would flash to summon the man on the beat if there was a phone message and constables were required to keep a regular note of their activities during their shift in a journal kept inside the box which would be monitored by the sergeant. Sometimes a box would serve as a temporary holding cell pending the arrival of a police vehicle.

A conscientious officer would deal with whatever occurred on his beat, whether it was a break-in, a street fight, a lost child, a traffic problem or some unforeseen drama. Acting on the principle that prevention was better than cure, he would go round with his torch when on night shift, checking that shops and offices were secure, which they often weren't. In 1947, the nightly patrols reported an average of fifty business premises per week where doors or windows were not properly fastened. Knowing this regular routine, malicious boys would sometimes scrape up dogs' mess from the street and put it on the padlocks in readiness for the nightly checks...

Filth of another kind kept officers occupied during a fourteen-day observation of the goings-on in a bookshop in Stobcross Street in July 1951. The owner was suspected of having on sale two indecent books entitled *Red Heads Die Young* and *Road Floozie*, the latter being a melodramatic story about a girl who packs in her dead end job, adopts a nomadic lifestyle with a succession of truck drivers and descends into prostitution and murder. By the standards of the day, this was one of the more lurid examples of the pulp paperbacks which, according to author and critic Clive Bloom, 'were sold on their "erotic" cover art or suggestive "blurbs" at every railway station newsstand, every corner newsagent, every back-street "bookseller" and every market book barrow, only to quickly and quietly disintegrate as they were passed from reader to reader in offices, army barracks (especially among those doing National Service) and mechanics' shops across Britain in the bleak post-war years'.

The punishment for the heinous offence of selling such material? A £10 fine for the shop owner, a £1 fine for his assistant and the confiscation of his stock of the titles.

Another occurrence largely unheard-of nowadays but not uncommon at the time was the runaway horse. Motor traffic had to weave its way round slow horse-drawn vehicles and tramcars and often a horse would take fright. Constable Jimmy Robertson was on duty directing the traffic in New City Road one day when a horse bolted and started running straight towards him. At the same moment a blind man walked across the road and Robertson's first action was to push him out of the way. As the horse-drawn cart charged past him, he tried unsuccessfully to grab hold of the tailboard and jump aboard. Many cars on the roads were of the pre-war type with a 'running board' – an elongated step running from the front mudguards along the side doors – so the intrepid constable leapt onto the side of a passing car and as it drew level with the horse, put his right arm round its neck and held its nose with his left hand, thereby calming the animal down. His actions won him a trip to Buckingham Palace to collect the King's Police Medal for gallantry.

A good constable had to be able to respond to such unexpected happenings. Above all, though, he would get to know his area and the people who lived in it and if he gained their respect he could often defuse a potentially threatening situation with an authoritative warning or by administering a cuff round the ear of some incipient juvenile delinquent. Though discipline within the force was strict, when constables were out on the streets they had considerable freedom to exercise their own judgement in deciding how to deal with whatever circumstances arose. A small minority of officers even seemed to relish the prospect of a fight, perhaps the most extreme example being PC Stewart, nick-named 'Big Hitler'. An oft-told story in police circles concerned the day when a group of 'neds' decided to take their revenge on 'Big Hitler' by pushing an iron grating off a roof as he passed. It missed the target who immediately charged after the culprits and laid into all five of them with his baton. They all ended up in hospital.

A potentially serious incident where a constable's familiarity with his district helped save lives occurred in November 1952. At around eight o'clock in the morning, Constable Andrew Cruikshank was patrolling his beat in the Plantation area of Govan when the wall of a tenement building started to crumble before his eyes. He fought his way through the dust and debris as bricks continued to cascade to the ground, leading terrified tenants to safety. He was awarded the BEM 'for carrying out his duties without thought for his own personal safety' but what makes the story still more remarkable is that he knew his beat so well that he could tell how many residents lived in the building and repeatedly went back in until he was sure they had all been rescued.

A beat constable worked long shifts for little money but there were a few perks that helped to make his lot a happier one. At the junction of Hope Street and Renfrew Street where the Royal Conservatoire of Scotland now stands there used to be a restaurant called the Savoy Café run by Joe Pieri, a well-known Scottish-Italian. The Northern Division HQ in Maitland Street were only a few minutes away and the 'polis' would invariably be found in the back shop of the Savoy enjoying a coffee or a plate of fish and chips. A similar haven for south side constables with sore feet was the Y.M.C.A. in Govan where they could always be sure of a cup of tea. This institution provided tempo-rary accommodation and meals for men in need and one former 'G' Division man recalls how, as a new recruit, he was called upon to break up a fight that broke out at breakfast one morning. Porridge had been thrown on the floor and as he dashed into the dining room he slipped on some of it and collided with the trestle tables, which immediately collapsed on top of him. The whole room burst out laughing at the sight of a policeman buried under the tables with his uniform covered in porridge and the cause of the brawl was soon forgotten.

There were even occasions when men on the beat who knew their clientele were not above playing the odd prank. A rag and bone man well-known to residents of the Garscube Road area once left his barrow at the roadside and went in for a refreshment or two. When he staggered out, he couldn't find the barrow until somebody eventually told him it was in a nearby backcourt. He stood there scratching his head in disbelief wondering how such a thing could have happened and, more importantly, how he would get it out again. The cops had taken off the wheels, carried the barrow sideways through the narrow close entrance and reassembled it in the yard behind.

More often, though, the target of a policeman's humour would be one of his colleagues. One former officer recalls joining the police cadets as a teenager. The sergeant in charge assigned him the job of looking after the mortuary, giving him half-a-crown [12.5p] for the work, though, of course, he himself was being paid a good deal more to carry out this duty. The youngster had the grim task of going out to the nearby Kirkintilloch railway line to gather up body parts from suicides who had thrown themselves under passing trains. This sergeant's idea of a joke was to hold up a severed head in front of an unsuspecting young policewoman, who promptly fainted. Her fiancé did not see the funny side and, in a rage, came up to see the sergeant and punched him. Looking back on the incident more than half a century later, the young cadet (by then a retired Chief Superintendent) reflected that such men had been through the war or had done National Service, where they had no doubt witnessed all kinds of brutality. 'There was less sensitivity in these days,' he said, 'and it would never have occurred to them that their actions might have a traumatic effect on somebody young and inexperienced.'

The same senior officer recalled many other episodes of banter and practical joking from later in his career. On one occasion, he and his colleagues had carried out a search for a gun in a house that was in a very dirty state. Back at the station, one cop went into the washroom and stripped to the waist to clean himself up. Suddenly, someone yelled, 'Hurry up, everybody – the bank's being robbed!' A dripping, half-dressed figure emerged moments later, asking 'where's the bank robbery?', only to be greeted by a chorus of laughter from the rest of the team.

In a similar vein, Joe Beattie, a former wartime RAF pilot who ended up as a Detective Superintendent, told the story of a rather straight-laced colleague who always sported a handkerchief in the top pocket of his jacket. In the course of enquiries into a robbery at a warehouse, the owner expressed his gratitude to the detectives and gave them a token of appreciation from his stockroom – a trade box of condoms. These were left in the CID office for any member of the team who happened to want some and, when the dour detective had hung his jacket on the back of his chair, someone decided to slip one into his top pocket. Later, he and Joe were visiting a house to take a statement and, as expected, the officer pulled out his handkerchief, letting the contraceptive fall to the floor. Less than amused, he asked Joe on the way out, 'Who put that in my pocket?' As ever, Beattie had a ready response: 'It's a tribute to your prowess!'

Every officer had a fund of similar anecdotes, some of them no doubt embellished at each retelling. Another prolific source of stories of law and order – or, rather, law and disorder – in the streets and tenements of post-war Glasgow was the column in the *Daily Record* entitled 'Looking for Trouble', which appeared daily under the pseudonym 'Pat Roller'. Reporters who had struck up a rapport with the local constabulary would bring the previous night's misdeeds to the breakfast tables of Glaswegians by the following morning and it's said that some of the 'neds' would eagerly read these reports to see if their exploits had made it into print. No other journalism brings the period to life better than these little vignettes, which, even after six decades, still have a freshness and immediacy about their style.

A couple of examples must suffice:

You wouldn't call Harry McGovern a lucky man. When life doled out slices of misfortune Harry was right there at the receiving end.

His wife died ten years ago and Harry brought up a young family all on his own at the ground floor house at 16 Raglan Street, up by the Round Toll.

His only son, now eighteen, is fighting guerrillas in Malaya with the Cameronians. Harry's on the sick list. His two daughters are only thirteen and fifteen. Not a lot of money comes in to No. 16.

What else could happen to Harry? Just this: last night thieves called at Harry's house while the family were out, burst open the door and hacked off Harry's gas meter with Harry's axe.

Gas escaped and swirled through the house. The thieves pulled down bed curtains and tied them round the gas pipe to save themselves. Then they dragged the meter into a back court, broke it open and made off with the pennies.

Unlucky Harry came in to find the meter gone and the gas still escaping. Last night, when the plumbers had fixed up the leak, Harry was told more bad news: he'll have to pay for the damage himself and refund the money stolen. It's the law.

Like Harry's gas meter, the old, tightly packed tenements of Raglan Street disappeared long ago, to be replaced by newer housing developments.

On another occasion, Pat Roller picked up the tale of a youth's late night dash through the streets of the East End with no shoes on and his hands handcuffed together:

Nineteen years old and an army deserter for several months past, the culprit was first spotted in a public house. When policemen entered he exited the bar and sped from a rear exit.

An hour or two later two constables called at a dance hall at the corner of French Street and Norman Street and again saw the wanted man – doing a quickstep. Next moment he was doing a quicker step out of the back door.

, This time, however, the fugitive ran into a cul-de-sac and after a scuffle in which he lost his shoes he was overpowered by the policemen and handcuffed.

One Bobby stood guard while the other went to phone for a Black Maria.

Suddenly the young soldier leapt to his feet and struck out and dashed back into the dance hall. Hot in pursuit, the policeman was hampered in his chase by dancers who packed themselves tightly in the doorway of the hall.

Two men were arrested on a charge of obstructing the police in the execution of their duty – but the original prisoner vanished.

Even when culprits were apprehended and made their appearance in court, they could still manage to bait the forces of the law. In November 1950, a man was on trial before Lord Strachan in the sombre setting of the Glasgow High Court after a razor-slashing incident in Radnor Street. The accused decided to conduct his own defence – as the mass-murderer Peter Manuel would do some years later. Faced with his victim in the witness box, the attacker asked him, 'You do love me, don't you?' 'Not as much as you love me,' was the reply. Laughter rippled around the courtroom. By the time the victim told everyone that on the night in question he was 'as sober as a judge', his Lordship had had enough and threatened to clear the public benches. 'People who come here for entertainment will not be allowed to remain,' he thundered.

Lighter moments notwithstanding, the man on the beat in Glasgow knew only too well that, to paraphrase the words of the poet Norman MacCaig, there was only a thin tissue covering violence. At any moment he could find himself in danger and there are plenty of stories of extreme courage being shown in situations where officers found themselves under attack.

One August night, just after midnight, Constable John Gunn of the Northern Division was on duty in New City Road. Hearing the sound of breaking glass, he spotted a man standing on a railing trying to break the window of a pub. Gunn knew the warren of lanes and closes in his district like the back of his hand – and the locals knew their constable. Some were even leaning out their windows to help him by pointing out his quarry. As the policeman cornered the man, he noticed something glinting in the darkness and moments later felt a knife sink into his stomach. His assailant fled and it was only the chance appearance of a group of passers-by that saved Gunn's life. He spent ten days on the danger list in the Western Infirmary but he was able to give his CID colleagues a vital clue: his attacker had kicked off his shoes at the scene of the break-in. This was enough for the detectives to track him down and he was eventually committed to Carstairs Mental Institution.

John Gunn was awarded a medal for bravery but when this previously fit and active constable returned to work after months of recuperation he was a broken man and the only suitable role that could be found for him was as a police librarian.

The odds were even more heavily stacked against PC William Hazelton of the Central Division when, late on a Saturday night, he and his younger 'neighbour' found themselves confronted with a jeering and swearing mob of twenty-five youths in the Gorbals. A bottle flew and the gang set upon the two cops. Though the younger man was knocked unconscious, the blows kept coming but Hazelton managed to struggle to his feet and lash out with his baton. Again, only a timely intervention from a courageous resident saved their lives. The man helped Hazelton carry his mate into a close where they were able to take refuge in one of the flats. The thugs had nearly battered the door down when police reinforcements arrived and six arrests were made. When Constable Hazelton was awarded a BEM for his heroism, he said that he only acted in the same way as any other officer would.

At the Sheriff Court in Glasgow in February 1951, a sheriff condemned the 'savage and uncivilised attitude' towards the police in many districts of the city. The case before him that day was typical. An inebriated twenty-two-year-old had been arrested by two policemen in Govan. As they were attempting to take him to a police box a hostile crowd gathered and tried to release him, but a passing police car came to the rescue. Once inside the car, the drunk attempted to smash the back window and assault one of the officers with a bottle, the car swerving wildly from side to side while they tried to subdue him. He later told the court he had been drinking and had no recollection of what he was doing.

To a Glasgow policeman, it was all in a day's work.

In spite of these dangers, some stalwarts of the force were happy enough to carry out the task of pounding the beat throughout their careers, and, while they may not have received promotion, many ended up with numerous commendations. Others were more ambitious. When Percy Sillitoe took charge of the Glasgow force in 1931, he observed that 'the average constable could not hope ever to be more than a puller of padlocks, doomed to spend thirty years or so shaking hands with doorknobs.' One of his first measures was to ensure that older senior ranks took the pension due to them in order to make way for new blood – a move which, predictably, alienated some of the old guard as much as it appealed to the younger men. Sillitoe was always ready to reward able officers who showed initiative and the first three post-war CID chiefs, William Ewing, Gilbert McIlwrick and Robert Colquhoun, were among them.

In the early post-war period, CID skills were largely learned on the job. There was little in the way of specialised preparation until October 1947 when the first training course for detectives in Scotland took place at the Oxford Street Training School. Participants were addressed by eminent speakers from medicine, forensic science, the legal profession … and by 'one woman', though it was hoped that in future more women would take part in CID work. The course lasted for four weeks and was attended by forty officers from across Scotland.

After four years' experience, a constable who was keen to get on could sit the Elementary Certificate examination, which would qualify him for the rank of sergeant, entry into the CID and other 'inside' administrative posts. He could then progress to the Advanced Certificate, which again tested the candidate's general educational level as well as his knowledge of police duties. But passing the exams didn't automatically get him the job. Promotion came by selection or, on occasion, by invitation if there was a need for a specific post to be filled. Otherwise, the officer's name would go on 'the list' and he would wait his turn to move up a rank. If this had the advantage that his turn would come eventually, it also meant that some individuals were promoted simply because they were on the list, and not because of their suitability for the job. One retired officer recalled an occasion early in his career when three colleagues were tragically killed in a road accident; the senior officer took out the list and solemnly scored out the three names, allowing the others to move up.

It was a big event in the force when a 'promotion parade' took place. Expectant officers would go home and tell their wives not to make any lengthy phone calls that evening in case a message came through. The successful candidates would be called and told to attend Headquarters the following day and not to tell anyone. At HQ, they were lined up outside the office of the Chief Constable who summoned them in one by one to tell them which division or branch they had been promoted to.

For some, moving into the CID and subsequent promotion occurred quickly – but this was by no means true in every case. Even those who reached the very top of the ladder did not necessarily ascend it rapidly. Of the post-war CID chiefs, William Ewing had nine years' service prior to being accepted into the CID and Tom Goodall eleven, whereas Robert Colquhoun and Bob Kerr became detectives within three years and Gilbert McIlwrick, exceptionally, in just two. On the other hand, it took Goodall twenty-four years to go from constable to sergeant. Even David McNee, who ended up as Commissioner of the Metropolitan Police and the recipient of a knighthood, remained a constable for more than sixteen years. 'That may seem a long time by present standards,' he later reflected, 'but it meant that I learnt my craft by hard experience and later on, when in command of men, those years enabled me to know the problems encountered by serving officers and how they should be dealing with them.'

A common factor shared by those who became Chief Superintendents is that they had usually clocked up between twenty and thirty years' CID experience so that when they reached the top job they were in their mid-fifties, with William Ewing and Tom Goodall being relatively young when they took charge, at the ages of forty-six and fifty-two respectively. Ewing served in the role for fourteen years, initially as Superintendent and then, from 1951, with the enhanced rank of Chief Superintendent. The four CID chiefs in charge between 1951 and 1969 each served in the role for a briefer period, lasting between three and six years. The unremitting nature of the duties was such that few men could have carried the burden for a lengthier spell.

One thing guaranteed to start an argument in the police canteen – whether in the 1950s or today – is to talk about someone being 'promoted' from uniform to CID. Levelheaded officers are well aware of the value of the mutual benefits to be gained from maintaining good relations between the two branches. The ideal situation was outlined by *The Police Journal* in the forties:

> If the best results are to be obtained the uniform branch should be made to feel that crime detection is as much their responsibility as that of the CID. There are many ways of doing this, but primarily it depends on the friendly attitude adopted by the CID. A CID office ought never to be barred to members of the uniform branch and discussions on interesting cases, points of law and the like should not be confined to the CID. The important thing is that each branch should know what the other is doing in the common cause.

That, at least, was the theory. But cops are only human and, as in every other business or organisation, harmonious working relationships largely depend on the individuals concerned. There have always been uniformed officers who feel they make the arrests only to be side-lined while CID does the follow-up – as used to happen in the classic 1950s radio serial *PC 49* when the hero regularly solved crimes which baffled his superiors only to be told, 'Back to your beat, 49.' Some senior CID figures made a point of being present while the uniform team mustered for duty in order to keep them fully informed; on the other hand, there would be the occasional detective with a big ego who considered himself to be – as one retired Glasgow officer memorably put it – 'Sherlock Holmes on steroids'. Generally though, problems could be defused by the exercise of good humour. Uniforms would often greet CID arriving at a crime scene with 'here come the brains' – even if later on they would tell you that 'CID' stood for 'Clowns In Disguise'!

The way Glasgow CID was structured in the 1950s was that an Assistant Chief Constable had overall supervision of criminal investigation. Under him were two senior officers with the rank of Chief Superintendent, one being the hands-on CID boss whose name would regularly be referred to in the daily press. He in turn had a deputy with the rank of Superintendent. In addition, each of the divisions had a CID with a Chief Inspector in charge and these departments would carry out murder investigations on the ground.

The other Chief Superintendent was in charge of the Identification Bureau. By the mid-fifties there were 120,000 sets of fingerprints and 150,000 criminal profiles in the files and a collection of 40,000 photos known in-house as 'the family album'. The laboratories of the Scientific Branch could provide expertise in such areas as ballistics, blood specimens, hairs and fibres and even laundry marks.

Nowadays forensics are crucial in the fight against crime but in the early 1950s that science was only in its infancy. As the CID Chief at the time, Gilbert McIlwrick, said, 'Scientific evidence is particularly valuable in providing evidence which will help to convict a suspect, but it very rarely answers the two questions which are the basis of all criminal investigation – "Who did it?" and "Where can I find him?"' Nevertheless, as a later chapter shows, there were a number of exceptional cases where the work of the forensic experts provided the solution to a crime.

Between the uniformed men patrolling on foot, on horses or in cars, and the CID men carrying out investigations, Chief Constables in postwar Glasgow had a force of about 2,000 men at their disposal. And in these days it was essentially a man's job. In the mid-fifties Glasgow had just forty-four policewomen, mostly employed behind the scenes to take evidence from women and children in assault cases or to deal with issues such as criminal abortion or concealment of pregnancy.

In a force the size of Glasgow's it was inevitable that there would be the occasional reprobate. The most notorious was the disgraced PC James Robertson, sentenced to death in 1950 for murdering a woman with whom he had been involved in a relationship. Criminals were always ready to accuse the police of planting evidence and officers could always be counted upon to back each other up in the face of such accusations. The daughter of one long-serving and thoroughly reliable constable married a minister but her father refused to become a church member until he retired from the force as the moral compromises he was required to make on a daily basis weighed heavily on his conscience. There were also instances where police officers were accused of theft or found guilty of using violence against those held in custody.

Occurrences like these, combined with a worrying rise in violent crime, led Shettleston MP John McGovern in 1950 to ask the Secretary of State for Scotland to set up an enquiry into the force and its discipline 'with a view to restoring public confidence'. McGovern had experienced his own battles with Glasgow police in the early 1930s when he was arrested for fighting for the right to free speech on Glasgow Green. In Parliament, the Secretary of State, Hector McNeil, dismissed his request for an investigation of the police force out of hand:

> I must affirm that I have no reason to doubt the efficiency of the City of Glasgow Police, nor have I criticism of substance to make on their supervision or their discipline. Nor have I any evidence that they have forfeited the confidence of the citizens of Glasgow. I therefore lack reason to institute any inquiry or to convene any conference of the kind suggested by my honourable Friend.

Perhaps Chief Superintendent William Ewing had McGovern in mind when he said the following year that 'Destructive criticism is easy but I consider that some of the critics would really be doing a service to the community if they endeavoured to assist by giving practical help and encouragement instead of apparently condoning the defiance of law and order'.

For it was clear that, no matter how hard they tried, the police couldn't tackle crime on their own – help from the wider community was vital. Sometimes it was forthcoming. At other times, the public deliberately hampered officers in their investigations.

This is where the '500 pairs of eyes' came in. If the public fully assisted the police, declared Gilbert McIlwrick, Glasgow's crime rate could be cut dramatically. 'Co-operation by the ordinary citizen is one of the most valuable aids to the police in the detection of crime,' he said. 'At any one time there are only about 500 policemen on duty in Glasgow – 500 pairs of eyes to watch against the 25,000 crimes committed in the city last year. If only the adult population of Glasgow would co-operate fully with the police, it could be 500,000 pairs of eyes.'

# 3

## 'The Big Fella'

### Detective Chief Superintendent William Ewing, CID Chief
### 1937–51

The public perception is that CID men are 'plain clothed', but for much of the post-war period their familiar garb of hat and raincoat almost constituted a uniform in itself. Even in the late sixties, Joe Jackson recalled joining the CID and being told to go out and buy himself a hat. 'The only choice left to me,' he said, 'was whether it would be a fedora, trilby or soft bowler.' There used to be jokes about 'the Ralph Slater Discount Overcoat Society', a reference to the well-known outfitters in Glasgow's Howard Street.

The get-up was so recognisable that it's said that certain unscrupulous newspaper reporters would dress in a similar fashion, drive around in the same type of car used by CID and pull up alongside a young uniformed constable doing his rounds, all in the hope of being first to pick up a good crime story.

One CID man who *didn't* look the part was Chief Superintendent William Ewing, in charge from 1937 until 1951. Seeing him on the street, said one journalist, you would probably take him for a doctor or a successful businessman, as he was always immaculately dressed.

This tall, courteous and distinguished-looking man was born in 1891 in Wigtownshire, where his father was a police inspector in Stranraer. The police station had four cells and kind-hearted Mrs Ewing would often give the prisoners a share of whatever the family were having for their meal. As a boy he witnessed an early form of community policing in action – his father was often consulted by local people if any trouble occurred so that problems were invariably solved without 'official' police intervention. Young Willie was employed at a local creamery for a time but it was inevitable that he, like his brother Tom, would follow in his father's footsteps and he travelled up to Glasgow in May 1911 for an interview at police headquarters – the first time he had ever visited the city. He hadn't expected to be told that he would be starting his duties the very next day and had to find himself suitable lodgings that night. Forty years later, at a dinner to celebrate his retirement, he joked that he still had the return half of his railway ticket.

The year Ewing started pounding the beat Glasgow police had a fleet of motor vehicles amounting to a grand total of one, used for the transportation of prisoners rather than for investigating crimes or pursuing criminals. It was only five years since the first detective constables had been appointed in the city and areas such as Govan and Partick were still served by their own separate Burgh forces. His starting pay was twenty-five shillings and one penny per week.

One of the more unusual tasks carried out by police constables in that far-off era was to act as a human alarm clock. Ewing's beat took in the area around Glasgow Cross railway station and hundreds of workmen who lived nearby could be seen rushing to catch their trains at 5 a.m. Often he would 'knock up' as many as thirty men to ensure they arrived at work in time. Another slice of Glasgow life that made a big impact on a lad more accustomed to the bracing seaside air of South West Scotland was the 'little armies of barefoot youngsters and children suffering from rickets who used to play among the grim tenements'.

By 1920 Ewing had joined the CID – just in time to take part in the investigations into the dramatic Sinn Féin shooting of May 1921. Frank Carty, a leading figure within the Irish Republican Army (IRA) also known as Peter Somers, had escaped from prison in Sligo and made his way to Scotland, where he was tracked down and arrested in a house in Springburn. On 4 May, Carty was being transported from the Central Police Court to Duke Street Prison in a police van when, close to the Cathedral in High Street, an armed gang attempted to free him, killing one of the escorts, Inspector Robert Johnstone, and wounding Sergeant George Stirton. Many years later, Ewing recalled the incident: 'It so happened that I was one of the first detective officers to arrive on the scene and I assisted in the subsequent enquiries. Over fifty persons were taken into custody. Eventually, thirteen men appeared for trial at the High Court in Edinburgh, but all were acquitted.'

Once in the CID, Ewing progressed rapidly through the ranks. He was promoted to Sergeant in 1921 and Inspector two years later. In 1929, he transferred from the Central to the Southern Division as Detective Lieutenant and took charge of Govan CID. By 1937 he was back in Central Division as Superintendent of the city's CID in succession to Adam McLaren and in 1944, at the age of fifty-three, as a result of the ever-expanding responsibility of the job, became the first to hold the newly created rank of Chief Superintendent with a salary of £625. At that time he was described as 'one of the ablest detectives in Scotland'. He left the force in March 1951 after forty years' service and undertook security work for some years before enjoying a decent period of retirement, often playing golf at Glasgow Golf Club in Killermont, Bearsden, of which he was a member. He is also said to have enjoyed reading detective novels! William Ewing was a bachelor, a fact that allowed journalists to sign off articles about him with the inevitable cliché: he was married to the job.

'The Big Fella', as his men liked to call him, died in Mearnskirk Hospital in March 1970 at the age of seventy-nine.

★ ★ ★

Given the time that has passed, it can be difficult to form an impression of what these prominent detectives were like as individuals, but in Ewing's case one journalist wrote a very perceptive portrait of him at the time of his retirement. 'He's quiet, unassuming, dislikes limelight shining on him ... That quiet, almost diffident voice of his puts penetrating questions which are not calculated to make an uneasy listener any easier.' He never lost his soft-spoken Galloway accent and had a habit of whistling to himself in a quiet, if tuneless, manner when thinking his way through a problem.

That tuneless whistle must have been heard many times when Ewing was working on the two major cases which made his name: the Scottish Amalgamated Silks fraud of 1932 and the Buck Ruxton murders of 1935.

Cases involving financial irregularities are rarely as dramatic as murders or daring bank robberies and, when reported in the press, interest in them tends to be restricted to those in business and legal circles. But, by any standards, the Silks fraud was breath-taking in its audacity. The sums involved were huge and the trial itself, involving 192 witnesses, set a new record at the time for being the longest ever in Scotland, lasting for thirty-three days.

A group of businessmen based in Scotland and England were accused of issuing a prospectus inviting the public to subscribe for shares in a new company with the aim of acquiring a controlling interest in Scottish Artificial Silks Limited, which was in fact on the verge of bankruptcy. The main charge was that they had 'defrauded the public of £439,000 by issuing a false prospectus and misappropriated a further £362,000 by false allotment of shares in the company's stock'. Two mills in England and two in Scotland – one of them in the huge abandoned Argyll car factory at Alexandria which, to this day, is still something of a white elephant – were purchased with the aim of spinning artificial silk according to a 'secret process' which one of the accused, Alexander Young, had purchased from a German scientist and resold to Scottish Amalgamated Silks for £25,000. At the trial in the High Court in Edinburgh during March and April 1932 it became clear that no-one in the company knew anything about artificial silks and an expert witness described the proposed manufacturing method as 'valueless'. 'They could search the minute books from beginning to end,' the Lord Advocate told the jury, 'and they would not find in these another reference to the secret process. It might have been a formula for anything. It might have been sheep dip.'

On top of that, some of the business practices of the organisation were so shambolic that letters sent out from the Alexandria premises did not carry the full Scottish address, with the result that correspondence sometimes ended up in Alexandria, Egypt! Two members of the respected J. and P. Coats family of Paisley had been appointed to positions in Scottish Artificial Silks at a very high level of remuneration and, although a disclaimer was published stating they had no connection with the famous thread manufacturing firm, the implication was that they were there to provide the venture with a veneer of respectability.

By mid-February 1931, Glasgow police had accumulated sufficient evidence to round up the culprits from their home addresses in a co-ordinated series of raids involving detectives from the various city divisions. On 16 February, Detective Lieutenant Ewing arrived at the home of Alexander Young at Kilhey Court, Worthington, near Wigan, an imposing Victorian mansion set in ten acres of ground. Ewing took Young into custody and spent two hours searching the premises, including the wine cellar, leaving with 'several thousands of letters'. Among them was one from a business associate who mentioned the research carried out on the secret process and added:

> I was thinking that owing to the amount of experimental work we had done here in the last two months you should add another £5,000 to the selling price of the mill.

Young told Ewing, 'I want you to take great care of this. They are all trying to make me the scapegoat but this will prove they are not all so innocent.' Hearing that another of the accused businessmen was at that moment at a mill in Leigh, near Manchester, Ewing and his colleague Detective Inspector Paterson arrested him as well and took both men back to Glasgow.

When Ewing appeared as a witness at the trial in March of the following year, he was questioned by Young who by that stage of the proceedings had decided to take over his own defence. Their exchange, referring to Ewing's visit to Kilhey Court on 17 February 1931, sheds light on Ewing's precision and attention to detail and even reveals something of his sense of humour:

> YOUNG: I put it to you that what I was telling you was to this effect: 'They [his fellow directors] tried to make me the scapegoat for the losses at the shareholders' meeting and although I had been off the board for over a year they all sat on the platform like a lot of innocent lambs'. Wasn't that what I told you?

> EWING: No. What you said was noted at the time. I recollect you said a lot about the directors being at the shareholders' meeting and not speaking up. That was said afterwards.

> YOUNG: You recollect I said a great deal during the time you were in my house – a period of two hours?

> EWING: Oh, you spoke all the time.

The trial traced in exhaustive detail the dubious valuations given to the numerous factory sites and the complex interconnections between the various companies, whose plausible names were memorably described at one point as 'wonderful garments for the skeletons they covered'. The verdict endorsed the Lord Advocate's allegation that Alexander Young was indeed the ringleader in a concern 'not only tainted but saturated with fraud from start to finish'. He was sentenced to three years' imprisonment with hard labour (this would involve, for example, working in a quarry – the sentence of imprisonment with hard labour was abolished in Scotland in 1950).

Though there was some concern, particularly among socialist Members of Parliament, that only one other of the original eleven businessmen was found guilty, the conviction of Young was a tribute to the months spent by Ewing and his colleagues wading through mountains of letters, minute books, cheques and certificates, 1,584 of which were produced as evidence in court. The judge himself acknowledged that 'the detail of it was far beyond the capacity of the human mind to carry and to retain'.

By the time the process finally reached its end, the business prospectus of Scottish Amalgamated Silks Ltd. had been shown to be as artificial as the silk itself.

* * *

In 1935 William Ewing was back in England investigating a crime of a very different type: a gruesome double murder. For more than eighty years, the case of Dr Buck Ruxton has provided a textbook example of the use of forensic medicine in solving crime, but the important role played by the Glasgow detective has been largely forgotten.

On 29 September 1935, a young woman called Susan Johnston was on holiday in Moffat, a small country town situated on the River Annan in Dumfriesshire, about half an hour away from the border between Scotland and England. She was walking with her mother over the bridge at Gardenholme Linn, two miles outside the town. 'Linn' is a Scots word referring to a waterfall or ravine, and Susan paused to look down at the water below. Convinced that she could see what looked like a human arm, she turned back to bring her brother, who climbed down the bank to take a closer look. The family immediately reported the matter to the police who searched the area and located four bundles of dismembered and decomposing human remains.

This was hardly the sort of affair that a small country force was used to handling and the local officers sent for outside assistance. Glasgow was the natural place to turn since, as one newspaper said, the city's CID was 'rapidly gaining a reputation as the Scottish Scotland Yard'. On the afternoon of 2 October, Chief Constable Keith of Lanarkshire and four Glasgow officers – Ewing, fingerprint expert Bertie Hammond, CID boss Adam McLaren and Assistant Chief Constable Warnock

– arrived to inspect the ravine, going thereafter to the mortuary at Moffat Cemetery, where the remains had temporarily been taken for examination by Professor John Glaister, from the Forensic Medicine department at Glasgow University.

Fairly quickly, Glaister was able to say that there were two victims, probably an elderly man of about 5 feet, 8 inches in height and a stockily built 5 feet, 2 inch female aged between thirty and forty. What was particularly chilling was that the bodies had not simply been cut up but systematically mutilated to erase any identifying features and pieces from different bodies were mixed together in the same package. This, said the journalists, required surgical skill and suggested that 'no mere madman' committed the outrage.

Though such care had been taken in dismembering the bodies, the killer was surprisingly lax in the materials he used to gather up the remains. Distinctive items of clothing – a child's romper suit, a woman's blouse and a bed sheet – were recovered and sheets of newspaper used to wrap other body parts were also easily identified as originating in the North of England. A local joiner constructed special wooden containers for remains relating to 'Body No.1' and 'Body No. 2' and these were taken in a trailer attached to a police car to Edinburgh University, where Glaister and Professor Gilbert Miller could begin the grim task of trying to piece them together.

John Glaister had been the first specialist in his field to be appointed to give lectures to the Glasgow police force in Medical Jurisprudence and Toxicology and, as a young detective, William Ewing had attended these. He could never have imagined that he would end up working closely alongside the great man in a case that would be a turning point in both their careers.

Back at Gardenholme Linn, exhaustive searches for further clues continued and the atmosphere at the scene was vividly captured by a reporter for the *Glasgow Herald* on 3 October:

Rain fell during most of the day and the surrounding hills presented a gloomy and forbidding aspect as the officers tenaciously pursued their search for remaining parts of the bodies, including the man's torso and legs. The weather was bitterly cold, and those engaged in the investigations, particularly the men groping among the stones of the stream, worked in acute discomfort. Despite the wintry conditions, a large crowd watched the proceedings from the parapet of the bridge.

The following day the items collected so far were laid out for the journalists to look at. Working on the theory that the remains had been brought by car from either Glasgow or Edinburgh, Ewing and his colleagues checked lists of missing persons and questioned some 900 motorists.

By 8 October, as many as thirty different packages had been located and, as a final check, bloodhounds were brought in to follow the scent. Ewing watched for two hours as the dogs sniffed their way around the location, without result.

As his work on the forensic jigsaw continued, Glaister issued more precise descriptions, which police announced to the press at their Dumfries headquarters on the evening of 9 October. The woman was not older than twenty-six and probably came from a working-class background. The man was about sixty and 'lantern jawed'. This intensified speculation about the relationship between the two victims, and the possible motive for the crime. Was it a case of father and daughter?

Simultaneously, police were narrowing down the search to Lancaster as one of the newspaper fragments found with the body parts was traced to a special edition circulating only in a defined area. The revision of the possible age of the younger female victim to under twenty-six brought the enquiry into closer relationship with a girl of twenty-one reported missing in Lancaster.

Then Ewing had a flash of inspiration while sitting in his Moffat hotel. Everything so far had been based on the assumption that this was a case involving a man and a woman. What if the victims were *both* women? From that moment, events moved rapidly. By the time the new theory appeared in the newspapers on 12 October, Ewing was already in Lancaster where Chief Constable H. J. Vann charged Dr Buck Ruxton with the murder of Mary Jane Rogerson, his young maid. Ruxton's wife Isabella was also missing, but he was not charged with her murder at this stage.

It might appear strange that in spite of the painstaking clinical examination carried out by the most eminent authority in the field of forensics, the identification of the second victim as female ultimately came about through the intuition of a policeman. But it must be remembered that Glaister had very little to go on and, of course, modern discoveries such as DNA lay far into the future. The killer had gone to extraordinary lengths to eliminate every possible feature that could assist identification: the feet, fingers and entire torso were missing and Glaister later said in court that, 'the eyes, the eyelids, ears and all the scalp tissue bearing hair had been removed. The lips had been cut out, and a portion had been cut from the tip of the tongue.' Special attention had been devoted to removing organs that could help determine the sex of the victims, such as the larynx. Few outside the medical profession would be aware that the male larynx is usually larger than the female. Forty-three out of a total of eighty-six 'soft pieces' of flesh could not be assigned to one body or the other.

Glaister's scientific expertise and pioneering analytical techniques were beyond reproach, but there was still a place for the detective's hunch. It would be fascinating to know how this figure who had attained almost god-like status in his profession reacted to the policeman telling him he might be on the wrong track . . .

Buktyar Rustomji Ratanji Hakim was a thirty-six-year-old doctor from Bombay who changed his name to Buck Ruxton and opened a practice at 2 Dalton Square, Lancaster in 1930. Isabella (his common law wife) previously worked as manageress of an Edinburgh restaurant and had separated from her Dutch husband before living with Ruxton. They had a stormy relationship; as Ruxton later said at his trial, they could neither live with, nor without, each other. Previous maids had seen him threaten her with a knife and police had been called to the house on two occasions. An obsessively jealous man, he once followed her to Edinburgh in a hired car when she went there with friends as he had convinced himself she was having an affair.

Neither Isabella nor Mary had been seen since 15 September 1935 and Ruxton told a series of inconsistent stories to his cleaners and to his maid's parents: the two women had gone on holiday; Mary was pregnant and had gone for an abortion; Isabella had left him, and so on. Unsatisfied with his explanations, the Rogersons reported the disappearance of their daughter to the police. Plenty of witnesses could testify to strange goings-on at Dalton Square – Ruxton had a serious cut on his hand, carpets soaked with blood had been removed, the bath in which the bodies had been drained of blood and dismembered was heavily stained and various items had been burnt in the backyard.

The case was now in the hands of the Lancashire force, but Ewing was seconded south of the border to continue helping with the enquiry. The doctor's premises were meticulously examined by Ewing and Hammond, and Glaister had the bath, the staircase and even blood-stained wall sections transported to Glasgow where he reconstructed the scene of the crime.

For the case against Ruxton to stand up in court, it was essential to prove that the bodies were indeed those of his wife and servant which, given the state of the remains, was no easy matter. As outlined in Blundell and Wilson's *The Trial of Buck Ruxton* (1937), the final grim inventory of body parts comprised the following:

> Two heads, each with a portion of neck attached; two trunk portions – an upper part including chest and shoulder girdle, and a lower portion including a complete bony pelvis; seventeen limb portions and forty-three pieces of soft tissue. The soft tissues included three female breasts, two portions of female external sex organs; and a uterus.

It was here that the groundbreaking forensic work of Glaister was crucial. He enlarged photographs of the faces of both victims and superimposed these over images of the skulls to establish their identity. He also studied samples of maggots found among the fragments of human flesh in the ravine and from their stage of development was able to narrow down to a two-day period the time when the remains were placed there.

Glaister later revealed that Crown counsel was unhappy about him using this evidence at the trial – they considered it would be too much for the jury members to stomach.

In spite of the overwhelming accumulation of evidence, Ruxton denied everything, frequently breaking down and sobbing during the trial. His response was simply, 'I have never done anything wrong to anybody, sir, and they come and tell these stories.' But the verdict was a foregone conclusion and Buck Ruxton went to the gallows at Manchester's Strangeways Prison on 12 May 1936.

The house in Dalton Square, Lancaster, where the killings took place was never again used as a dwelling-place and is today occupied as business premises. It is said that the bath where Ruxton cut up the bodies was subsequently used as a horse trough at Lancashire police headquarters.

William Ewing had been a key figure at every stage of the enquiry, from his first arrival at Moffat on 2 October until his return to normal duties in Glasgow twelve days later. During this period he made frequent trips back to Glasgow to consult with CID bosses, to Edinburgh for conferences with Crown officials, and to Lancaster where he was present in the police office when Chief Constable Vann formally arrested Ruxton at 5 a.m. on Sunday 13 October. Ewing returned to Glasgow the next day.

Ewing received many tributes for his work on the case. The *News of the World* was one of the more sensationalist British newspapers, but there is no reason to suppose it was exaggerating when it described him as 'one of the most brilliant investigators of the Glasgow CID'. After the trial, the Director of Public Prosecutions in England, E. H. Tindal Atkinson, wrote to Glasgow's Chief Constable Percy Sillitoe to highlight 'the excellent work carried out by [his] officers, Detective Lieutenant Ewing and Detective Lieutenant Hammond'. In 1937, he was not only promoted to Superintendent but received an MBE in the

Coronation Honours List. The Lancaster officers didn't forget the man they referred to as 'the big Scotsman' either. As a token of appreciation, they took up a collection for a silver rose bowl and donated it to their colleagues in Glasgow to use in police bowling competitions.

The second year it was awarded, the winner was William Ewing.

★  ★  ★

In March 1946, the King's Theatre in Glasgow's Bath Street staged a now forgotten play by St. John L. Clowes entitled *Dear Murderer*. A melodrama about a husband who decides to dispose of his wife's lover and make it look like suicide, the production was described by one critic as 'a new exercise in polite murder'.

Only a few minutes away from the plush red seats of the grand circle, murders of a far less polite kind were regularly being committed in the less salubrious areas of the city. Chief Superintendent Ewing's department did, however, have considerable success in clearing these up. Between 1946 and 1951, for example, the Chief Constable's annual reports list fifty-eight cases of murder, attempted murder and culpable homicide and only three of these remained unsolved.

It's commonly thought that if you had murdered someone in the fifties, you'd have been hanged. Until 1957, the death penalty was indeed the statutory punishment for murder, but it was comparatively rare for the execution to be carried out. Juries would often make a recommendation of mercy and the sentence would be reduced on appeal. Between 1946 and 1963, when the final hanging in Scotland took place in Aberdeen, only fifteen hangings took place in Scotland, ten of them at Barlinnie Prison in Glasgow.

It might well have been eleven had it not been for a brother's last-minute confession. After a brawl in the backcourt of a Govan tenement in July 1950, thirty-eight-year-old Martin Dunleavy was taken by a friend to the police station near where he lived in Neptune Street. He received first aid but later died in hospital. By 3 a.m. three men had been charged with his murder including two brothers, Claude and Paul Harris. At the High Court in Glasgow in September the third man was found not guilty, though he was sent to prison on a separate assault charge. Both the Harris brothers were sentenced to death but, before he went to the gallows, Paul confessed that it had been his hand that struck Martin Dunleavy in the throat with a broken bottle and as a result Claude's execution was delayed for a week to allow the Secretary of State to consider this new information. He sat anxiously in the condemned cell at Barlinnie until 2 November when he was told that his sentence had been commuted to life imprisonment.

Paul's parting gift to his brother was an extra thirty-five years of life – even though he did spend much of it behind bars.

In his career as CID Chief, William Ewing would direct enquiries into many similar random and often inexplicable acts of violence which ended in loss of life. In September 1947, for instance, he was called to a tenement flat in Alexandra Parade where a joiner, George Hay, came home from work to find his sixty-three-year-old sister Christina lying dead. Years of experience enabled Ewing to reconstruct the sequence of events and his comments on the scene reveal his careful, methodical approach. 'She had been struck a blow or blows to the head with a blunt instrument,' he said. 'The doors of the house are fitted with Yale locks and the keys were found on the kitchen table. It would appear, therefore, that she had opened the door to her assailant who on leaving pulled both doors behind him.' The body was found at 5.50 p.m. and door-to-door enquiries went on far into the night. By 1.30 a.m. Ewing had found out what he needed to know and he and three other officers set off for Leith where they arrested an eighteen-year-old former member of the Merchant Navy – just ten hours after the discovery of the murder.

One current Dennistoun resident vividly recalls her mother telling her a story in connection with this case. During the war years a lady lived in a ground floor flat in nearby Meadowpark Street with her young daughter, her husband being away on military service. She frequently saw a man looking in the window and, naturally frightened, reported this to the police on more than one occasion, only to be told, 'Here, Missus, dae you no know there's a war on? We've better things tae dae than search for folk lookin' in windaes!' After the murder had taken place, she went straight back to the police office and asked, 'Well, what do you say now?'

Medical experts could find no motive for the killer's behaviour. There were no signs of robbery or disturbance in the flat. The assailant had already undergone treatment in a mental institution and he was found insane and unfit to plead. Sir David Kennedy Henderson, a specialist from Edinburgh, said that 'he appeared to have been dominated by impulsive action and could give no explanation of the tragedy. Throughout his life he had been lacking in emotional control … and was a danger to his fellow men.'

When unstable individuals got their hands on guns, the consequences could be even more horrific, such as in December 1945 at Pollokshields East railway station on the south side of the city.[1] Ewing described the crime committed that night as 'one of the most callous and cold-blooded that had ever been perpetrated in Glasgow'. On a cold, foggy evening, three members of the L.M.S. (London, Midland and Scottish) railway staff were keeping warm in the stationmaster's office when a man burst in, saying, 'This is a hold-up!' There had been plenty of incidents of that kind across the city in the previous few months since the end of the war, but this one was different. Without further warning, the gunman successively shot clerk Annie Withers, fifteen-year-old porter Robert Gough and forty-two-year-old clerk William Wright. Withers, still

---

1. Several well-known murder cases have been covered in detail in a number of other books and are only discussed briefly in these pages in relation to the role played by prominent CID men. For a fuller account of cases such as the Pollokshields East Station murders, the killing of John Brady in Washington Street (October 1945), the shootings in Hyndland (August 1952), the murder of Betty Alexander in Garnethill (October 1952), the murder of Ellen Petrie in West George Street Lane (June 1956) and of John Cremin in Queens Park (April 1960), see *The Book of Glasgow Murders* by Donald M. Fraser (Neil Wilson Publishing, 2009).

screaming, was shot again twice. The junior porter who moved to help her received a bullet in his stomach.

The gunman then raided the office next door and made off with wages from the safe to the value of £4 3 shillings and 8 pence [approximately £4.19]. When he had left, Wright was able to crawl out and phone for help. He later recovered from his injuries but Annie Withers died on her way to hospital. Young Robert Gough lay in the Victoria Infirmary with detectives keeping a thirty-six hour vigil by his beside. Before he died, he managed to give them a description of 'a ginger haired man in a light raincoat', this being the type of coat supplied to demobilised soldiers.

With little else to go on, CID followed up a report from Oban of a man fitting the description who had arrived on an early morning train from Glasgow and was seen in a tearoom reading an account of the crime in a newspaper. He mentioned it to the waitress and appeared worried about it. Next, Ewing authorised the printing of a cryptic message in the press. It simply said: 'RIGHT. The full significance of this word is known to the party concerned.' This proved to be a reference to an anonymous letter sent to the police and the idea was to signal to the writer, who signed off with the word 'RIGHT', that his or her communication had been received. A further line of enquiry involved teams of detectives questioning city landladies as to whether any of their lodgers had departed suddenly after the murders.

Whether the contents of the letter were of any help was not revealed. Even an offer of £1,000 reward failed to elicit anything more definite. Newspapers resorted to stating that Ewing's men were working day and night on the case – which really meant the journalists had nothing new to tell their readers.

The mystery was unexpectedly cleared up in August of the following year, not as a result of a detective's brilliant hunch or even by patient footslogging enquiries but because a recently recruited PC happened to be at the right place at the right time.

On 10 October 1946, William Ewing issued a dramatic state-ment: about 10 o'clock that morning two constables of the Southern

Division had telephoned their headquarters to request assistance with a man they had detained in Spean Street. Detective Lieutenant McDougall and Detective Sergeant McKenzie were sent to take the individual to the Southern police office where he was charged with the murder of Anne Withers and Robert Gough and the assault of William Wright.

The man in question was twenty-year-old Charles Templeman Brown, a railway fireman and former soldier. He approached Constable John Byrne who was on points duty in Newlands Road and confessed to the Pollokshields murders. The astonished Byrne, who had only been in the force for seven months, took him to the nearest police box where Brown handed over a Luger automatic revolver and a box of ammunition with the words, 'you might as well have it'. He explained how he had tried to commit suicide that morning on the banks of the River Cart. In the police box, he wrote a note on the telephone message pad to a friend in the Highland Light Infantry, in which he said, 'I woke up knowing I had to give myself up. I hope by this rotten crime I have not lost your friendship.'

At his trial in December, five specialists in mental illness testified that Brown was someone of 'gross mental abnormality' and, if not insane, was only a hairsbreadth away from it. One expert diagnosed him as a schizophrenic. In interviews, Brown talked about his interest in Mussolini, Hitler and the Belsen concentration camp and reckoned that the authorities were dealing with him in far too lenient a manner, saying that he wanted to be 'shot in the back and finished'.

He was indeed sentenced to death and no appeal was lodged, but the leniency of which Brown complained continued to be shown to him: he was reprieved at the last minute and went on to serve only ten years of his sentence before being released in 1957.

Chief Superintendent Ewing was personally handling murder enquiries right up to the last few days before he retired in 1951. On a Saturday night in early March, he was on the scene when a man's body was discovered in Gallowgate and he worked all through the night along with Gilbert McIlwrick, his close colleague since the 1920s and the man who would soon take over from him as CID Chief. By Monday, the culprits were in court.

Willie Ewing was someone who did not seek the limelight, but as he approached his retirement he received several accolades. In February 1951, he was invited to be a member of a newly formed dining club for the most eminent figures in the medical-legal field. Named 'the Half Century Club', its president was John Cameron, KC, Dean of the Faculty of Advocates and others in this select band included experts with whom Ewing had visited many a crime scene – Professor Glaister, Dr Imrie, the chief medical officer to the city police, and Chief Inspector George Maclean of the police scientific bureau. The following month, colleagues gathered at police headquarters to listen to Ewing deliver his retirement speech. The script of this has survived and, instead of the usual collection of reminiscences, it proved to be a rather formal lecture in which he reviewed how policing had changed over the previous four decades. He took advantage of the occasion to make clear what he thought was needed to halt the ever growing crime rate, making a plea for more men on the beat and tougher sentences. 'Leniency has had a fair trial and in some instances has been overdone,' he said. Nevertheless, he drew some comfort from the fact that forty years of experience had taught him that crime does not pay. Having done a careful analysis of the criminal returns, Ewing noted that 'almost without exception these law-breakers have died either in a poorhouse or in destitution or they have committed violence, been hanged for murder or have themselves been murdered. Very few have died in their own beds'.

Maybe Ewing recalled that statement when he learnt of the fate of Charles Brown, convicted of the Pollokshields Station murders. In 1960, three years after his early release from prison, he was killed in a car crash.

# 4

## *The Cop Killer and the Killer Cop*

*John Caldwell (1946) and James Robertson (1950)*

Two high-profile murder cases during William Ewing's period as CID Chief involved police officers from the Glasgow force – one as the victim and the other as the killer. The murderers came from very different backgrounds and became caught up in situations that quickly moved beyond their control. In the end, though, both shared the same fate.

Edinburgh Road is a long, wide dual carriageway, which starts at the end of Alexandra Parade in the Dennistoun area of Glasgow and makes its way through Carntyne, Barlanark and Garrowhill until it eventually joins the motorway towards Edinburgh. The 1930s Glasgow Corporation houses are now mostly owner occupied and have a lighter exterior appearance than their earlier drab grey roughcast finish, but in most respects the scene today is much as it would have been in 1946 – except, of course, that there's a lot more traffic.

Traffic was particularly light on the evening of Tuesday 26 March 1946. James Deakan, who lived at no. 524, had enjoyed an afternoon off work that day and he and his wife were on their way back from a local cinema at about 8.30 p.m. Most of their neighbours were indoors listening to the radio, laughing along to one of Richmal Crompton's 'Just

William' stories on the Light Programme. As the couple approached their semi-detached house, they noticed a light was on upstairs – and in these days people didn't usually leave a light on when they went out. Thinking an intruder had entered, Deakan sent his wife to ask the man next door to come and help him investigate what was going on.

He had the ideal neighbour for the job, for James Straiton was a retired Detective Sergeant from the Eastern Division who had received ten commendations during his police career. Like many other officers, he had left the force to take up more lucrative security work, in this case as an investigator for a hire purchase scheme operated by the furnishing firm of Gow and Sons of Hope Street. Mr Deakan was also in the furniture business, being employed as manager of Jay's in Sauchiehall Street. No doubt they had plenty to chat about over the garden fence on summer evenings.

Former sergeant Straiton had been looking after his three-year-old granddaughter who was asleep upstairs but, drawing on instincts honed by decades of experience, he at once armed himself with a baton and went next door. Mrs Deakan tried to unlock the front door but the key would not turn. Going round the back, the two men discovered that the scullery window had been forced and Deakan managed to squeeze through, switch on the lights and open the front door from the inside. As he did so, he said to Straiton, 'it looks as if the birds have flown'. It was a tragically mistaken assumption. At that point, two men rushed down the stairs brandishing four guns, one in each hand.

Deakan and Straiton were certainly no cowards: they barred the intruders' way in an attempt to stop them leaving the house. Even when the gunmen threatened to 'let them have it', the two neighbours didn't flinch, telling them, 'Drop your guns, boys. You're not getting away tonight.' According to Deakan's own account, one of the men then fired at him and missed. He and Straiton grappled with the pair on the doorstep, in the course of which the former policeman struck one of them with his baton. This man then shot Straiton in the stomach at a distance of three inches, and when Deakan bent down to assist him, the duo made their escape down the garden path.

Mrs Deakan showed considerable courage, too. A bus was stopped nearby and she had gone to tell the driver and conductor what was happening. She returned to her garden gate as the two men were fleeing and threw her husband's coat at one of them. They pushed her aside and ran down the street, turning round to fire in her direction as they did so. The bus set off in pursuit, but the fugitives turned down a street too narrow for the vehicle to enter, so the crew headed back to their depot to contact the police while Mrs Deakan sent for medical help. By the time Straiton reached hospital, he was pronounced dead.

This was clearly a major incident which called for investigation at the most senior level, involving not only William Ewing but two rising stars who, in due course, would succeed him: Superintendent Gilbert McIlwrick and Detective Lieutenant Robert Colquhoun, at the time in charge of the Eastern Division where the killing took place. One or other of these detectives would oversee every major murder enquiry in Glasgow over the next fifteen years.

For a number of reasons, the Straiton case is one of the best documented of the period. All the newspapers had their crime reporters, of course, but in this instance one of them gained an exclusive – a man called Hector McSporran. There were those who thought that sounded very much like a pseudonym, but it was in fact the real name of a reporter who, having shown promise as editor of the *Campbeltown Courier*, secured what he called his 'entry into big-time journalism' when the *Glasgow Herald* took him on in 1944. The *Daily Record* had six reporters and the *Scottish Daily Express* had ten, all of them looking for leads on the Carntyne murder, but somehow McSporran managed to win McIlwrick's trust and on this occasion it was the *Herald* that provided the best coverage. As well as that, there is Colquhoun's own account of the enquiry in his memoirs, *Life Begins at Midnight*, published in 1962. Yet another perspective can be found in the original criminal case file, which provides a chilling insight into the state of mind of the killer.

Colquhoun, who lived only minutes away, had just settled down to relax with a book for the evening when a police car arrived at his door to take him to the crime scene. It didn't take him long to find some useful evidence. To start with, there were good descriptions of the two suspects, one of whom was wearing a blue suit and a distinctive white scarf. A search of the garden and surrounding streets turned up some of the stolen goods – a camera, cigars and an unusable antique revolver – while the discovery of Deakan's fountain pen in nearby Abbeyhill Street shed further light on the culprits' escape route.

In addition, a pair of shoes had been left in the back garden near the drain pipe, belonging to one of the gunmen who had climbed in through a window before admitting his confederate through the front door which he then locked from the inside. A description of the shoes was issued: 'brown grain Derby, size 7½, with Goodyear diamond pattern rubber soles. There was evidence that the heels had been replaced.' Then there were the cartridges found in the garden, which came from a .45 Colt automatic pistol, hundreds of which had been left behind by American servicemen after the war. Ewing put out an appeal to the public: 'Surely any person with any knowledge of the men who committed such a dastardly deed will come to us with their information.'

Colquhoun quickly linked this evidence to several other recent housebreakings in the Dennistoun area.

A week before the killing, a burglar had entered a flat in Whitehill Street by climbing up the drain pipe, returning to the same property a few days later. This time the tenant had taken the precaution of locking an inner door but, instead of trying to kick it open, the trigger-happy housebreaker put a bullet through the lock.

Then, on 25 March, the day before the incident in Edinburgh Road, an elderly woman found herself confronted in her home in Golfhill Drive by an intruder wearing a white scarf threatening her with a gun.

The painstaking process of following up the clues began. Shoe shops and shoe repairers were systematically visited and eventually the man who purchased the shoes was traced – but he had given them away months before. The trail had gone cold.

Forensic evidence proved more promising. A fingerprint would eventually trap the killer in what one *Daily Record* journalist described as 'a classic piece of scientific detection'. While examining the house at Golfhill Drive, detectives noticed a small piece of glass missing from the front door where the burglar had broken in. Eventually it was found in the backcourt – and there was a partial fingerprint on it.

Meanwhile, the Lanarkshire police were investigating a spate of break-ins in the Mount Vernon area. The method of entry was the same as in Edinburgh Road: climbing up a drainpipe. A heel mark with a diamond pattern was found at one crime scene, and a fingerprint at another. As soon as he heard about the Straiton murder, Inspector William Muncie (who many years later would end his career as an Assistant Chief Constable in Strathclyde Police) immediately contacted his Glasgow colleagues, providing a key link in the chain of forensic evidence. The print matched up with the one found in Golfhill Drive and the experts in the Glasgow Police scientific headquarters in St Andrew's Street came up with a name from their thousands of files of prints: John Caldwell.

Colquhoun's account of what happened next captures all the drama of the event:

> Life begins at midnight on a manhunt. It's a cop's favourite time for a swoop or a round-up – from midnight on is the time when a crook or a killer is most likely to be resting up. The time, too, when the quarry is likely to be tired and sleepy, his resistance at bottom.

Scoring off addresses from a list of places across the city where the wanted man had relatives or associates, a team of armed detectives led by Colquhoun and Ewing eventually arrived at a tenement in Fielden Street in the Mile End district where they found Caldwell asleep in bed.

'At 2.20 this morning,' reported the *Glasgow Herald*, 'a patrol waggon, followed by three police cars, drove to the Central Police Station where Chief Superintendent William Ewing of the CID was waiting. It was announced subsequently that a young man would appear at the Eastern

Police Court, the initial charge being only for the Golfhill Drive break-in. Shortly afterwards, his fifteen-year-old accomplice was picked up.

John Caldwell was a twenty-year-old from a troubled background who had a track record of housebreaking. At the age of eleven, he had been sent to Thornly Park Approved School in Paisley. In 1945, he was sentenced to three years at Polmont Borstal, Falkirk but was released to serve in the army after twelve months. He then deserted from the Seaforth Highlanders and made his way back to Glasgow.

Honesty was never Caldwell's strong point and he initially told Colquhoun an unconvincing version of events and tried to pin the murder on someone else before finally admitting, 'It was me who shot the man.'

The trial at the High Court of Glasgow before Lord Stevenson began on June 25. It was not a long one. The father of the accused, fifty-seven-year-old James Caldwell, explained how his son and a fifteen-year-old boy came to his house after 9 p.m. on March 26. John was in his stockinged feet and had to borrow a pair of shoes. The next day, Caldwell Senior read in a newspaper about the events in Carntyne and went to see his son in his lodgings. When he asked him if he had a gun, John replied, 'Aye, it's in my pocket.' His father took it and threw it in the Clyde. In spite of extensive searches near Rutherglen Bridge using electro-magnets, it was never found.

There was a brief hiccup in proceedings when a juryman left the court room at the lunch interval. His disappearance was condemned as 'inexcusable' but the court agreed that the trial could still continue. Advocate Depute Douglas Johnson argued that 'an overwhelming body of evidence against the accused' had been presented. 'He was carrying those weapons for no other reason than that he set out to commit the offence of housebreaking and intended to use them either to intimidate any householder or to facilitate a getaway.' Professor John Glaister gave a detailed account of the injuries which killed Straiton, while Detective Lieutenant George Maclean of the Scientific Bureau not only confirmed that the bullet extracted from the former policeman's body was the same calibre as the three empty cartridge cases found at the scene but even gave the court a demonstration of what was involved in 'shooting from the hip'.

If there was to be any hope for Caldwell, it would lie in an examination of his state of mind. But Dr Angus MacNiven, physician superintendent of the Glasgow Royal Mental Hospital, maintained that he could not certify Caldwell insane, though he added rather vaguely that 'there is something peculiar in his attitude', which MacNiven put down to 'a kind of toughness that he has built up in the course of his life in order to get along. I think this man has had a very hard life.'

In the absence of any convincing medical evidence to the contrary, the Advocate Depute told the jury: 'Steel your hearts and do your duty as citizens of Glasgow and return a verdict – the only proper verdict in this case – that the accused is guilty as libelled.' The jurors took only fifty minutes to reach a majority verdict: guilty of murder, though they added a rider recommending mercy on account of his age. Lord Stevenson pronounced the death sentence, fixing the execution for 17 July at Barlinnie Prison. He said the jury's recommendation of mercy would be 'forwarded to the proper quarter'.

The unnamed 'fifteen-year-old lad' who accompanied Caldwell was by this stage 'an inmate of an institution'.

Notes kept by the warders who guarded the prisoner at Barlinnie reveal a good deal about his family relationships and state of mind in the last few weeks of his sorry existence.[2] The visit from his father on 28 June did not go well. Smelling of drink, James Caldwell told his son not to worry – the hanging would only involve five minutes of pain. John replied that he was the one who would hang, not his father. A more sympathetic bond existed between the young man and his sister, Mary. On a visit on 1 July, she told him that 'Mr Colquhoun had been up to the house getting particulars of his past life and she had told him of how their father was hardly ever sober.' There was also a visit from a friend called Mrs Moffat of Kilmun, John's landlady when he had worked in Argyll for eighteen months,

2. Criminal Case file, John Caldwell, Crown copyright, National Records of Scotland (HH16/642/1)

who perhaps provided the care and affection the young killer lacked in his childhood. She had written to tell him that she was praying for him and that good times might come again, and when she visited, she said that 'his home will be across the water when he comes out of Peterhead' – it's clear that throughout his final weeks Caldwell convinced himself that he would not hang but would serve a spell in the Aberdeenshire prison.

His appeal against conviction was heard on 23 July but the judges held that 'The fact that Caldwell fired the fatal shot was established beyond doubt and the jury were entitled to find criminal intent.' The defence had argued for 'diminished responsibility on the grounds of peculiarity of mind amounting almost, but not quite, to mental disorder' yet the medical evidence indicated that 'Caldwell was completely callous about the consequences of his actions on other people' and, in the opinion of Lord Normand, Lord Justice Clerk, 'evidence of ruthlessness, of callousness, and of disregard for others is, in fact, evidence of a criminal character and not evidence of diminished responsibility'. Even in his final weeks in prison, Caldwell showed little sign of regret.

At the same time as the appeal process, preparations for the execution were going forward remorselessly. The Barlinnie Governor wrote to the Lord Provost's office, intimating that 'the necessary ropes and straps have been received from Wandsworth Prison'. By 5 August, prison officers described Caldwell as very quiet and worried. If he was not reprieved, he said, he would 'swing' on 10 August. He added that his ghost would wander round Barlinnie Prison – but he still showed no sign of any remorse. He went as far as saying that he was sorry for 'not cutting up Straiton's body, as he would have been proved insane and that he would have got clear'.

A letter from the Scottish Home Department dated 7 August confirmed the inevitable: there were no grounds for a reprieve.

On 9 August, the prisoner received a last visit from his family. Mary cried most of the time but John was 'composed and cheerful'. After a 'slight outburst' against detectives, he told her not to come up to the prison next day and wished goodbye to his father and sister.

John Caldwell was executed at 8 a.m. the next day.

There was one thing left for the authorities to do. Deserter though he was, Caldwell had still been wearing his army battledress, trousers and greatcoat and these were duly returned to Maryhill Barracks. Whether they were subsequently issued to some unsuspecting recruit is not recorded.

The wife of the murder victim had to rebuild her life as best she could. Praise had been lavished on former Detective Sergeant Straiton, a 'conscientious and courageous police officer' whose actions on that fateful night in March had been prompted by 'a high sense of citizenship'. That was all very well, but it didn't help look after his widow who had been awarded a pension of just £30 a year. Her application to Glasgow Corporation for a special pension under the terms of the Police Pension Act in view of the circumstances of her husband's death was rejected on the grounds that such payments could only be made to widows of serving officers. Straiton's former colleagues stepped in to make up the shortfall. Policemen throughout Scotland subscribed their support and a football match and a 'variety and cinema show' organised by the Glasgow force also contributed 'a substantial sum'.

As has happened so often before and since, the police were left to look after their own.

★ ★ ★

The murder of a policeman is something that takes place all too regularly in the annals of crime; cases where the murderer is himself a member of the force occur much more rarely.

On 6 November 1950, the public gallery at Glasgow High Court was packed and more than 100 people had gathered in the street outside, though they had been told there was no chance of admission. Inside the court, thirty-seven reporters jostled with each other for the fourteen seats allocated to the press. In the dock was a 6 foot 2 ½ inch policeman dressed in a blue double-breasted suit. James Ronald Robertson, known to many as 'Big Ronnie', was charged with murdering Catherine McCluskey on 28 July. He was alleged to have 'struck the deceased on the head with a truncheon and by that or some other unknown means rendered her insensible and thereafter driven a motor car bearing a false registration over her'.

This was – to put it mildly – a slightly different version of events from the one which Robertson recorded in the police box on his beat in the Gorbals area when he was on nightshift. Timed at 2.10 a.m., his entry read: 'At 12.50 a.m. today a woman was knocked down and fatally injured in Prospecthill Road at Aitkenhead Road . . . The car did not stop and was last seen driving citywards.'

The reality was that thirty-three-year-old PC Robertson, a married man with two children, had been carrying on a relationship with Catherine McCluskey and was believed to be the father of one of her two sons. He was in the habit of calling in for a quick visit while on duty and his activities were not unknown to his colleagues in the force. On the night in question (according to Constable Douglas Moffat, who was on the neighbouring beat), he had excused himself at about 11.15 p.m., saying he was 'going to take a blonde home' – though Robertson later dismissed that remark as a joke that wasn't meant to be taken literally. He did not reappear until nearly two hours later, sweating profusely and claiming that the exhaust pipe on the car he was driving had broken.

Fifteen minutes before Robertson returned to his duties, a taxi driver on his way back to Rutherglen discovered a woman's body lying on the roadside, her face matted with blood. He immediately called the police and when Constable William Kevan of the Traffic Department arrived he quickly realised that he was not dealing with a simple accident of the hit-and-run variety. In his evidence at the trial he described the grisly scene that confronted him: 'The whole way up the road there were flesh, blood, fatty substance and skin tissue ground into the road surface. A dental plate had been broken up. There was no substantial pool of blood.' In Kevan's judgement, the injuries were too severe to have been caused by a road accident and when he noticed two converging tyre marks across the body, he began to suspect that it had been placed on the road before it was run over.

This was clearly a matter for the CID. Neighbours of the dead woman confirmed that a policeman regularly called on her, sometimes arriving in a car and taking her for a run down the coast. Robertson was on duty on his next shift when Detective Chief Inspector Donald McDougall and Sergeant McAllister of the Southern Division met him in Eglinton Street.

'Is there any need to tell you who this is?' asked the Sergeant.

'Oh no,' replied Robertson. 'It's Mr McDougall.'

He was duly cautioned and charged and the detectives searched his home where they found two car log books, a wireless set and a ring with eighteen car keys on it. Robertson claimed he had found these items in a backcourt; as for the Austin he was driving about in, it had been abandoned in Hillington Road and he had managed to start it and drive it away. However, when he turned up to his shift driving the car, he told Constable Moffat it belonged to a friend. It later emerged that Robertson had fitted false number plates.

In other words, the policeman was a car thief.

When Robertson entered the witness box on 11 November he clearly had some explaining to do. Medical expert Dr Andrew Allison endorsed Constable Kevan's opinion: the injuries were 'more gross' than any that might have been caused by a private car. He identified as many as thirty external injuries, some made before and some after death. The nature of these indicated that the woman could not have been standing when the vehicle struck her. But throughout two and a half hours of cross-examination, Robertson maintained that 'it was an absolute accident'. He resolutely denied being involved in any sort of relationship with Catherine McCluskey. Did he take her out with the intention of murdering her? 'No, sir, I certainly did not.' He conceded she had been in the car with him and that they had had a row. He pushed her out and left her on the kerb, shouting at him but then decided it was unfair to leave her to find her way home alone in the darkness and reversed the car to go back for her. He felt something underneath and realised he had run her over.

In the absence of eyewitnesses, the key piece of evidence was the Austin and, at one point, the jury members were taken out to inspect the car. Forensic examination confirmed that hairs retrieved from the underside of the vehicle were those of Catherine McCluskey. Furthermore, the propeller shaft was enclosed in such a way that if the car had knocked down a pedestrian, clothing would not have become entangled in it.

Summing up, Lord Keith said that 'by no accounts was it an ordinary accident and it was a very unordinary accident if the accused's story were accepted . . . If the Crown case was right, then it was a deliberate and diabolical murder.' He added that the jury needed to consider whether 'this was just a casual acquaintanceship with an occasional lift in a car as an obligement, or whether there was more to the relationship.'

It was the opinion of his lawyer, Laurence Dowdall – a name which crops up in many prominent Scottish murder trials of the fifties – that if Robertson had admitted his relationship and had come clean about whatever argument or fight took place before the murder, then the possible existence of an element of provocation might have saved him from his fate. But he publicly denied the liaison in the belief that this would stop his wife Janet being shamed and stared straight ahead with a blank expression on his face when the death sentence was passed.

Afterwards, Janet also stood by her husband. 'We often went for walks with the children along the beat Ronnie patrolled,' she told a reporter. 'Was that the action of a man who was carrying on a double life?'

If John Caldwell, the killer of ex-Sergeant Straiton, was a young man whose descent into a life of crime had a certain predictability about it, the opposite was true of 'Big Ronnie' Robertson. He had a strict upbringing in a Christian Brethren family in Clydebank and an unblemished record of employment in Beardmore's engineering, the Singer sewing machine factory and Rolls Royce at Hillington where he was an inspector of aircraft engines. It was a standing joke among work colleagues that he had no interest in women, but in 1942 he surprised everyone by marrying the daughter of a Canadian policeman with whom he had two children. The newspapers summed him up as a 'teetotal, non-smoking, church-going family man'. Yet Robertson started to change after joining the police in 1945. The needs of the job required assertiveness and, at times, aggression, and he began to conduct himself in a similar manner off as well as on duty.

At 6.33 p.m. on 13 November 1950, Robertson was officially received into Barlinnie Prison, in preparation for his execution scheduled for 4 December. Thereafter, he followed a parallel course to that of Caldwell four years earlier and, in some respects, revealed a similar mindset as his fate loomed ever closer.

He and another condemned prisoner, Matthew Graham, were asked if they minded sharing a cell and both welcomed the chance of company. Robertson is recorded as having talked to Graham about 'making a run for it' and heading for Edinburgh though such an escape would have been highly unlikely. Like his cellmate, and Caldwell before him, Robertson appealed against his sentence but he was unsuccessful.

A new date of 16 December was set for the execution and while he awaited the inevitable the disgraced constable adopted an attitude typical of many in his position. His prison guard reported to the Governor that Robertson told Dowdall that 'he thought his counsel did not cross-examine enough the witnesses who were against him and also stated that the buzz that was going on about him did much to influence the jury in their findings'.[3] Similarly, he wrote to Janet that 'the Jury and Judges were very obviously very biased against me' and condemned 'those press hounds' who 'have done enough damage already'.

Yet, even after the failure of his appeal, he remained optimistic that the Secretary of State would grant him a reprieve. On 4 December, he wrote to Janet (whom he called Nettie): 'Please try and bear up Nettie darling. I know it is nearly unbearable at times but I'll come back from this and we will all be together again.' He was heartened to hear on 9 December that his cellmate Graham had been reprieved and told his brother that he, too, hoped for good news soon.

---

3. Criminal Case file, James Ronald Robertson, Crown copyright, National Records of Scotland (HH16/642/17 and HH16/643).

Four days later, however, he was informed that the Secretary of State had decided that he could 'find no grounds to interfere with the due course of law'.

Although Robertson saw the prison chaplain regularly, he rejected a request for a visit from an evangelist of the Church of God in Clydebank, a congregation with which he had at one time been associated. He was also sent a letter from a Church of Scotland minister who had retired to Cambridge. Enclosing a tract and a copy of St John's Gospel, the minister urged him to repent of his sins and wrote that 'God has laid upon my heart a burden for your soul's salvation. I have been praying for you and feel that I must write to you.'

But the well-meaning gesture came to nothing: the prison authorities never passed on the communication. Across the envelope they scrawled the words 'No' and 'From Stranger' in red pencil and put the letter in the prisoner's file where it remains to this day.

Robertson's last recorded comments come from a conversation with his wife and brother on 15 December. He told his visitors that he 'was framed by the police and he wondered how the policemen felt now who had given evidence against him. It would be on their conscience all their lives.' The only thing he admitted feeling guilty about was stealing the car – in a final letter to his wife, he wrote that 'I'm praying for your Mum too that she might forgive and forget my car episode but I know she knows that was my worst mistake, the running around in the stolen car.'

At 8 a.m. the next morning Constable Robertson, whether penitent or in denial, went to meet his Maker.

Once again, former police colleagues collected money to help a widow. They raised enough for her to go abroad and start a new life.

# 5

## *The Quiet Man*

*Detective Chief Superintendent Gilbert McIlwrick, CID Chief
1951–57*

On Friday 10 December 1937, four inches of snow fell on the city of
Edinburgh. It was turning to slush by the late afternoon when a senior
police officer left the High Court and made his way down to Waverley
Station. He was in a hurry because he had been delayed at the end of
the day's proceedings and was rushing to be in time for the 5.30 p.m.
train back to Glasgow Queen Street.

If he had caught it, Detective Lieutenant Gilbert McIlwrick might
not have lived to become boss of Glasgow CID some fourteen years
later. The train to Glasgow, travelling at an estimated seventy miles
per hour in whiteout conditions, plunged into the rear coaches of a
stationary local train near Falkirk, resulting in the loss of thirty-five
lives. This tragic event would go down in history as the Castlecary
disaster, Britain's worst ever snow-related railway accident.

That narrow escape was just one remarkable episode in a life packed
with drama. Yet, although McIlwrick had been a respected figure in
police and legal circles since the late 1920s, few members of the general
public had heard of him until he took over as head of Glasgow CID
in 1951. Part of the reason lay in his personality: one journalist at the

time described him as 'self-effacing and publicity-shy' while a colleague characterised him as 'a quiet-spoken man with a remarkable memory for detail'. In these respects he was not unlike his predecessor William Ewing, six years his senior, and both men often worked on investigations together.

Born in the village of Cronberry near Cumnock in East Ayrshire in 1897, McIlwrick, like Ewing, came from a family with a tradition of police service. His father, John McIlwrick (1871–1954) was a police inspector in Ardrossan and Gilbert attended the Academy there. He subsequently saw action during the First World War with a motor transport unit, joining Glasgow police in 1919.

Publicity-shy he may have been, but, in his first few years as a constable in the Southern Division, McIlwrick carefully cut out newspaper reports of cases he was involved in and pasted them into a scrapbook which he also used to keep magazine cuttings and advertisements relating to his hobby of stamp-collecting. The crimes reported on occurred almost a century ago and they seem to belong to a different world. Much of the young constable's time was taken up dealing with minor offences relating to drink which, on account of the licensing laws of the era, took a very different form from today. In this period there was a proliferation of unlicensed drinking premises known as shebeens, particularly in areas with a high proportion of Irish immigrants. These would often be run by a woman working from her own tenement. A typical case from June 1920 reads as follows:

> Having supplied a woman with a glass of whisky, for which she was paid 2 shillings, in a house at 286 Mathieson Street, Glasgow, Elizabeth McAvoy or Russell was fined £5, with the option of 30 days' imprisonment, in the Divisional Police Court, where she admitted a charge of shebeening.

Much police activity also related to illegal gambling. There were no betting shops and until 1961 betting could only be carried on at racecourses, by telephone or by post. As a result, in working-class areas, street bookies would set up temporary pitches in tenement closes or on vacant ground near factories, aided by watchers and runners.

Many stories are told of the ingenious ruses employed in connection with these activities – and not just by the perpetrators. In February 1920, Constable Dawson, disguised as a plumber carrying a kit of tools and a blowlamp and accompanied by his labourer (aka PC McIlwrick), apprehended Joseph Donnachie, who was 'loitering in Thistle Street for the purpose of receiving bets', for which he received a fine of £10 at the police court. On another occasion McIlwrick had a man under observation in the Gorbals but when he arrested him could find no betting lines on him, though he was carrying a large sum of £23 cash on his person. It was only when McIlwrick examined the suspect's hands that he found the names of the horses written there in ink.

In the same vein, a man claiming to be a dock labourer was caught loitering in Eglinton and Bedford Streets. McIlwrick and a colleague had watched the accused taking something from several workmen during their lunch hour but once again, he had nothing on him when arrested. The explanation soon became apparent: a girl came up every few minutes, received 'something' from the man and then quickly disappeared. The usual penalty for these activities was a fine of £10 or sixty days' imprisonment if this was not paid – something that the bookies would cover as a necessary business expense. There were, in fact, occasions where the police chose to turn a blind eye to street betting or even, if it suited their purposes, tip off a bookie about a forthcoming raid.

Another amusing incident from McIlwrick's early days involved a beggar with a disappearing arm. One day in September 1920, an elderly man appeared at the Southern Police Court charged with having procured alms on the 'false and fraudulent pretence that his left arm was injured or deformed'. The observant young constable saw him take up a position on Victoria Bridge, draw his arm out of the sleeve and pin the sleeve to his jacket. After waiting until several passers-by had taken pity on the beggar and given him some money, McIlwrick and his neighbour went up to him, pulled out the pins from his jacket and revealed the missing arm!

Some top detectives spent many years on the beat but, after just two years, the quick-thinking recruit from Ardrossan had made such a good impression that he was able to join the CID, where he was involved in the arrest of Frank Carty, the escaped IRA leader who was tracked down in a house in Springburn on 30 April 1921. Unlike his colleague William Ewing, McIlwrick is not recorded as being present at the sensational sequel on 4 May when armed supporters unsuccessfully attempted to free Carty from a police van on its way to Duke Street Prison.

In addition to his ability to make arrests, a more cerebral skill noted by McIlwrick's superiors was his flair for mathematics, which led him to be entrusted with a complex fraud case in 1927, even though he was still a comparatively inexperienced detective. As a result, he was promoted to Detective Sergeant. His success in this area proved to be the turning point in his career as Chief Constable Percy Sillitoe turned to McIlwrick to take charge of a new commercial section within the CID to deal with fraud. Over the next four years he oversaw a significant clean up in crimes of embezzlement, fraud and bankruptcy, with eight solicitors being among those arrested.

Now with the rank of Detective Lieutenant, he led the enquiry into what came to be known as the Oriental Rug fraud case of 1936. Numerous businessmen across the country had been swindled out of a total of a quarter of a million pounds, yet none was prepared to name the individual responsible. Eventually a Glasgow man who had lost £20,000 provided McIlwrick with the necessary evidence to convict the culprits and reports of the trial at the High Court in Edinburgh filled many newspaper columns in December 1937. It appeared that the wealthy victim had, in the words of the judge, 'parted with his money with a lavishness and light-heartedness that seem simply astonishing', purchasing carpets, rugs and tapestries for exorbitant prices from the conmen who, among other underhand tricks, persuaded an unemployed man to disguise himself as a 'Colonial from Canada' in an attempt to sell goods to the gullible victim. Thanks to the efforts of McIlwrick and his colleagues, the four men behind the fraud received sentences ranging from eighteen months in prison to four years' penal servitude. In passing sentence Lord Aitchison, Lord Justice Clerk, considered it important for the Court to demonstrate that to condone fraud would be 'a blow struck at the integrity of our business life'.

Lack of integrity in local government can be even more difficult to root out. During the 1930s, the police frequently received anonymous communications alleging 'graft' in Glasgow Corporation with regard to licensing matters, housing and the operations of the ratings and valuations department. In 1933, a trader in the city's meat market reported that she had been offered a stall in a more favourable location in exchange for a payment of £25 to two magistrates (bailies). This led to the conviction of one of these officials but a further enquiry into the extent of corruption in the Corporation could not gather sufficient evidence.

Some years later a better opportunity presented itself and Gilbert McIlwrick played a key role in an exciting piece of undercover work . . . although the operation did not quite go according to plan.

In Sauchiehall Street, there's an imposing building that has been described as Glasgow's first skyscraper. Now divided into private apartments, this was originally the Beresford Hotel, opened in 1938 to accommodate visitors to the city's Empire Exhibition. During the war, it was a popular meeting place for American servicemen who must have felt at home in the splendour of its Art Deco surroundings.

In the early forties, a licensing problem arose but the hotel's managing director, Hugh Fraser, was told by Bailie Hugh Campbell of the Corporation's licensing committee that he could ensure the hotel's licence would be renewed without any difficulties. All he had to do was hand over £120.

Fraser promptly informed the police. The required sum of money was prepared in marked notes and a hidden microphone installed in Fraser's office where the handover was due to take place, with McIlwrick listening in on the floor above.

The subsequent series of mishaps is related by Sillitoe in his autobiography *Cloak Without Dagger*, published in 1955 and now long out of print. First, the listening equipment didn't work and though police engineers quickly arrived on the scene, they could not repair it. A Plan B was hastily devised and the engineers rigged up an extension to the office's telephone intercom – not a moment too soon, for the dishonest bailie's car had just drawn up outside and he strode into the hotel foyer telling the porter to 'show me Fraser's room'. Unfortunately, the porter misunderstood and took him instead to one of the hotel's conference suites known as 'the Frazer Room' – the very place where McIlwrick was sitting surrounded by wires and listening equipment. Campbell took fright and fled, but ran into Mr Fraser on his way out. Fraser tried to convince him that engineers were simply testing the hotel's phone system and eventually the handover of the money did take place, outside in Campbell's car.

But there was a war on, and at this moment an air-raid siren sounded and Campbell hastily drove off. Disappointed but undaunted, McIlwrick and William Ewing obtained a warrant and turned up at his house early the following morning, though with little hope that he would still have the marked notes. Ewing and McIlwrick were two of Glasgow's most determined detectives and, in spite of Campbell's denials, they made a thorough search of the house and found the money hidden up a bedroom chimney. Campbell served a six-month prison sentence for his dishonesty, and he also started naming names, resulting in the conviction of a further three Corporation members. One of them was the convener of the Police Committee.

McIlwrick's reputation was such that when Glasgow CID received requests from other forces for assistance with difficult investigations, he was often the one chosen. In August 1941, for example, Moray and Nairn police called for help in tracking down the killer of a seventeen-year-old baker's shop assistant whose body was found in a wood by two children on their way to help with potato digging. Her skull had been crushed and a bloodstained stone lay nearby. McIlwrick, accompanied by Detective Inspector W. Barron, was sent up to investigate and he arrested a young soldier four days later.

A much greater challenge was presented by the murder of Gertrude Canning, a Wren (i.e. a member of the Women's Royal Naval Services) whose body was discovered with four bullet wounds at Inveraray in July 1942. Witnesses had seen the young Irish girl going into the town to post a letter and had also observed a soldier following her down a wooded path on her way back to base. She had been shot with a standard British Army .38 revolver and there were thousands of men stationed nearby with just such a weapon. In spite of a mammoth effort to test every available weapon and transport all the sample bullets to Scotland Yard for analysis, the killer was never found. This case is discussed in more detail in chapter eight.

It led McIlwrick to recommend to the Chief Constable that a scientific bureau be formed so that such testing could be carried out more quickly. Since 1926 the Glasgow force had been building up records of the *modus operandi* (M.O.) of known criminals and after being promoted to Detective Superintendent in 1943 McIlwrick developed this system further to include in-depth descriptions of distinctive personal features – scars, tattoos, peculiarities of speech, and so on. Its value was demonstrated in the speedy arrest of the murderer of former Detective Sergeant James Straiton during the burglary in Carntyne in 1946.

Yet, while McIlwrick was ready to employ the latest methods where appropriate, he was sometimes impatient with the notion that crimes could be solved in the laboratory. Most detection, he said, is done 'by simple question and answer, painstaking enquiry and meticulous searching for information'. It was by such means that McIlwrick usually got his results. 'If there is a more painstaking officer around than Gilbert McIlwrick, I've yet to meet him,' observed one journalist who knew his methods, while another memorably described him as 'a monument of suspicious watchfulness'.

One intriguing story from the early war years clearly illustrates his thoroughness and is also remarkable for having a supernatural dimension. The sisters of a young woman in Perth were worried that she had not been seen for two days. They became more worried still when a fortune-teller reading tea leaves told them, 'Something has happened to your sister. Go to her house and look under the bed.' The sisters took the woman's advice and found their sister lying there naked, with a scarf tied round her neck in a reef knot. The local police asked for McIlwrick's assistance and he and Professor John Glaister carefully examined the scene. After carrying out an autopsy, Glaister would go no further than saying that 'the ligature found around her neck could have been applied suicidally or by another'.

McIlwrick agreed that there was no evidence to indicate murder rather than suicide but, with typical thoroughness, he then carried out an experiment of his own. He rounded up fifty male and fifty female volunteers and asked each of them to tie a scarf around his or her own neck and then around someone else's. However, the results did not settle the matter, as he discovered that in both cases the knots were tied in the same manner.

As in the Gertrude Canning case, wartime conditions made it impossible to carry out a proper investigation. The young woman's husband was away on military service and in his absence she had struck up friendships with soldiers from a local base but by the time the body was discovered the unit was on its way to North Africa. Many years later, though, McIlwrick was asked about the case and he said, 'I was quite satisfied it was murder.'

McIlwrick's career culminated in his appointment as head of Glasgow CID in April 1951 on the retirement of William Ewing. The role did not allow for the luxury of a honeymoon period as, in a matter of days, he was orchestrating the finale of a saga which had been running since the previous December: the recovery of the Stone of Destiny, removed from Westminster Abbey by four Glasgow University students who were ardent supporters of Home Rule for Scotland.

Just before Christmas 1950, the young nationalists drove down to London in two cars with the intention of bringing the Stone back to

Scotland. Unfortunately, in the process of removal, the Stone split in two and they temporarily stored it in locations in England before returning to collect it a couple of weeks later. Rumours about the culprits and the whereabouts of the Stone filled many newspaper columns over the next few months and one of the first jobs for the new Chief Superintendent was to dampen down speculation about imminent arrests. 'There have been no new developments,' he told reporters two days after his appointment.

The only news seemed to be that there was no news – until, on 10 April, the Stone was ceremoniously draped with a saltire and delivered to the curator of the ruined Abbey of Arbroath where the Scottish Declaration of Independence had been signed in 1320. From there it was taken into custody, as it were, by police in Forfar and then removed to Glasgow police headquarters where McIlwrick made a statement to the effect that two Scotland Yard officers would be arriving by train at 9.30 a.m. on 12 April to carry out a positive identification, after which the Stone would make the journey back to London.

During the following night an elaborate game was played out between police and reporters. McIlwrick was giving little away, saying only that the Stone was in the strong room and that he had the key. At 5.15 a.m. a black Jaguar slipped out of the yard at police headquarters but attracted little attention from the pressmen keeping vigil outside. However, when the gates opened again to allow a convoy of three police cars to make their exit, the CID chief was spotted in one of them and the journalists, convinced that he was escorting the Stone on its journey, immediately gave chase.

The scene, said one observer, was like the start of a Grand Prix race. The patrol cars roared through the darkened streets towards Bellshill, Harthill, and then pulled up at some huts at the Police Training Centre in Whitburn, West Lothian. The pressmen dived for their cameras but McIlwrick and his two Scotland Yard colleagues quickly got back into their car and set off again. By the time the reporters had returned to their vehicles, another police car had blocked the narrow roadway, stopping the press pursuit of the Chief Superintendent's Wolseley, which was, of course, a decoy. The Stone had been in the Jaguar.

The journalists seemed happy enough to admit they had been hood-winked. After all, that was a story in itself. 'Press lost the scent,' was the sub-heading on the front page of the *Evening Times*. Just after 8 p.m. on 13 April, the Stone of Destiny arrived back in Westminster Abbey and Wendy Wood, President of the Scottish Patriots' Association, was arrested for trying to hold a public meeting in Trafalgar Square to demand the return of the precious relic to Scotland. Her timing was perfect: thousands of tartan-clad Scots were already in London, for Scotland was playing England at Wembley.

And, just to add another dimension to this extraordinary sequence of events, the final score was England 2 – Scotland 3.

By removing the Stone of Destiny, the students had caused conster-nation for the authorities, but ultimately common sense prevailed. Sir Hartley Shawcross, Attorney General, deplored the theft but decided that criminal proceedings against the perpetrators would not be in the public interest. 'Rightly or wrongly, Scottish feeling is running very high on this matter,' observed the Very Rev Dr Charles Warr, Dean of the Thistle and Chapel Royal, and even that archetypal pillar of the establishment expressed the hope that agreement could be reached over the future resting place of the Stone in Scotland.

Eventually the government did agree that, except when required for a coronation, the Stone should be kept north of the border – but not until 1996.

★ ★ ★

McIlwrick's early reputation had been built on his successful investiga-tions of corruption, and the issue occupied him once more in 1952. This time, however, the accused were two of his own colleagues.

In May of that year, two Southern Division CID officers, Detective Sergeant Joseph Kay and Detective Constable Bernard Strain, appeared at the High Court of Glasgow on conspiracy charges. It was alleged that they had conspired to remove a fur coat belonging to the wife of

Mr Jack Feldman of Braidholm Road, Giffnock, the idea being that Feldman would then submit a fraudulent insurance claim for £700 and share the proceeds with the accused. The trio met on several occasions to discuss the scheme at The Kind Man pub on Pollokshaws Road in the Strathbungo area and at business premises Feldman shared with his partner at the Hillman Fur Company in Oswald Street. Hillman had been annoyed to see Feldman deep in conversation on the landing with two men, apparently doing business with them. When he challenged his partner about it, Feldman told him that the officers had suggested the fur coat scam and as a result the two businessmen decided to go to the police with their story.

On 1 February, they met with Robert Colquhoun (now promoted to Detective Chief Inspector) who asked them to repeat their statement in front of McIlwrick. He came up with a plan: Feldman should keep his next appointment at The Kind Man while detectives put both the business premises and the pub under observation. At one point Colquhoun had a narrow escape while watching the pub and hastily jumped onto a passing tram to avoid being recognised by Kay and Strain who knew him by sight.

Acting on the information passed onto them by Feldman, the CID warned his wife that her house would be broken into on the evening of 9 February, though they refused to reveal any further details. Mr and Mrs Feldman went out to the cinema and returned to find their home full of police. Near the front door lay a suitcase containing the fur coat. For nearly two hours, six detectives had kept a vigil outside the premises until the burglars were seen to enter just after 7 p.m. After giving them time to ransack the house, one officer – who sounds like he was enjoying the assignment – approached the open window at the back of the house and called, 'Come out, Barney and Joe!' Kay was apprehended but Strain ran off down the street, though he was soon captured, and both were charged with breaking and entry with intent to steal.

It seemed like an open and shut case, but the two accused reckoned they could explain everything. They claimed to be onto a 'fraud of some magnitude' and believed they were justified in not fully adhering to the proper rules of conduct. When asked the obvious question about why they had not informed their superiors, Kay told the court: 'I thought we were capable of carrying out the investigations ourselves.' His version was that the planned fraud was entirely Feldman's idea. The court was already aware that Feldman was a less than honest individual who had served two prison sentences. Kay maintained he had gone along with the faked burglary with the intention of delivering the fur coat in the suitcase to Giffnock police station so that when Feldman subsequently came in to report the theft the police would know it had been a set-up. Strain had run away when the police officers arrived because he thought they were neighbours of the Feldmans and, when eventually caught, he tried to give the impression that he was in the house because he was a police officer in pursuit of a housebreaker.

It was an ingenious story but the jury didn't fall for it. Kay was sentenced to five years' imprisonment and his sidekick Strain to four.

★ ★ ★

The saga of the Stone of Destiny and the case of the fur coat fraud had their lighter moments, but they were hardly typical of the cases that would keep McIlwrick fully stretched over the six years when he was in charge of the CID between 1951 and 1957. During that period the Annual Reports of the Chief Constable of Glasgow record a total of seventy-one cases of murder, attempted murder or culpable homicide.

The procedure was that the CID Chief would oversee the progress of murder investigations while enquiries on the ground would be led by senior officers from the division in which the offence occurred. Murders are not necessarily carried out by individuals with a criminal record, nor do all such cases involve lengthy and complex investigations. The type of incident where excessive drinking leads to a fight in which someone is stabbed or struck with a broken bottle occurred with monotonous regularity across the city, and often the culprit would be quickly apprehended.

On occasion, a depressing mixture of intoxication, bungled criminal intent, aggression and sheer panic could have unforeseen and tragic results. In March 1954, police received an anonymous tip-off that a body was lying under a pile of blankets in the locked storeroom of a model lodging house in Centre Street in the Kingston area of Glasgow. The following day a twenty-five-year-old man was charged with the murder. Under the influence of drink, the pair had broken into the store with the intention of stealing shirts and a waistcoat. Some kind of argument ensued, in the course of which one man took off his leather belt and strangled the other. While police were searching for the killer he walked into Govan Police Station and gave himself up. His explanation, that he strangled his accomplice who had passed out, made little sense and at the High Court of Edinburgh in April he was ordered to be detained in the State Mental Hospital at Carstairs.

In these days, too, there were numerous cases where an unfortunate woman would dispose of an unwanted baby. In March 1952, the body of a newly born child was found on the south bank of the Clyde and, nearly two years later, another baby, strangled with a stocking, was found floating in the river. In May 1952, a woman left a bag containing the body of an infant at the Left Luggage office the railway station in Gourock. She told a friend what she had done and later received a prison sentence of nine months for culpable homicide.

Similarly, the murder of a wife by her husband was not uncommon. On 27 February 1952, forty-four-year-old labourer Patrick Deveney stood in the dock at Greenock Police Court, holding his cap in his hands and looking down to the floor, while the charge was read out that on the day before, at 115 Blackburn Street, Glasgow, he 'did assault Jean Todd or Deveney (37) your wife, strike her on the head with a hammer or similar instrument, and strangle her with a necktie, whereby she received injuries from which she has since died, and you did thus murder her.'

At the trial in Glasgow Sheriff Court in May, details of their unhappy marriage emerged: endless arguments, milk bottles being thrown, occasions when Mrs Deveney had to go to stay with her mother, and threats from her husband that he was going to kill her. At the scene of the crime, there was blood on the sink and on the wallpaper, on Deveney's shirt and on his trousers. After the murder, he went down to Greenock where his brother lived. For the defence, Hector McKechnie, QC, said that the Crown had to prove that Deveney did commit the murder, and not simply that he could have committed it: 'The accused may have come into the house, found that somebody had killed his wife and got such an emotional shock that he lost his memory and went to Greenock.' Lord Keith directed the jury that 'it is for you to consider whether the accused is mentally diseased or whether he is just a man like many others who are not able sometimes to restrain their impulses.' It took the jury no more than forty-five minutes to reach a unanimous decision: Deveney was guilty of murder. He was sentenced to death and executed at Barlinnie Prison on 29 May. He left five children, who were taken into care.

A comparable case with a different outcome occurred in December 1954 after the son of a woman who lived in Taylor Street, Townhead, called on his mother and found her lying seriously injured with a head wound. Detectives kept vigil by her bedside but she died a week later. Her husband, a sixty-two-year-old dock worker, was tried at the High Court in Glasgow in February of the following year where it emerged that some weeks before the attack he had attempted to commit suicide by inhaling gas, possibly as a result of having appeared in court for a minor offence which had left him deeply ashamed of himself. Medical evidence showed that he had been a heavy drinker for over thirty years and that his mother was also an alcoholic. He could give no explanation of why he had attacked his wife and in the opinion of Dr Angus MacNiven, physician superintendent of Glasgow Royal Mental Hospital, 'was suffering from organic disease of the brain and melancholia and both these diseases were present in severe form'. As a result, he was declared unfit to plead, found insane and ordered to be detained during Her Majesty's pleasure.

Even in the popular press, some of these cases attracted relatively little coverage. The same could not be said for three murders from the

1952–54 period: the Hyndland shootings of August 1952, the murder of Betty Alexander in Garnethill two months later and the killing of George McNeill in Govan during the summer of 1954.

The first of these episodes involved an eighteen-year-old youth called Edwin Finlay. Far from being a knife-wielding hooligan from the slums, Finlay was a former pupil of Glasgow High School, a Sunday school teacher and a conscientious young bank clerk. He helped himself to a four-figure sum from his workplace, went to Renfrew Airport and took a flight to Dublin where he somehow managed to buy an automatic pistol without arousing suspicion. He had previously acquired two other supposedly 'antique' guns from an auction and these he had left in a suitcase at the left luggage office in St Enoch station. The diffident youth was known to be an admirer of a girl who was a member of a tennis club in Hyndland and police officers who were looking for him in connection with the bank theft kept an eye on the club in case he made an appearance.

Heavily armed and with his pockets full of cash, he was in fact soon spotted by two constables in the Hyndland area. Oblivious to the fact that Finlay was carrying guns, the two officers approached him. Without warning, he immediately killed one of the policemen with a shot in the chest while the other received bullets in his leg and arm. A third officer, having heard the shots, arrived on the scene, blowing his whistle and further reinforcements were quickly summoned. Firing random shots as he ran, Finlay was eventually cornered in a lane and as police closed in he shot himself in the head.

If the short and dramatic West End siege was over before any detective work began, the opposite was true of the search for the killer of four-year-old Betty Alexander in Garnethill in October 1952, which became one of the most extensive ever carried out in Glasgow. Betty was last seen playing outside near her home in Buccleuch Street at about 5.30 p.m. on Tuesday 7 October. Her body was found three days later in a back yard just 200 yards away and the secluded nature of the location led McIlwrick to announce that 'there is a strong possibility that it is someone with local knowledge who has committed the murder'. The area was sealed off and over the next couple of days some 3,000 local people were spoken to by a team of forty detectives led by Detective Chief Inspector Neil Beaton, a Gaelic-speaking former Gordon Highlander from Skye who had taken over responsibility for the Northern Division CID the previous year.

There was one clue to go on: a fingerprint found near the body, and McIlwrick decided to ask every adult male resident in the Garnethill area to allow his prints to be taken – an estimated 800 men. Such was the public revulsion at the crime that the police were overwhelmed with possible sightings and descriptions, many of them contradictory. Time after time, hopes were raised only to be dashed. A dog hair found on Betty led to a search for a dog she had patted; its owner was traced but, after questioning him, Beaton announced, 'We have decided not to proceed any further in this direction.' CID were contacted by a man who declared, 'I killed Betty,' but it was another red herring. On several occasions individuals were pulled in for interview, but in the end the killer was never brought to justice.

The Betty Alexander case was the first murder enquiry that Joe Beattie, then a Detective Constable, had been involved in. More than forty years later, he told the author that he was certain of the identity of the killer but was never able to prove it. He moved to another part of the city and whenever Beattie happened to encounter him, he would remind him: 'We know it was you, you bastard.'

But the murder which attracted more newspaper coverage than any other of the era was the case of George MacNeill, whose body was found in August 1954, some three weeks after he had been brutally killed in his flat in 1 Water Row, Govan. This came to be known as 'The McFlannel Mystery' as the dead man was a minor celebrity, having played a small part in the radio series 'The McFlannels', an early soap opera about an ordinary working-class family first broadcast in 1939. Concerned that he had not heard from him for weeks, McNeill's brother contacted the police and Detective Inspector Alexander Calder and a constable accompanied him to the flat. There they found the body in an advanced state of decomposition, buried under a pile of bedclothes and boxes. McNeill was wearing his pyjamas and his left temple and eye socket had caved in as a result of a severe head wound.

The likely weapon, an axe, was discovered and fingerprints found in the flat matched a known criminal, twenty-four-year-old John Gordon. McNeill, a lay preacher employed as a welfare officer at Fairfield's Shipbuilding and Engineering Company, had met Gordon through his involvement in schemes to assist ex-convicts. Gordon, who liked to describe himself as a 'freelance journalist' though he had little success in getting his material published, could not be found and while police continued routine enquiries at his known haunts in Glasgow, McIlwrick told the press on 5 August, 'We are almost certain Gordon is no longer in Britain.' A few days later, he made the dramatic announcement that Gordon was being held by the Spanish authorities in a prison in Gerona for entering the country illegally. He had been arrested after turning up penniless at the British Consulate in Barcelona where a member of staff realised he was the man mentioned in British newspapers in connection with the murder.

Glasgow officers were standing by to receive Home Office clearance to fly out to Spain but, said McIlwrick, 'the matter is out of the hands of the police for the time being.' It was not in fact until November that Gordon was handed over by Spanish police on the Royal Mail steamer 'Alcantara' at Vigo, and he was charged on board the ship.

The trial at Glasgow High Court lasted from 21 February to 2 March 1955 and the newspapers devoted page after page to verbatim coverage of the evidence. In the course of tracking Gordon's movements, Chief Detective Inspectors McAulay and Calder had travelled to Paris, Madrid and Barcelona and a truly diverse and cosmopolitan array of witnesses were cross-examined at the trial, including an Inspector from the Sureté Nationale in Paris, Inspector Gonzalez of Gerona police, Chief Superintendent John Capstick of Scotland Yard and Douglas Roche, Vice Consul of Barcelona. In addition, the Rev Dr George MacLeod, the founder of the Iona Community who knew both the victim and the accused, spoke of Gordon's childhood instability and his genuine wish to reform. The distinguished churchman also praised McNeill for his commitment to youth work and told of how he had counselled him in his struggle with 'personal tensions of a homosexual kind'.

Though some of the jury members harboured doubts, they took just fifty-eight minutes to find Gordon guilty and he was sentenced to death. No clear motive was established and the fact that Gordon had apparently panicked and fled abroad counted against him. However, two days before he was due to be executed, a reprieve came through and he served a prison sentence of nearly nineteen years.

Gilbert McIlwrick's role in the case involved a constant round of conferences and press briefings in addition to close liaison with legal experts as the CID found its way through the complexities of the extradition process. He did not travel to Spain to arrest Gordon, though he did manage to take his summer holiday (in Scandinavia) during August 1954. After the trial, he received a letter from Chief Constable Malcolm McCulloch, expressing 'how great has been my pride in the members of the Criminal Investigation Department on the successful conclusion of the investigation of the murder of George McNeill'. McCulloch continued:

> The chain of evidence against the accused man was built up in a manner which has evoked universal admiration in legal circles. Long after we have left the Police Service, I feel perfectly certain that succeeding generations of Police Officers will point to this case as an outstanding example of the co-ordinated application of all branches of criminal investigation.

By this stage of his career, McIlwrick had long since given up cutting out newspaper reports of his cases as he had done as a keen young constable in the 1920s. But the Chief Constable's congratulations must have meant something to him, as he stuck the letter into the back of his old scrapbook and it was still there when he died thirty-one years later, at the age of eighty-eight.

Yet, when asked for his verdict on his formidable record of achievement, the self-effacing sleuth simply said, 'The few unsolved cases — these are the ones you remember most.'

# 6

## *Too Young to Hang*

### *The Problem of Juvenile Delinquency*

'What's the younger generation coming to?'

'We'd never have got away with it when we were kids.'

Those who make such comments are generally looking back fondly to the 1950s or 1960s, that golden age of social stability when children treated their parents with respect and the mere threat of a dose of the belt from the teacher was enough to ensure good behaviour in school.

The newspapers of the time suggest a very different picture. The post-war generation was in a rebellious mood and there was a resurgence of the gang culture that had so often blighted the poorer areas of Glasgow. Petty hooliganism was widespread: in February 1951, it was estimated that in half of the 300 telephone boxes in the city window panes had been smashed or cables cut. In 1950, 37% of all crimes in Glasgow were carried out by those under the age of seventeen.

Even more worryingly, young offenders were also becoming involved in serious violence and murder and several cases occurred which led to much agonising about what should be done. Two particularly shocking incidents brought the problem to public attention during 1953.

In the course of an evening in June spent drinking in a park, three youths from the Provan district of Glasgow met up with nineteen-year-old Ronald Cairns who lived in their neighbourhood. The gang headed for Hogganfield Loch to meet with a couple of girls but they didn't turn up so the youths decided to break into the Corporation boathouse to steal some oars and take out a couple of the rowing boats for a moonlight cruise. Once inside the hut, Cairns boasted that he knew where the proceeds of the tearoom were kept and started to hammer on a locked door in an attempt to break it down. One of his cronies told him to stop and hissed, 'That noise will land us all in jail!' But the hot-headed Cairns turned on the other youth and took a swipe at him with the hammer. 'Defend yourself!' shouted one of the gang, tossing him a knife. As Cairns lunged forward, the frightened youth held out the blade in front of him but his assailant did not stop and ran straight at him. Blood surged from the head of Cairns and he fell on one knee, screaming in agony. 'You are mad,' he cried. 'My eye is pouring out of my head.'

Sobering up to the horror of what had happened, the panic-stricken trio dragged Cairns outside into Cumbernauld Road where they stopped a passing car and told the driver to take the injured youth to hospital, claiming rather unconvincingly that they had found him lying at the side of the road. One of the gang went with them in the car and when they reached the Royal Infirmary, the motorist informed a passing policeman. By this time it was late at night and Chief Detective Inspector Neil Beaton of the Northern Division was phoned at home, arriving at 1.30 a.m. to take charge. Fingerprints were taken from the damaged pavilion door and throughout the night detectives rounded up the other youths who were present. By morning Beaton issued an update: 'This man is gravely ill. We have detained a man in connection with the incident.' But Cairns never got the chance to tell his side of the story. Although officers kept a vigil by his bedside at the Royal Infirmary, he never regained consciousness and died seven days later. A post-mortem revealed the blade had penetrated an inch into his brain.

What had started as petty theft was now a case of culpable homicide. At the trial four months later the judge, Lord Keith, accepted there had been 'a considerable degree of provocation' and sentenced the

eighteen-year-old youth who had stabbed Cairns to a year's imprisonment, adding, 'It is important you should try to get a grip of yourself
and in future carry on a decent, respectable, honest life and avoid
unsuitable companions.'

If events at the loch side ended in disaster for one of the would-be
burglars, a couple's late night walk along a canal towpath was to have
a similarly tragic outcome, for, only a few weeks after the Cairns case,
Glasgow's High Court was the scene of another trial involving even
younger culprits whom the press quickly dubbed 'the Boy Murderers'.

One Saturday evening in May 1953, Mrs Jean Muir left her tenement home in the St George's Cross district and took a short tramcar
ride to the Cowcaddens area with the intention of visiting her mother.
As she walked round the corner of Milton Street, she met a friend
called Tom who worked as a wheelwright at the Albion Motor Works
and, by a curious coincidence, happened to share the fairly unusual
surname of the then head of the CID: McIlwrick.

The couple spent the evening drinking in various pubs before
walking home after closing time, taking a shortcut via the banks of the
Forth and Clyde Canal. Meanwhile, two youths – one aged seventeen,
the other fifteen – had bought a couple of bottles of V.P. wine at a
licensed grocer's in nearby Grove Street and had gone off to drink them
on the canal bank at South Speirs Wharf. The initials V.P. stood for
nothing grander than 'Vine Products' and the cheap concoction was
notoriously potent, being brewed from husks to which red colouring
had been added to give the bogus appearance of vintage port. It was as
popular in the 1950s as Buckfast Tonic Wine is nowadays.

When the two intoxicated youths saw the couple approaching, one of
them asked for a cigarette and then pulled Mr McIlwrick aside while the
other pushed Mrs Muir to the ground and tried to tear off her clothes.
A violent struggle ensued during which the thirty-five-year-old woman,
who was five months pregnant, was brutally punched and kicked. She
heard one of the boys shout, 'For goodness sake, stop it or you'll kill her!'
She also noticed that the attackers called each other Dusty and Steve.
She then lost consciousness and awoke to find herself lying on the canal

bank with her coat draped over her. In the meantime, McIlwrick had staggered home where he collapsed in a chair. At first his wife thought he was drunk and incapable but he told her: 'I haven't had as much drink as you think I have.' She undressed him to put him to bed and found the wound in his stomach. He was taken by ambulance to Oakbank Hospital where he died three days later, though he did manage to give a full account of the night's events to detectives.

After the attack, Mrs Muir, dazed, bleeding and unable to see through swollen eyes, had 'half walked and half crawled' to a close in Wigton Street behind Possil Road. Knocking on the first door she came to, she tried to relate what had happened but had been curtly told, 'Ye'd better get the police then – and clear out of here!' She collapsed at the close entrance where she was found at 6 a.m. by a lamplighter going his rounds who took her to Oakbank Hospital where she remained for three weeks.

Enquiries in local cafes soon pointed detectives in the direction of Dusty and Steve and, a few nights later, the two youths were hanging about their usual Garscube Road haunts when a patrol car pulled up and Chief Inspector Beaton quickly bundled them into it.

Mrs Muir was able to identify them, but the police had another witness as well. The day after the murder, a young boy had been repairing his bicycle near his home in Civic Street when he was pulled into a close by one of the youths who gave the frightened youngster an eight-inch blade and told him, 'Get rid of it – or I'll do you!' The boy duly cycled off and threw the weapon into a field somewhere between Bishopbriggs and Torrance. Later Beaton and Detective Constable Joe Beattie called at his home and, although it was 2 a.m., they took him back to the area where he had dropped the knife. In spite of the darkness, Beattie – 'through sheer luck', he later said – retrieved it.

At the trial in October, High Court Judge Lord Russell carefully explained to the jury the decision they had to make:

Let me give you a word as to what murder is . . . If the facts disclose that the injury which caused death was the result of serious and reckless violence, and if that was caused by the use of a lethal weapon and unprovoked, then that is murder and nothing less than murder.

The jury unanimously agreed with that definition. Both youths were sentenced to be detained during Her Majesty's Pleasure since, being under eighteen, they could not be hanged. It had been more than a hundred years since anyone as young as fifteen had been sentenced for murder in Glasgow. 'I did not think he would be convicted on the murder charge,' said the father of one of the boys. 'It has come as a great shock to me.' He described his son as a 'timid boy' and 'a happy, laughing youngster [who] never gave trouble to his parents'.

Max McAuslane of the *Daily Record* saw the conviction as evidence of a wider social problem. 'Where was your son or your teenage daughter last night?' he asked. 'If you don't know, you're a failure as a parent . . . and remember, thousands of adolescents live just like the Glasgow Boy Murderers.' He lashed out at 'the morons dressed in short-cut drainpipe trousers exposing yellow socks over a pair of thick-soled suede shoes. You'll see them in the cafes, clustered around the juke boxes, as brassy and crude as the music they get for their coin.'

The diatribe continued in the best tabloid fashion:

> Of course, some are brought to justice right enough. I've been having a look at a few of the unlucky ones in the city juvenile courts. All nice and informal in case little Johnnie's susceptibilities might be hurt . . . They ask questions about his schooling, his home background, hoping to find some excuse for Johnnie's misdemeanours. But no magistrate ever seems to ask if anyone has tried leathering the hide off the little sinner.

This drew an interesting response from a young reader, himself a resident of the area where the crime took place, who saw things from a different perspective:

> The picture Max McAuslane painted of night life in Glasgow's Garscube Road summed it up pretty well – but he forgot one thing. He forgot to

mention that the youngsters who hang around the cafés and corners find them better places than the squalid homes most of them come from. These kids don't need a hiding – a decent home would be much better. So please don't hound them – help them.

The City Fathers would largely have endorsed that. It was widely recognised that living conditions within much of the city provided the breeding ground for hooliganism and violence. While many pleasant residential areas could be found in the West End, as many as 700,000 people were packed into overcrowded tenements in an area of central Glasgow measuring three square miles. Glasgow Corporation saw the solution as decentralisation, which they believed would, as one planner put it, 'emancipate people from the thraldom of congested squalor'.

An ambitious plan of slum clearance had already been on the drawing board before the war and, with the return of peace, building work proceeded as quickly as possible on four huge peripheral housing developments at Pollok, Drumchapel, Castlemilk and Easterhouse, each designed to accommodate in the region of 50,000 people. Such a massive undertaking, however, would take the best part of twenty years and though understandably seen in the 1940s as the answer to many social problems, this exercise in social engineering ended up replacing one nightmare with another. Modern housing blocks might have offered more space and better sanitation but the downside was that community spirit was lost and insufficient thought was given to the provision of shops, play areas and other social amenities. Out of this background a different type of juvenile delinquency would emerge in the 1960s.

Even in the early fifties, though, research was suggesting that poor housing was not the only, or even the main, explanation for teenagers getting into trouble. In 1952, Professor Thomas Ferguson of Glasgow University published a survey based on a study of 2,000 boys and one of his findings was that 'the rehoused boys were almost as prone to crime as they were when they lived in the slums.' The professor felt that 'low scholastic ability' and 'parental neglect' were equally significant factors in the rise of juvenile crime. During the war years, home life had been severely disrupted as so many fathers were away on military service for extended periods, leading to a lack of discipline in the home.

It was, of course, easy enough to express outrage and Lord Provost Sir Victor Warren duly obliged. When a Maryhill doctor and his wife, whose son had been attacked in daylight by youths on the banks of the canal, demanded an interview with him, he told them that 'The only way to put down hooliganism is the strap or the cane.' The parents were grateful for Sir Victor's sympathetic response but felt that some action had urgently to be taken to address the issue.

Finding a solution was more difficult and the best that anyone had to offer was to blame delinquency on poor parenting. Journalist Henry Cockburn of the *Scottish Daily Express* related an incident that seemed to show that without proper guidance children would go off the rails at a very young age. He was in a cinema when he saw two girls aged about seven and eight with a boy who was only about three years old. They left after the film but the older girl came back in and handed the commissionaire a military cap with a badge, saying, 'Here ye are, mister, the wee fella knocked it off in the seats but it's no worth onything.' 'What is the answer to this sort of thing?' enquired Cockburn. 'Some way must be found to jerk erring parents back to a sense of their responsibilities.'

One social worker offered the same simplistic solution: 'Let parents re-establish their authority and face up to their responsibilities and the term juvenile delinquent will pass out of the language.'

Glasgow has changed in many respects since the crimes at Hogganfield Loch and on the banks of the Forth and Clyde canal grabbed the headlines in 1953. The Garscube Road tenements have mostly gone and some of the streets no longer exist.

But the problem of juvenile delinquency is still with us and the social worker's hope is as far from fulfilment as ever.

# 7

## *Crime Takes No Holiday*

### *The Summer of 1955*

Even today, when budget airlines can whisk you off on vacation at any time of the year, there are still Glasgow folk who talk about 'going away for the Fair'.

There really was such an event, held during the second half of July, with origins dating as far back as the twelfth century when horses and cattle were traded at market. By Victorian times, it had evolved into a holiday fortnight where the buying and selling was supplemented by entertainment. In a heavily industrialised area like twentieth-century Glasgow, it made sense for the factories and shipyards to schedule their annual shutdown for the 'Fair fortnight', when thousands of workers would crowd onto trains and steamers for a trip 'doon the watter'.

Brilliant sunshine greeted the masses of holidaymakers setting off in July 1955. British Railways laid on 200 extra trains and the Automobile Association reported that twice as many people as the previous year were touring by car at home or abroad. A couple of hours away from Glasgow, business was booming in the popular resort of Rothesay on the Isle of Bute; with 40,000 visitors on the island, there was not a spare bed to be had in any hotel or boarding house. As *The Bulletin's* headline on Saturday 16 July put it, 'The Outlook is Fine for the Fair'.

The extraordinarily hot weather would last all summer – but the men of Glasgow CID would have little time to enjoy it, for that year's Fair fortnight ushered in a summer crime wave. In seven days, a succession of five killings occurred in the city and these coincided with the largest and most complex bank raid investigation that a Scottish police force had ever dealt with.

No wonder Gilbert McIlwrick called it 'heatwave madness'.

While thousands of Glaswegians crowded into the rail and bus stations for day trips to Ayr, Largs, Gourock and Wemyss Bay on Fair Monday, 18 July, three of their fellow citizens were appearing at the Central Police Court on charges of murder or attempted murder. On the previous Friday night, a street fight between two men in the Gorbals left one lying bleeding in Crown Street near Adelphi Street. He was arrested and charged with breach of the peace but later collapsed and was rushed to the Royal Infirmary where he died the following day. The other man was charged with murder but at his trial in September he was found guilty of a reduced charge of culpable homicide and sentenced to six months' imprisonment.

Then, on Saturday 17 July, a woman was battered to death in her flat in Bath Street opposite the King's Theatre. While theatre-goers enjoyed a performance of *Time Remembered*, a romantic comedy starring Margaret Rutherford, police photographers and fingerprint experts carried out their painstaking work at the crime scene across the road. The thirty-five-year-old husband of the murdered woman was taken into police custody and at the High Court in November claimed he had acted in self-defence. During a vicious row, his wife had told him she was fed up with him and was going to kill him. She lifted an ashtray stand to strike him but at that point, the husband says, 'I became violent and took it from her and hit her on the side of the head.' He admitted he had a tendency to 'explosive violence' when he had been drinking. By a majority verdict, the jury found the husband guilty of culpable homicide and he was sent to prison for fifteen years.

The third violent death of the Glasgow Fair weekend occurred on 18 July when a forty-five-year-old Sunday school teacher collapsed with a dagger in his back a few feet from his own doorway on the second floor of his tenement home in Logie Street, Govan. A twenty-four-year-old worker in a Royal Ordnance factory was arrested. At his trial in September, psychiatrist Dr Hunter Gillies told the High Court that he had no doubt the killer was 'dangerously insane'. He seemed unconcerned with the gravity of his position, telling the psychiatrist that he was learning new things every day and now knew what it was like to be in danger of hanging. Other conversations ranged over subjects like the workings of the brain, the psychology of Teddy Boys and the nature of good and evil. He was ordered to be detained during Her Majesty's pleasure when he no doubt had plenty of time to pursue his philosophical speculations.

All these incidents were soon to be overshadowed by a daring crime which attracted nationwide attention. On Wednesday 20 July, a bank raid in Ibrox lasting all of sixty seconds triggered a complex investigation which continued for months and involved CID men travelling thousands of miles up and down the country.

At 9.30 a.m., fifty-nine-year-old bank messenger Lindsay Currie was sitting inside a maroon Bedford van outside the Paisley Road West branch of the British Linen Bank while his two colleagues delivered a consignment of banknotes to the value of £6,000. Four men descended on him, knocked him out and drove off, with some of the money spilling out of the van's back doors. Helpfully, the driver had left the key in the ignition.

The gang headed straight for an unoccupied villa opposite Bellahouston Park in nearby Dumbreck Road where they switched the loot to another waiting vehicle. Currie was left tied up in the back of the van but the robbers removed his gag and he was able to shout to neighbours for help. Under the direction of Detective Inspector Mackie of Govan CID, teams of detectives began questioning people in the Ibrox, Govan, Dumbreck and Mosspark areas, while McIlwrick told reporters they were looking for a black Austin A40 saloon, believed to be the getaway car.

Early reports suggested a haul of £10,000 but by the next day the sum had been considerably revised in an upward direction to £40,000 and eventually to £44,025. Numerous leads were quickly followed up, such as the sighting of four men walking through the park, but McIlwrick was uncharacteristically negative in his press comments. After spending four hours in conference with senior colleagues, he announced, 'so far we're stumped'. 'The descriptions we have of the men at the moment are very hazy,' he said; in spite of checks at garages and car hire firms, the Austin could not be located and, as McIlwrick said, 'We haven't even a fragment of a registration number to give us a lead.'

On the other hand, police press releases can't always be taken at their face value and McIlwrick may have had his own reasons for giving little away. After all, this was the man who was fond of saying, 'Tell me this, and tell me no more.'

In the absence of any tips from underworld contacts, the CID was working on the theory that the gang may have come up from England. Cars crossing the border were stopped and searched, though detectives remained open to the possibility that the robbers could be lying low in Glasgow for the time being. One detective who clearly understood the workings of the criminal mind wryly commented that 'There are quite a number of "neds" in the city who are capable of pulling a job like this but I don't think any of them would be capable of keeping their mouths shut afterwards or resisting the temptation to throw money around extravagantly.'

As many as 200 possible sightings of the culprits were reported and they all had to be followed up. Detectives trailed round shops and other retail outlets showing samples of the tape and rope used to gag and bind the bank messenger but there was nothing distinctive about the materials from which these were made. It all took up man-hours and it wasn't producing any results. Equally frustrating was the fact that most of the banknotes were in smaller denominations whose serial numbers could not be traced.

By the end of the week, *The Bulletin* reported that 'rain is badly needed to refresh the land everywhere in Scotland'. Glasgow's hard-pressed CID men felt in need of some respite as well.

Instead, the weekend brought yet another murder investigation which, as so often, began with a group of men returning home after an evening's drinking. A twenty-two-year-old woman was waiting at a bus stop in Shettleston Road with her boyfriend when she heard a noise on the other side of the road and saw a man slump to the ground but she did not go across to help him. If she had, she would have discovered he was her own father, a forty-seven-year-old steelworker known to everyone as 'Wee Joe'. The young woman saw her boyfriend onto his bus and returned home, where her father had already taken to his bed. It seems that two men had helped him home and one of them kept saying that he was sorry he had hit Joe. During the night his condition deteriorated and he was taken to hospital at 5 a.m. but never regained consciousness.

One of the city's most tenacious detectives, Chief Inspector Alex Brown of the Eastern Division, took charge and he told the press that while the victim showed no visible signs of injury he may have fractured his skull. After intensive enquiries throughout Saturday, Brown made a high-speed sixty-mile car journey to Cockenzie, East Lothian where the twenty-six-year-old killer was picked up and by 2.45 a.m. he was in custody in Glasgow, charged with murder. His defence was that an altercation had arisen and he had struck Wee Joe in the face, causing him to fall backwards. The jury at his trial accepted this version and he served a four-month prison sentence for culpable homicide.

It seemed that murder enquiry number five was looming after an incident late in the evening of Sunday 24 July, when the windows of a ground floor flat in Pollok occupied by a baker were broken. He emerged later with his son-in-law and went to the local police station to report that three men had forced their way into the house and assaulted him. Soon after returning home, however, he collapsed and died. The three were arrested and charged with murder but when they appeared at the Sheriff Court some days later, the charges were reduced to assault, breach of the peace and malicious damage.

This case was handled by Detective Inspector Robert Kerr of Govan CID who remained at the flat in Pollok until 1 a.m. on the Monday.

After that, it was straight back to the Ibrox bank raid enquiry and, two days later, Kerr was on his way to London – the first of many similar gruelling journeys. 'During that fortnight I had an average of two hours' sleep a night,' he later recalled. 'When I came home my wife hardly recognised me.'

Thanks to Gilbert McIlwrick, there had been an unexpected breakthrough. The man who in his younger days had set up secret tape recordings to catch a corrupt councillor now became the first Scottish CID chief to exploit another form of technology in the fight against crime: television. In spite of meticulous planning the raiders had slipped up in one respect as they left behind some brown overalls of a type commonly worn by many shopkeepers and warehousemen (known as dustcoats) with initials on them, and McIlwrick had the idea of screening a nationwide television appeal for information.

It was a long shot, but it worked. Mr F. H. Buckingham, an A.A. patrolman from Fulham, London recognised the coat as being his own. This provided a new lead, and Govan detectives James McAulay and Robert Kerr sped south to carry out the task of 'co-ordinating links between Glasgow CID and Scotland Yard'. Their work ultimately led to the arrest in a Fulham flat of John Blundell, who greeted officers of Scotland Yard Flying Squad with the words, 'How the **** did you find out I was here?'

Other clues were emerging, too. A black Rover left in a car park in Perth was found to have been stolen from London in May and fitted with false number plates. Enquiries next focused on the Rob Roy Roadhouse near Aberfoyle, about an hour's drive from the scene of the bank raid. Staff had no suspicions at the time but now they began to put two and two together. Ten men, several of them with English accents, stayed there in mid-July. The hotel proprietor later recalled that they did not sign the visitors' book individually but only wrote 'George and party'. Four were absent on the morning of the robbery and the entire group hurriedly departed the day afterwards in two cars, the Rover and a Riley. One guest made a particular impression – a sociable individual whom his companions addressed as 'The Major', and a witness remembered passing by one of the chalets and seeing him counting a pile of banknotes of a bluish colour like those issued by the British Linen Bank.

Now occurred one of the lighter moments of the investigation, when heat wave and crime wave momentarily coincided.

On 29 July, Detective Inspector Colquhoun and two colleagues were pursuing their enquiries at the Aberfoyle hotel when staff mentioned that members of the gang had been spotted throwing what might have been a set of car number plates into the nearby River Forth. A keen swimmer who regularly used the Dennistoun Baths in Glasgow, Colquhoun borrowed a pair of swimming trunks and spent an hour searching in the water while his sergeant sweated it out on the river bank. Neither of them noticed a press photographer hiding in the bushes and his snap of Colquhoun emerging from the river 'wearing short trunks and a startled expression' found its way onto the front pages next morning.

The underwater search proved fruitless but in other respects the pieces of the jigsaw were coming together as a result of Kerr's travels throughout the UK and Ireland which took him to Belfast, Dublin, Southend, Gloucester, Scarborough and Middlesbrough as well as London. By September four arrests had been made, including two men brought back from Ireland and one who had already been arrested the previous month, though police had not made that public.

A total of six men went on trial at the High Court in January 1956 and the daily proceedings received much detailed press coverage, especially when one of the witnesses was a ten-year-old girl, 'an attractive child with a shock of curly hair' who had been playing near the bank at the time of the raid. She smiled to the court as she described how 'two men came from a telephone box and they jumped in the van and drove it away'. Witnesses and hotel staff were able to identify the men in the dock and there was further amusement when one was referred to as 'Gumsy' on account of his lack of teeth. A bank teller from Dublin confirmed that one of the men had deposited some of the cash in British Linen Bank notes and the London A.A. man identified one of the robbers as the man to whom he had lent his dustcoat.

One figure constantly mentioned who was not on trial was the apparent ringleader, the sociable military type called George Grey who, because he had occasionally been seen at the Roadhouse wearing a monocle, was inevitably dubbed 'the monocled Major' by the press. There was a good reason for his absence: he was in Brixton Prison serving a sentence for another robbery. It was not until 1957 that he stood trial in Glasgow for his role in the Ibrox raid and a further six years were added to his existing sentence. Of the original six gang members tried in January 1956, three received prison sentences – six years in the case of Englishman John Blundell and Scot Charles McGuinness, and eight in the case of Australian-born John Lappen – with the charges against the other three being found not proven – an option available in Scottish courts when the jury is not convinced that the accused is innocent but does not have sufficient evidence to establish his or her guilt.

Lawyers involved in the case were surprised at the comparative leniency of the punishment for Grey, 'the monocled Major' considered to be the ringleader. Many years later Sheriff J. Irvine Smith QC made some interesting observations about the sentence in his autobiography *Law, Life and Laughter*:

> I have recently been given information, which if correct, would explain the lenience of the sentence on Grey. It is that when he came to be sentenced the defence plea in mitigation, apparently not challenged by the Crown, was that 'the Police no longer regarded Grey as the leader and he did not take an active part in the crime'. If this is correct, I for one would certainly be fascinated to learn who was nominated for the allegedly vacant role of leader in this robbery. If there is any substance in this story I am satisfied it would not be the opinion of the then head of the Glasgow CID, who investigated the case.

Irvine Smith was referring to Bob Kerr (who was head of Govan Division CID at the time and took overall charge of Glasgow CID in

1960). There is no doubt that Kerr was a key figure in the lengthy enquiry into the robbery, which lasted for over two years. Between July and October 1955 he had only three days off duty and it's reckoned that he clocked up something like 3,000 miles travelling throughout Britain and Ireland. For months, newspapers carried headlines like 'City CID man goes to [Scotland] Yard' and 'Travelling CID man comes home'. During the trial, he had the additional job of looking after the witnesses who had to travel north to give evidence, meeting about 100 different people from trains and booking them into city hotels.

McIlwrick was entitled to feel satisfied with the performance of his department. 'The investigation was our most extensive ever,' he said. 'Above all, it was an example of teamwork at its best. There is hardly a member of the entire city police force who was not engaged on inquiries at some stage.' Lionel Daiches QC agreed: 'I cannot recall a case where so much remarkable and meritorious police work has been effected.'

It was a generous tribute, considering he was acting for the defence!

As for the effect of the case on the CID boss himself, the *Evening Times* commented towards the end of July that 'five murders and a £40,000 bank raid in the space of seven days would surely bow any ordinary man. Mr McIlwrick simply looks slightly tired – and that is hardly astonishing when you consider he hasn't had an undisturbed night's sleep for weeks.' The reporter noted with astonishment that among the utilitarian pieces of furniture in his office there was a camp bed. He had not been required to use it since the Stone of Destiny business but, he said, he may well have to if the crime wave did not cool off soon.

There was no sign of that happening. July 29 saw another attempted murder case – a particularly harrowing one whereby a mother tried to kill her four-year-old daughter and commit suicide by inhaling gas. The woman was certified insane and sent to Stoneyetts Mental Hospital. Other senseless incidents, partly attributable to the weather, occurred: gangs of youths wantonly uprooted plants and stripped the bark from trees in Ruchill Park while on the other side of the River Clyde in Victoria Park the keeper disarmed a nine-year-old boy carrying an axe.

A gang fight in Shettleston led to a tram conductress being slashed with a broken bottle.

Academics reckon there's a close correlation between crime and temperature. The hotter the weather, the more easily angered people become as levels of adrenalin and testosterone rise. They are also more likely to be outside and to gather in public places, increasing the possibility of aggressive encounters, especially among the young.

A summer when hardly a day passed without some serious crime being reported led to some soul-searching on the part of the citizens of Glasgow, and this was reflected in the correspondence columns of the newspapers. Some pointed the finger at those at the top of the police force. In response to Chief Constable Malcolm McCulloch's assertion that Glasgow had never been so free of crime, one letter writer exclaimed, 'O, for a Sillitoe!' – a fond reference to the 1930s when Sir Percy Sillitoe took robust action against the scourge of the razor gangs. Surely, he continued, 'the gangster menace could be ended in a month if the police were released from watching private cars and permitted to perform their duty of policing the city.' The writer (who signed off with the pseudonym 'Wake Up') further suggested that the police should be armed.

Others detected a deep-seated malaise affecting the city's populace. 'Who can raise his hands in horror at the street fights of the Teddy Boys when a mob of 100 "honest citizens" of Govan attacks two young police constables doing their duty to keep the peace?' asked 'Shocked'. 'How can a city be kept decent when it does not want to be decent?'

Rain fell on Glasgow on 2 August for the first time in nearly three weeks. The heatwave came to an end, the factories reopened but the litany of crimes continued.

In the course of the first weekend of August, a twenty-one-year-old man smashed a whisky bottle against a window of Govan police station. 'I just wanted to see inside a police office,' he said. Fining him £3, the judge in the Police Court remarked that it was lucky that the bottle shattered, not the window.

Meanwhile, thieves broke into a public house in High Street. They smashed a hole in a close, entered the cellar of a shop, exited the premises, forced the door of an upholsterer's and broke through the floor, which allowed them to enter the pub below via the ceiling. After all that effort, they blew the safe in the pub but the door jammed and they left with almost nothing.

Further along the same street, a thirty-year-old dock worker was found dead in a doorway. A scuffle between some men had been witnessed by passers-by shortly before. 'We have not ruled out the possibility of murder,' said McIlwrick.

It was no longer a matter of 'heatwave madness'. It was just madness.

# 8

## *'Life Begins at Midnight'*

*Detective Chief Superintendent Robert V. Colquhoun,*
*CID Chief 1957–60*

A teetotaller famous for impersonating drunks; a keen swimmer and judo expert; a friendly cop with a boyish smile – just three of the various descriptions applied to R. V. Colquhoun in the course of his long police career.

Of all the CID bosses featured in this book, Colquhoun – generally known as Bob, though his wife considered his middle name of Vernon to have more gravitas – was the only one who published his memoirs in retirement, thus preserving for posterity both the details of his cases and his own opinions and insights. The book, which appeared in 1962 under the stirring title *Life Begins at Midnight*, was in fact ghosted by one of the best crime journalists of the day, the late Bill Knox (1928– 99). As well as working for numerous newspapers and presenting the Scottish Television series *Tales of Crime*, Knox was a prolific writer of crime fiction, and he no doubt drew on his considerable powers of imagination when recounting Colquhoun's career, which involved the investigation of more than fifty murders over a period of nearly four decades. Copies of this highly readable volume are so scarce today that even the finest detective would have difficulty tracking one down.

Like William Ewing and Gilbert McIlwrick, his two post-war predecessors as CID chief, Colquhoun had a family connection with the police force, though in his case it was not through his father but his grandfather, Hew Colquhoun, a native of the remote Highland village of Duror, Appin near Loch Linnhe and Glencoe, who joined Glasgow police in 1860 and ended up, as his grandson would do, as a Superintendent. Bob Colquhoun's father worked for the Discharged Prisoners' Aid Society and his mother was known as Sister Vernon, employed by the Church of Scotland as a home visitor in the city slums.

In common with many others of his generation, young Colquhoun was desperate to take part in the First World War. Born in 1900, he was just old enough to join up before hostilities ended in 1918. He then began an engineering apprenticeship but this was a time of industrial depression and there seemed little future in such a career choice. As a result, he applied to join the police and, even though he was technically half an inch under the height requirement, soon found himself patrolling the streets of the tough Garngad area in 1923 – a year he described as 'a vintage year for Glasgow's gangs'. His ambition was to join the CID and after only a year and a half's experience he had passed both the elementary and advanced certificates in preparation for the time when the opportunity would arise.

It came more quickly than he expected. His abilities in the written examinations had been noted and he was given the role of temporary uniformed clerk in the Chief Constable's Office. This was effectively an office job though for some weeks he was back in the thick of the action when the General Strike broke out in 1926 and every available man was drafted in to control the mayhem in the streets – something that, as a keen boxer and wrestler, Colquhoun was well able to handle. In the autumn of that year, having proved himself in his clerical role, he was invited to join the CID under Superintendent John Forbes – a notable achievement for someone whose total amount of police service amounted to only three years.

This rapid ascent of the ladder would continue throughout his career. In 1931, the year he was promoted to Detective Sergeant, he was the youngest officer to be presented with an award for arresting and securing the conviction of the greatest number of criminals. In 1936, he became a Detective Inspector. And in 1943 he took on the role of Detective Lieutenant (a rank later regraded as Chief Inspector in 1948) in the Eastern Division CID where he led the enquiry into the murder of former policeman James Straiton. He returned to the Central Division as deputy to Gilbert McIlwrick with the rank of Superintendent in 1951 and succeeded him as CID Chief in 1957. He held the post for three years and at the time of his appointment was described as 'the automatic choice' for the job.

The pattern for so many top CID men has been to take up a security role on leaving the force and the same was true of Colquhoun. The Monday after he left the police he took over as area manager of the Glasgow branch of Security Express Ltd., a subsidiary of Wells Fargo which specialised in the transportation of valuable cargoes, especially large amounts of payroll cash – salary payments by bank transfer were still a long way off. There was a neat symmetry about this role for Colquhoun, as the UK head of Wells Fargo was none other than Sir Percy Sillitoe, the Chief Constable under whom the ambitious young detective had worked in the 1930s.

In recognition of his distinguished police service, Robert Colquhoun was awarded an MBE. Though he had the reputation of being one of the fittest men in the police force, he died suddenly at the relatively early age of sixty-eight when visiting a friend in Portobello, Edinburgh in September 1969.

★ ★ ★

Detective fiction generally focuses on the way a perpetrator is tracked down and caught. Real life detective work is rather different. Colquhoun remembers his mentor John Forbes telling him, 'The Sherlock Holmes stuff is fine to read, Robert. But you can't bring a man to the dock by using his methods. It's one thing to solve a crime, and know who should be arrested – but it's twice as hard a job to gather the evidence to satisfy a jury that they've got the right man before them.'

Colquhoun had certainly absorbed that lesson by the time he headed an enquiry into the activities of the Irish Republican Army, soon after becoming a Detective Inspector. If William Ewing's reputation was founded on his work on the Ruxton murders and Gilbert McIlwrick's on his pursuit of fraudsters, Robert Colquhoun made his name with this complex investigation, which severely weakened the IRA's support network in Scotland.

The IRA was implacably opposed to the partitioning of Ireland and in 1939 carried out a bombing campaign in the UK as part of what it regarded as a war against Britain to secure an Irish Republic. These attacks took the form of tear gas in cinemas, incendiary bombs in hotels, letter bombs in post offices and many similar explosions in public places, creating a climate of fear. One of the most serious attacks occurred in a shopping area of Coventry, killing five people and injuring many more.

A considerable amount of support for the IRA existed in Scotland as a result of the steady influx of Irish immigrants since the mid-nineteenth century. While the guerrilla war was being waged in England, police noticed an increase in the theft of explosives from mines in Scotland. It seemed likely that this material was being supplied to the IRA and Colquhoun was given the task of monitoring meeting places such as clubs and dance halls frequented by the Irish community in Glasgow. Particular attention was given to Irishmen who had found jobs in mines and quarries where explosives were used and, using intelligence supplied by the Royal Ulster Constabulary, the list was gradually narrowed down to a number of suspects whose every move was tracked. Colquhoun described a typical episode during this operation:

> One day I followed a small, grey-haired figure we had labelled The Commandant, a natural leader of men in appearance. All unsuspecting, he led me across the town, out into the country, and finally walked into a quarry site. The Commandant had landed a job which gave him direct access to an explosives store!

By May 1939, enquiries focused on the comings and goings at 132 Trongate, the venue for meetings of the Celtic Literary Society. Colquhoun was given the go-ahead to make a raid and it soon became apparent that the company gathered inside the hall had other purposes in mind than studying the poetry of W. B. Yeats. Eight arrests resulted, and Colquhoun gave evidence at the trial later that year. He told how 'two detectives who went under a platform in the hall called out that they had found a locked suitcase, and when one of them cut a hole in it, he saw it contained gelignite'. In total, 540 sticks were found and further stashes of explosives and detonators recovered when the houses of the arrested men were searched. Much of it had been stolen from the premises of the Garngad Brick and Sand Co. Ltd.

This carefully planned CID operation ended with three men receiving sentences of ten years' penal servitude – including the one nicknamed The Commandant. But the trio remained defiant to the last. 'If it is a crime to love Ireland and hate British rule in Ireland then I am a criminal and always will be,' said one after being found guilty. 'God bless the IRA.'

Chief Constable Sillitoe later pointed out that arresting these conspirators might actually have done them a favour as they had erroneously stolen a large supply of white tape fuse which burnt almost instantaneously and not, as they thought, the ordinary slow-burning variety.

The IRA's war against Britain coincided with the even bigger threat of a German invasion and the consequent blackout conditions provided a convenient cover for all kinds of criminal activities in the centre of Glasgow. From this period date the famous stories of Colquhoun and his men disguising themselves as drunken sailors on leave. Having drawn attention to themselves by their behaviour in pubs, they would stagger out into the night, invariably followed by pickpockets and thugs who saw them as easy targets. A punch-up would ensue and the unsuspecting thieves would soon be bundled into a waiting police van.

A far more serious aspect of wartime crime was the difficulty of investigating murders when military personnel were involved. In July

1942 Colquhoun was awakened by a knock at his door at 1 a.m. It was Detective Sergeant Alex Brown with the news that CID assistance was requested in investigating the murder of a member of the Women's Royal Naval Service (Wrens) at Inveraray. A car sped north through the night containing four of Glasgow CID's most capable detectives – Colquhoun, Brown, McIlwrick and scientific expert George Maclean.

Twenty-year-old Gertrude Canning originally came from County Donegal in Ireland but was brought up in Milngavie where she attended St Joseph's Primary School. She joined the Wrens and in 1942 was based at No. 1 Combined Training Centre at Inveraray where, on the afternoon of 30 June, she went out to post a letter to her family in Ireland. She was never seen again.

Five days later, two boys who were collecting wild flowers found her body in a ditch in a woodland area. She had been shot four times, three of them at close-range, but what was unusual was that the other shot had gone through her wrist which had then been bandaged with a handkerchief. Colquhoun suggested a possible explanation:

> Perhaps she began to struggle, and . . . the gun was produced as a threat of what would happen if she didn't allow her attacker his way. The first bullet, the one which went through the wrist, could have been fired by accident. That allowed for the wound being bandaged.

A story of this kind usually hits the headlines, but wartime conditions meant that the crime was only reported in the vaguest of terms. In addition, the odds were overwhelmingly against the detectives. The shots came from a standard British army .38 revolver which could have been accessed by any one of several thousand servicemen stationed in the area. Worse still, the day before the CID men arrived an infantry brigade had finished its training and left for the south of England.

Undaunted, George Maclean started firing a test bullet from every gun in the area that could be traced. Glasgow did not have the resources to analyse the results at this time and the bullets were taken down to Scotland Yard. Colquhoun personally travelled south in search of the men who had previously been stationed at Inveraray, visiting a host of military bases in the Buckinghamshire area and the Isle of Wight in the hope of testing as many weapons as possible before the troops departed on what turned out to be an unsuccessful raid on the German occupied port of Dieppe in Northern France in August 1942.

The murder investigation, it seemed, had been taken as far as it could go. This was Colquhoun's later verdict:

> My theory – and theory it must remain, nothing more – is that the Wren was killed by a soldier whom she knew; that that same soldier was later one of the men who poured ashore from the landing craft at Dieppe . . . In all probability, he died at Dieppe . . . and his secret died with him.

Yet that was not the last word on the case. A new generation of the Canning family has maintained an interest in the murder and Gertrude's nephew has recently unearthed information about troop movements at the time as well as about his aunt's life. To keep her memory alive, on the occasion of the seventieth anniversary of Gertrude's death in 2012 the family arranged for a plaque to be placed at the woodland path in Inveraray where she died.

In the last few years R. J. Mitchell, a writer of crime novels and former police officer, has also taken an interest in the story of Gertrude Canning. It was established at the time that two roadmen had seen her entering the woodland path, followed soon afterwards by a soldier. From his own police experience, Mitchell considers that 'It wouldn't have been difficult to get descriptions and get an artist's impression, then compare this with the soldier's mugshot and see which branch of the service he came from.' To Mitchell, the failure to do this 'had the whiff of a cover-up' and he speculates on whether the killer may have been a well-connected officer, a revelation of whose identity would have caused a scandal.

★ ★ ★

Colquhoun played a prominent role in many of the post-war murder hunts discussed in earlier chapters but the years when his profile was at its highest were between 1957 and 1960 when he was in charge of the CID, with Alex Brown as his deputy.

He had only been in the top job for three days before the first murder occurred on his watch.

The circumstances were familiar enough: a fight between men who had been drinking. The incident began outside a pub in Douglas Street after closing time with a chance meeting between two men who had served in Korea and who, apparently, had some unfinished business. The altercation only lasted one minute; the victim, James Craney, was struck on the side of his head and, according to his wife Mary who was present, left 'bleeding a wee bit'. But hostilities resumed later that night in premises up a close in Argyle Street when Craney was hit by a chair, dying the following day from a fractured skull. When his two assailants went on trial at the High Court in May, they argued they had acted in self-defence; the charge against one was found not proven and the other was acquitted.

Such occurrences were all too common in Glasgow when the pubs emptied. What made this one stand out was that James and Mary Craney had only been married for forty-eight hours.

That case was handled by detectives within the division where it occurred, but Colquhoun took personal charge when, in July 1957, a seventy-two-year-old woman was murdered in her flat in Hill Street, Garnethill.

Nan Wilson was a dressmaker who lived a quiet life with her cat Judy. As usual, she had spent Saturday evening with a close friend who came over from Springboig to visit her and left just before 10 p.m. Barely fifteen minutes later, an intruder climbed twenty feet up a drainpipe and entered her kitchen window. He cruelly gagged the old woman with a silk stocking and proceeded to ransack the flat. On the floor below, a neighbour was annoyed by a banging noise from the ceiling caused by the old lady frantically hitting her heels on the floor in an attempt to be heard, and she hammered back with a brush handle to tell her to stop. The burglar therefore ripped off his tie, tied it round her ankles and escaped through the window. Another neighbour spotted him running across the back green and jumping over a three-foot high wall, not realising that on the other side of it there was a sixteen-foot drop into the darkness. The first neighbour, now alarmed by groaning noises coming from the flat above, called the police who forced their way in, to find that the old lady had died from suffocation. The cat was found cowering behind a chair in terror.

The actions of Miss Wilson's intruder had been inept at every stage. He had left a trail of footprints, had almost certainly fallen and injured himself – and, of course, he had provided a clue in the form of his tie.

Colquhoun immediately set in train a number of lines of enquiry. First, neighbours were interviewed and an appeal issued for witnesses who had seen the fugitive. A tracker dog was brought in to follow his scent, without success. Hospitals were alerted in case the killer had sought medical help for injuring his leg in the fall. Door to door enquiries also led detectives to seek out window cleaners who had cleaned Miss Wilson's windows earlier in the week. It emerged that these were not the usual men; Colquhoun announced, 'they may be unlicensed window cleaners and afraid to come forward. Nothing will happen to them if they give us their help.'

But his best hope seemed to be the tie. A detailed description and a photo of a similar item were published in the newspapers. Blue-grey in colour with a pattern of red double diamonds, this was of a style then in fashion known as a 'Slim Jim' tie and, inevitably, the pressmen dubbed the wanted man 'the Slim Jim Killer'. Shops, suppliers and manufacturers were all followed up, but many hundreds of these ties had been sold.

Then something else came to light. A couple from Aberdeen staying in a nearby hotel came forward to say that they saw not one but two men climbing across a fence.

In the end, it turned out to be the window cleaners.

Colquhoun received a midnight phone call at home with a tip-off and one of his dramatic nighttime manhunts commenced. At 5 a.m.

police cars were seen leaving the Northern HQ in Maitland Street, one heading to a tenement in nearby Cowcaddens and the other to the Blackhill area. Colquhoun and Divisional CID head Neil Beaton brought back thirty-two-year-old John Reid and a seventeen-year-old youth and charged them with the murder of Miss Wilson and the theft of £4 10 shillings [£4.50] from her house.

Colquhoun had made a good start as CID boss. The *Evening Times* noted with approval: 'This is the second murder investigation led by Chief Superintendent Colquhoun since he took charge of the CID in January this year. The previous case also ended in an arrest.'

The trial promised to be an interesting one from a legal point of view as it was the first for capital murder in Scotland under the new Homicide Act, which came into force earlier that year. This was passed as a result of the growing opposition to the death penalty which now ceased to be the mandatory sentence for all murders, although it was still retained for certain killings defined as 'capital murders', particularly 'murder in the course of furtherance of theft' – a description that applied to the case of Nan Wilson.

However, in the High Court in September, the charges were reduced to culpable homicide in view of various mitigating factors. Miss Wilson was 'frail in the extreme' and this may have hastened her death. Furthermore, there had been no intent to kill: on the night of the robbery, the perpetrators had lost their last four shillings gambling and Reid suggested they should go to Miss Wilson's as he knew where she kept her money. At the time of the offence, he was an army deserter scraping a living doing odd jobs like caddying for golfers and window cleaning and he 'got a fright next day when he saw in the papers that she was dead'. But the most crucial factor was the medical evidence which suggested that one of the accused was 'mentally sub-normal' and the other 'a simpleton', though they were both deemed to be, in the words of the judge, 'responsible for their actions to some extent'. Reid was sentenced to twelve years in prison and his accomplice to five.

As for Judy the cat, she was taken into the care of the RSPCA.

The death of Nan Wilson took place only a few hundred yards

from where, in 1952, the body of four-year-old Betty Alexander had been discovered – an event still fresh in the memory of many locals. When, on 6 June 1958, the body of five-year-old Ann McKinlay was found in front of a coalbunker in a tenement in South Woodside Road, Kelvinbridge, the CID braced themselves for the nightmare of another similar enquiry.

Colquhoun had only two hours' sleep that night. While a crowd gathered outside, he and a team of officers led by Chief Detective Inspector John Johnston of the Marine Division searched the close and interviewed neighbours, including the little girl's friends with whom she had been playing an hour before her death. This led to the speedy arrest of a 'feeble minded' seventeen-year-old youth who lived up the same close. Described as being barely able to read or write and unable to foresee the consequences of his actions, he was found guilty of culpable homicide and detained in the State Mental Hospital at Carstairs.

The case raised some uncomfortable issues regarding the treatment of those who were mentally ill, as the killer had been released from an institution. 'I feel only pity for him,' said Ann McKinlay's mother, 'but I have a deep bitterness for the authorities.'

If such tragic cases involved individuals with a limited capacity to understand and control their behaviour, the murder of William Vincent followed a deliberate and protracted attempt by an older man to dominate an impressionable youth. This series of events reached its climax in Colquhoun's ninety-mile dash from Glasgow CID head-quarters to Longtown, just over the border between Scotland and England.

Robert Scott was a car-mad teenager who used to enjoy attending motor auctions in the Gallowgate where he met a second-hand car dealer called William Vincent in January 1954. They encountered each other again one night when Scott missed his last bus home and Vincent offered him a lift. The pair became friendly and Vincent, who dressed well and liked to flash his money around, took the impression-able youth to West End clubs, plying him with drink and introducing him into what journalists described as 'his strange and queer world'.

Eventually Scott ended up spending the night in the older man's flat above his garage in Park Terrace Lane. He later said he had drunk so much that he had no recollection of what happened.

In 1955, Scott was called up on national service and posted to the Royal Army Ordnance Corps (RAOC) at Longtown. During this time Vincent kept writing to him and even approached the Colonel in charge, portraying himself as a friend of the family and asking how much it would cost to buy Scott out of the army. In other letters, he claimed to be the employer and guardian of the young man and argued that he needed him discharged to help with his business.

On his return to Glasgow, Scott had had enough of Vincent's attentions and resolved to tell him that he wanted nothing more to do with him. One evening in April 1958 he went round to the fifty-year-old car dealer's flat where, as he later described it, 'Vincent tried to embrace me. I tried to push him away. I put my hand over his throat, squeezed and he dropped to the floor. There was blood coming from his throat. I took [his] sock off and held it round his neck to stop the blood. I dragged him into the garage.' Scott then bundled Vincent into the boot of his Sunbeam Alpine and drove through the night, heading south for Longtown where, from his period of military service, he knew there was a secluded area called Blackbank Wood where he could bury the body. But the Alpine got stuck in the boggy ground and Scott walked to the guardroom of the military base to ask for assistance. Then, it seems, he lost his nerve and called the police at Gretna with a blunt message: 'I've done a murder.' He asked the sergeant on duty to meet him at RAOC Longtown and then hung up. As the location lay 500 yards over the border in the jurisdiction of Cumberland and Westmoreland Constabulary, the message was passed on and it was one of their officers who drove to the scene. There he found the body in the boot of the car, cautioned Scott and took him to the tiny Longtown police station to await the arrival of Glasgow CID.

Writer Douglas Skelton includes the story of William Vincent and Robert Scott in his book *Bloody Valentine* (2004) as one of Scotland's 'crimes of passion', but the case is equally interesting for what it reveals about policing methods of the era and shows how procedures allowed for investigations to be wrapped up very quickly.

Colquhoun received the message from Cumberland police at 8 a.m. and arranged for a car to pick him up, along with Detective Sergeant Hector McDougall and Detective Inspector John Johnston of the Marine Division where the crime was committed. First they called at Scott's family home, then at Vincent's empty flat and set off on the drive south. After visiting the scene of the crime, Colquhoun interviewed Scott at Longtown where he said: 'I charged him myself with murder.' He was then taken to a waiting police car, his head covered with a blanket. In the interim, Vincent's convertible had been taken to a garage at the RAOC depot, filled with petrol and prepared for the drive back to Glasgow with Sergeant McDougall at the wheel.

At 12.35 a.m. a black police Humber and cream Sunbeam pulled up outside the Glasgow Central police station. Thereafter both cars drove to the Marine Division office in Partick where Scott was led into the CID offices on the first floor and formally charged with murder at 1.18 a.m. The next morning a police van took him to the Sheriff Court for an appearance that lasted barely ten seconds, after which he was transported to Barlinnie Prison. When an inquest had been carried out in Carlisle, Vincent's body travelled back to Glasgow in a hearse with a police escort.

Commenting on the difference between police procedures back then compared to current practice, one retired senior officer said simply, 'It's like chalk and cheese.' Today, the car would not have been instantly driven back to Glasgow. The whole scene would have been sealed off for forensic examination and interviews of the suspect, in the presence of his lawyer, recorded on tape or video.

At his trial at the High Court of Glasgow in July, further details of the relationship between the young man and the car dealer came to light, and much was made of Vincent's homosexuality. Scott said, 'he tried to ruin my life and make me the same as him'. To put this aspect of the case in context, it should be remembered that the trial took place a few months after the publication of the Wolfenden

MARYHILL
OR
F DIVISION

27 BEATS
47 SIGNAL BOXES

MARINE
OR
B DIVISION

46 BEATS
51 SIGNAL BOXES

GOVAN
OR
G DIVISION

36 BEATS
47 SIGNAL BOXES

SOUTHERN
OR
D DIVISION

36 BEATS
52 SIGNAL BOXES

THE CITY OF GLASGOW.
POPULATION          1,106,000
ACREAGE               39,725
VALUATION           £11,550,941
AUTHORISED STRENGTH OF FORCE
2331 OFFICERS & MEN.

NORTHERN
OR
E DIVISION

36 BEATS
51 SIGNAL BOXES

EASTERN
OR
C DIVISION

41 BEATS
55 SIGNAL BOXES

HEADQUARTERS
OR
H DIVISION

ADMINISTRATION
C.I.D. H'QUARTERS
TRAFFIC DEPT.
ETC.

CENTRAL
OR
A DIVISION

42 BEATS
45 SIGNAL BOXES

DIVISIONAL OFFICES  ⬤
SUB-DIVISIONAL OFFICES  •

1949 diagram showing the eight Glasgow police divisions and their headquarters.

Detective Chief Superintendent
William Ewing (in charge of
Glasgow CID, 1937–51).

Detective Chief Superintendent
Gilbert McIlwrick (in charge of
Glasgow CID, 1951–57).

Detective Chief Superintendent Robert Colquhoun (in charge of Glasgow CID, 1957–60).

Detective Superintendent Alex Brown – 'The man who caught Manuel'.

Detective Chief Superintendent Robert Kerr (in charge of Glasgow CID, 1960–63).

Detective Chief Superintendent Tom Goodall (in charge of Glasgow CID, 1963–69).

Superintendent George Maclean, carrying away a parcel of bed clothes for forensic examination after the murder of Mrs Minnie Wilson in her Pollokshields flat in October 1959.

Superintendent Joe Beattie during the Bible John investigation.

Police examine the van used in the 1955 Ibrox bank raid, discovered soon afterwards in the grounds of an unoccupied villa in Dumbreck Road.

Violence on the streets: Joe Beattie leads away a blood-stained man after an attack (mid-1950s).

Robert Colquhoun leads away a man arrested for the murder of Mrs Helen McGhee in her Cathcart baby linen shop in April 1959.

Photographs showing the various activities of the Identification Bureau in 1949.

BOTANY · BALLISTICS · CASTS · CHEMISTRY · COUNTERFEIT COINS · DOCUMENTS · HANDWRITING · TYPEWRITING

FINGERPRINTS · RECORDS · MODUS OPERANDI · GEOLOGY · HAIRS & FIBRES · INFRA RED · PHYSICS · SPECTROGRAPHY · U.V.

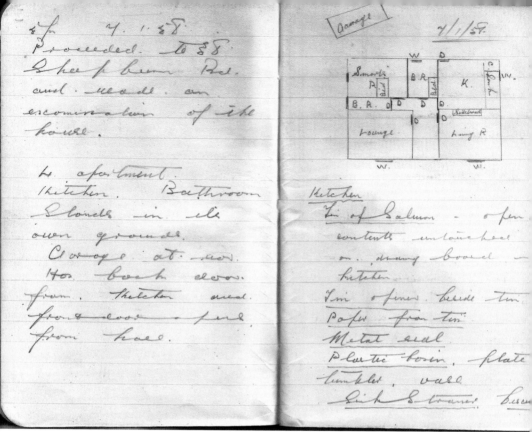

A page from Tom Goodall's notebook with notes made during his visit on 7 January 1958 to 38 Sheepburn Road, Uddingston, home of the Smart family murdered by Manuel. Note the reference to the 'tin of salmon'. Manuel returned to the house and is believed to have fed the cat.

SIX ISSUES IN ONE—PRICE ONE SHILLING & THREEPENCE

The Bulletin
and SCOTS PICTORIAL

NEWS FROM SCOTLAND

THE POPULAR WEEKLY EDITION

No. 1699

MONDAY, MAY 26, to
SATURDAY, MAY 31, 1958

MANUEL TRIAL CONCLUDING STAGES

Some of the people who waited to be admitted to the High Court in Glasgow during the sensational trial of Peter Manuel.

Cover of *The Bulletin*, showing crowds gathering outside the High Court of Glasgow during the trial of mass-murderer Peter Manuel in 1958.

Edward Heath (later to be Conservative Prime Minister between 1970 and 1974) visiting the new caravan designed for use by Glasgow Police as a temporary office at crime scenes, c.1968. Behind him is Detective Chief Superintendent Tom Goodall.

A 'Coup of a Lifetime': the *Evening Times* front page, 17 August 1966, reports on Tom Goodall's arrest of Gorbals-born John Duddy, wanted in connection with the shooting of three policemen in London.

Jaguar Mk.VII, as used by the Traffic Department in 1956.

A unique photograph taken in April 1964 on the occasion of the retirement of 75-year-old Edward 'Ned' McCartney, a veteran crime reporter for the *Daily Record*. It shows CID Chief Tom Goodall (left) with his five predecessors (left to right): Adam McLaren, who retired in 1937, William Ewing, Gilbert McIlwrick, Robert Colquhoun and Robert Kerr.

Report on Homosexual Offences whose key recommendation was that 'homosexual behaviour between consenting adults in private should no longer be a criminal offence'. It would be more than a decade before the law was changed in England and Wales, and considerably longer than that in Scotland. None of this, however, was reflected in the words of Lord Russell at the trial. He told the jury that 'however worthless an individual you may think the evidence has shown William Vincent to be, no person is entitled to take upon himself the role of Vincent's executioner'. By a majority verdict, twenty-one-year-old Scott was found guilty of murder and sentenced to life imprisonment.

Whatever emotional trauma he had gone through as a result of his involvement with Vincent is a matter of guesswork. Eighteen months later, though well behaved in confinement in Perth and apparently optimistic in his letters home, Robert Scott found himself briefly alone in the prison workshop and hanged himself.

The murder of William Vincent and the suicide of Robert Scott were the culmination of a tortuous relationship over a period of years; in another murder investigation conducted by Colquhoun in person, the victim and killer had only known each other for a few hours.

Detectives arrived at a tenement in Aitken Street in the Haghill district around 2 p.m. on 15 May 1959 as neighbours crowded round the close mouth watching events unfold. A woman had been found dead in one of the flats and detectives started door to door enquiries. A Mr and Mrs Daisley, who lived in the next close, described how they had been in a local pub the previous afternoon in the company of the woman and a number of other people. She went by the name of Margaret Blyth but had previously been known as Mrs Mary Whyte, wife of former Scottish welterweight boxing champion, William Whyte from whom she had separated some months earlier. Since then, she had been living in hostels and lodging houses.

After an afternoon drinking in several pubs, she and a woman friend had gone back with the others to the house of James Jackson in Aitken Street where the partying continued, with Jackson playing the piano while the others sang along. The Daisleys returned home but later that evening there was a knock at their door. Jackson stood there, his head and hands covered in blood, saying that he had fallen and split his head open. Janet Daisley helped to clean him up but when he took off his jacket and cardigan – he had no shirt on underneath – she noticed that there were two blood-stained handprints on his back.

The Daisleys went back with Jackson to his house where a trail of blood between the kitchen, bathroom and bedroom could be seen on the floor. 'Where the hell did this blood come from?' exclaimed Mrs Daisley. Then she saw Margaret Blyth lying on the bed and told Jackson to send for a doctor but he replied, 'Oh, she's all right, she's only in a drunken sleep.' Next morning, however, Jackson was at his neighbours' door again. Would Janet come and take a look at Margaret as she doesn't seem to be breathing? Then Jackson's mother arrived and insisted on phoning the police. In desperation, Jackson suggested that they should agree on a story about the woman falling and hitting her head on the bath.

By midnight, Colquhoun was able to announce: 'we have charged a man with murder'.

In September, Jackson celebrated his thirty-third birthday by standing in front of a jury in the High Court. He admitted that he and thirty-five-year-old Margaret Blyth had been drinking heavily. When he stopped playing the piano to go to the bathroom he noticed her bending over a chest of drawers and accused her of trying to steal from him. He slapped her face. She slapped him back. He pushed her and she fell. 'And that is really all the help you can give us?' asked his frustrated counsel. A bloodstained bottle was found on the scene but Jackson said he could not remember if he had hit her with it. Dr Imrie, the police surgeon, said that 'the general picture was more indicative of an assault than a fall'.

It was probably the evidence of consultant psychiatrist Dr William Blyth that saved Jackson from a long jail sentence. 'He had been drinking that day from about ten o'clock in the morning until two o'clock the following morning,' said Blyth. 'He was addicted to alcohol of the lowest type – that is, a mixture of cheap wine, cider, beer, etc.

He led a life that I do not regard as normal.' He added that Jackson was 'sane and fit to plead' but 'not fully responsible'. The verdict was 'guilty of culpable homicide'. The sentence: two years in prison.

In his memoirs, Colquhoun wrote that, 'If I said what I thought about some psychiatrists, I'd get done for libel'. It might have had something to do with the verdict in Jackson's case...

★ ★ ★

Murder hunts make the biggest headlines, and reporters relished stories that allowed them to produce eye-catching front pages like 'Killer Arrested in Midnight Swoop'. But CID work covered many other aspects of criminal activity as well.

Payroll robberies were an almost weekly occurrence in these days. Robbers would study the regular movements of couriers and work out the right moment to strike. In March 1957, two men assaulted a cashier of the Kelvin Construction Company as he left bank premises at the Round Toll, escaping with the £1,000 in cash. In September, daring raiders tunnelled through a brick wall and concrete roof to reach the strongroom of a Dennistoun bakery, making off with £7,000. A far more low-key, but equally successful raid took place in April of the following year when Colquhoun's deputy Alex Brown led the search for a nondescript individual who walked into a branch of the Royal Bank of Scotland in Royal Exchange Square, leant across the counter, helped himself to £1,000 in £5 notes and walked out before the theft had been noticed. In many cases, the proceeds of these robberies were never recovered.

Then there were the times when a crime had been investigated and the culprit tried, convicted and imprisoned – only for the prisoner to escape. It used to happen with monotonous frequency with the famous safe blower Johnny Ramensky, who found his way out of Peterhead Prison on no fewer than three different occasions in 1958. Colquhoun was involved in a more unusual incident in August of the previous year when two prisoners escaped through the window of a prison bus taking them to Barlinnie. One was found hiding under the floorboards of a house and CID men took no chances when he appeared at the Sheriff Court next time – they took up positions all-round the entrances. The second prisoner, however, had a flair for publicity. Safe blower Daniel Hynds wrote a letter to the police, announcing that he would give them another opportunity to (as he put it) 'illegally arrest and wrongfully imprison him' by turning up at the Sheriff Court on a Monday morning at 11.30 a.m. Crowds lined the street to see what would happen and CID men nervously patrolled the area as the time drew near. It wasn't until about 11.50 a.m. that he duly arrived in a taxi, handed the cabbie a generous tip and gave himself up to a very relieved Colquhoun and Brown who were there personally to receive him.

Colquhoun also took charge of the investigation into another attempt at a dramatic gesture. This time, it seriously backfired on the perpetrator who, as a result of a grudge against the owner, had decided to cause an explosion at a fish and chip shop in Castle Street. Screaming women ran out into the road as the bomb shattered the window. Unfortunately, the bomber had still been holding the stick of gelignite when it went off, as a result of which he suffered devastating injuries, losing an eye and both his hands. The following day – the day he had been due to appear in court on assault charges – it was announced that he had lost the sight of his remaining eye.

Perhaps Colquhoun's strangest enquiry dates from June 1957, when workmen in Adelphi Street on the opposite side of the River Clyde from Glasgow Green were digging down to a depth of seven and a half feet in preparation for the installation of a hydraulic garage ramp when they unearthed five skeletons, one of them a child. 'As far as we know just now, these bones could be five, fifty or 500 years old,' said Colquhoun initially. The matter was looked into with remarkable thoroughness: Tom Goodall was given the task of organising a team of detectives to sift through old cases of missing persons, and investigations were made into the use of the land in the nineteenth century and earlier. These revealed that there had once been a Leper hospital in the vicinity and the initial theory was that the remains of patients had been buried there.

Further research identified a mixture of human and animal bones and, when it was discovered that a doctor's house formerly stood on the site, police reached the conclusion that the bones must have been used for anatomical purposes and finally buried in the grounds.

An amusing incident occurred in relation to this dig. A reporter came up to the side of the hole and asked one of the officers busily engaged in the digging what it was all about. Straightening himself up after all the heavy exertion, he replied, 'I'm not sure what it's all about, but it's murder.' It was only with some difficulty that the reporter was persuaded that the cop was referring to the backbreaking nature of the task and did not mean it was a real case of murder.

Even the most dedicated detective needs some form of relaxation. For Willie Ewing it was bowling, for Bob Kerr it was golf and for Joe Beattie it was DIY. Bob Colquhoun, always fit and athletic, would dive into the swimming pool. When off duty he would spend much of his leisure time at Dennistoun baths; he had more than fifty proficiency awards for swimming and lifesaving, served as chairman of the Swimming section of Glasgow police and was a member of the Scottish Executive of the Royal Life-Saving Society. Judo was another passion. His interest started when he met a Japanese munitions worker who taught him some elementary moves and after the war he helped out in a youth club where he trained the boys to put on a judo display. This in turn led him to establish a police judo team and it used to be said that younger officers would take up the activity in the hope of enhancing their promotion prospects.

Once, when he was attempting an arrest, the suspect punched him on the nose and ran off. Further down the street, Colquhoun caught up with him and tried to hold him but the man continued to throw wild punches until the detective gave him a judo arm-lock. It was devastatingly effective. As he later recalled, his assailant 'stood twisted to one side as if paralysed'. By this time a considerable crowd had gathered and an old woman stepped forward. 'I don't know what that polisman wants, son,' she told him, 'but for God's sake do it, or he'll probably kill you.'

Top cop he may have been, but Colquhoun had a sense of fun and sometimes liked to catch his colleagues off guard and try out one of his arm-locks on them. And, as with every other famous detective, there were stories about him that found their way into police folklore. Searching a tenement flat for the proceeds of a bank raid, Colquhoun was continually warned by the anxious housewife to 'mind the wean'. Her endless repetition of this refrain started to puzzle him since the baby was lying there quite contentedly and no one was anywhere near it. He decided he'd better take a look inside the cot – and that's where he found the money. Another joke was that when the staunchly church-going detective was asked by his minister which psalm he would like, he is said to have replied without hesitation 'Sam McKay!' – a reference to the well-known Glasgow bank robber Sam 'Dandy' McKay.

But underneath the affable exterior, Colquhoun was a man who knew exactly how the criminal mind worked and held robust opinions on the need for disciplining the young, favoured the reintroduction of the birch and believed in capital punishment. Perhaps a former shoplifter who knew the detective got it right. 'Don't be taken in by his smiling face,' she told her son. 'Colquhoun would jail his own granny.'

The Chief Superintendent didn't contradict her . . .

# 9

## *The Man who Caught Manuel*

### *Superintendent Alex Brown, Deputy CID Chief*
### *1957–1959*

In November 2016, Scottish Television aired a three-part drama called *In Plain Sight*, telling the story of the gruesome killing spree carried out by Peter Manuel in Lanarkshire between 1956 and 1958. It made for gripping viewing and practically every word of the script was true to life. No effort was spared to get the circumstantial details just right: the clothes, the cars and even a copy of the *Eagle* comic which eleven-year-old Michael Smart was reading in bed the fatal night when Manuel broke into his family's home in Uddingston.

Yet in one key respect factual accuracy was sacrificed for the sake of good television. The programme portrayed the hunt for Manuel as a mind game played out between the man known as the 'Beast of Birkenshaw' and his nemesis, Detective Inspector William Muncie of Lanarkshire CID.

The truth turns out to be rather more complicated. The key figures in Manuel's final arrest were in fact seconded from the Glasgow force, Detective Superintendent Alex Brown and Detective Inspector Tom Goodall. Newspapers of the day dubbed Brown 'the man who caught Manuel', yet with the passage of time, his role in the story has been largely forgotten and his name has undeservedly slipped into obscurity.

It's time this quietly spoken, unassuming man received the recognition he deserves.

★ ★ ★

Unlike several other high-ranking Glasgow CID figures discussed in this book, the police was not Alex Brown's first choice of career. As a youth he had shown considerable promise as a footballer and at one time considered this as a profession. However, in 1926, as an out-of-work twenty-seven-year-old fitter from Girvan, he saw the police force as a means of obtaining steady employment. He signed up as a constable with Glasgow police in April of that year, a matter of days before the start of the General Strike. Uniform work didn't appeal to him and after another six years he joined the CID in the Eastern Division based in Bridgeton.

Frequently in a policeman's career, an opportunity arises for the officer to seize the initiative and show his potential. Brown's moment arrived when he was on the trail of a pickpocket who planned to stowaway on a liner and leave the country. The Detective Constable doggedly followed his quarry through the city from Bridgeton to Govan where he discovered that no suitable ships were scheduled to sail that day. Still with Brown on his tail, the man next headed to the Pollokshields area and attempted to break into a house. Seeking a witness for the arrest, Brown asked a passer-by to assist.

The passer-by happened to be Assistant Chief Constable David Warnock, who a few years later would became Chief Constable in succession to Sir Percy Sillitoe.

No doubt that incident had something to do with Alex Brown's promotion to sergeant in the Eastern Division in 1938 and after that his rise was rapid. After working in the Southern Division during the Second World War he became Detective Inspector at Central headquarters in 1946, thereafter returning to the Eastern Division as Chief Inspector before ending his career back at Central as Superintendent where, in 1957, he was appointed deputy to Bob Colquhoun. At one point he stood in as CID boss when Colquhoun took ill.

It was in 1958 that Brown became a household name when he assisted the Lanarkshire force in the pursuit of Peter Manuel, a year before he retired in March 1959 after thirty-three years' service. Though the most spectacular and widely publicised, the Manuel case was only one of many where Brown's quiet persistence helped track down his quarry. He found himself in the limelight for one final time in June 1959 when he collected the Queen's Police Medal 'for distinguished services'.

Two days after Brown retired, John Gray Wilson's book *The Trial of Peter Manuel* was published – the first of many which were to feed the public's fascination with the case, which has not abated over the last half century.

Sadly, ex-Superintendent Brown was not destined to enjoy retirement for long. He died suddenly of a heart attack at home in Gelston Street, Shettleston on 30 March 1963. Hundreds attended his funeral at Daldowie Crematorium, including Chief Constable James Robertson, CID Chief Bob Kerr and the heads of the city's CID Divisions. His son, at that time a Detective Constable in Central Division, went on to have a distinguished career in the force ending up, like his father, with the rank of Superintendent. He, too, played a role in the Manuel trial at Glasgow High Court when, as a uniformed constable, he had guarded the prisoner.

★ ★ ★

To the public, Alex Brown may have been 'the man who caught Manuel' but his colleagues within the force knew him as 'Faither Broon'.

Like the fictional priest in G. K. Chesterton's detective stories, he was infinitely patient: police drivers used to joke that if they delivered him to a tenement close to question someone and he came down again within the hour then there couldn't have been anyone in. For Brown, it wasn't enough just to knock. If the door wasn't opened to him, he'd peer through the letterbox, listen for movement from within, or go into the stairhead toilet and look out the window. If he was searching a house, he wasn't content to look through each drawer or cupboard: he'd examine every item inside. Those who worked with him maintained that 'if he doesn't find what he's looking for, he'll strip the wallpaper from the walls'. On one occasion he was systematically going through a drawer containing women's underwear. He picked out a bra and, after carefully examining the cups, turned to his colleague and uttered one word: 'falsies'.

Brown famously advised younger detectives to 'let the other fellow do the worrying; use the minimum of words and the maximum of action.' It was the Faither's favourite method and it could produce spectacular results. The psychological pressure would start as soon as he turned up at a house in search of his victim. There could be a party in full swing but he would simply stand there and say nothing. He would gaze at each person in turn and a tense, uneasy silence would gradually spread over the assembled company. Then, suddenly, he'd ask something like, 'Well, are ye working then?' The question might be followed up by another; then again, it might not. The suspect would be thoroughly unnerved.

When asked to describe their distinctive methods, detectives tend to brush the question aside and Brown's approaches are usually attributed to his personality rather than to any premeditated strategy. Yet there is evidence that his tactics were not simply a practical response to the needs of whichever enquiry was on-going but were founded on carefully thought-out theoretical principles.

Buried away in the yellowing pages of an old edition of *The Police Journal* from 1943 lies an article entitled 'Psychology in the Investigation of Crime', written by Brown himself, which reveals that he was fully conversant with the latest developments in that field. In it he argues that police work overlaps with psychology as it seeks to understand behaviour in terms of the inner life of thought and feeling. Hence, the best police investigators will be those who understand human nature. 'It has often been said of certain police officers that they have a remarkable aptitude for obtaining important evidence or information in connection with crimes under investigation,' he writes. 'It is not so much a matter of aptitude on the part of the police officers concerned as the bringing to bear on the enquiries the knowledge of human nature which they have cultivated or acquired.' In a particularly interesting section of the article, he goes on to explain a tactic that he must have used to good effect in many an interrogation:

> If we want to know how a person is affected towards a certain circumstance, all we have to do is to ply him with a number of words including a few connected with that circumstance and see how he reacts to them. From tests it has been found that with what we might call dangerous words, the time taken to reply was a good deal longer than in the case of innocent ones.

One can only speculate on some of the conversations that might have taken place between Brown and his boss Colquhoun over matters concerning the workings of the human mind. While Colquhoun's views on psychology as a discipline are not on record, he certainly expressed some robust opinions on experts in psychiatry: 'I sympathise with a disgruntled senior detective who once growled at me, "Psychiatry is the lowest form of medical life".'

From time to time within the police force, incidents occur when officers fall short of the standards expected of them and take advantage of a situation for personal gain. Few detectives would have handled an episode of this kind in quite the same way as Brown did. In November 1956, a police constable on duty discovered that a tobacconist's shop in Duke Street had been broken into. He immediately reported the matter from the nearest police box and a divisional patrol car soon arrived containing his Inspector and two other constables who proceeded to remove packages of cigarettes and put them in the car. Finding this somewhat unusual, the PC who made the discovery informed Brown, the Detective Chief Inspector in charge of the Eastern Division CID.

Then, some weeks after the event, an anonymous phone call was made to police HQ saying that officers had been seen stealing goods from the shop.

Brown went round to the houses of those involved. What is characteristic of his approach, though, is that he did so in the middle of the night. At 4.50 a.m., one of the constables involved heard knocking at his front door and peered out of the window to see the figure of Brown looming in the darkness, wearing his trademark coat, hat and scarf. He came inside to interview the suspect, who sat shivering uncomfortably in his pyjamas in a room with no fire.

Brown's boss Colquhoun used to favour midnight raids when the quarry would be sleepy and his resistance low, but his Deputy took that method to a new level . . .

The result of the interview was a full confession. 'I feel better now that everything is off my chest,' said the constable as he explained how twelve large cartons containing about 1,600 cigarettes had been taken back to the station and shared between an inspector, two sergeants and two constables. Later in court, though, he retracted the story and claimed he had no memory of that conversation. But Brown had it all written down in his notebook and prison sentences were imposed on three of the officers.

Joe Beattie, the Superintendent in charge of the Bible John investigation in the late 1960s, recalled another typical incident which illustrates Brown's methods. A crook who, on account of his slight build, had earned the ironic nickname 'Shooders' (i.e. Shoulders) was being questioned over the theft of a sum of money from a fruiterer's shop. There were no witnesses: the woman who kept the shop said it was Shooders and he said it wasn't. Brown left his men to handle the case but kept a discreet eye on their progress.

'So, you had a go at Shooders?'
'Aye, we had him in for an hour but he didn't admit it.'
'Ye had him in for an hour?'
A long pause.
'Get him in again.'
Next day:
'Well, did you have Shooders in?'

'We grilled him for two hours this time, but he says it wasn't him.'
'Ach, it was him all right. Bring him in again.'

The process was repeated perhaps half a dozen times, with the suspect becoming increasingly irked and making loud threats about what he was going to get his lawyer to do. But Faither Broon was completely unperturbed.

'Bring him in again. We'll gie him another nip.'

Shooders couldn't believe it when, for the umpteenth time, detectives turned up at the tenement where he lived. They didn't even need to ask him again. 'All right! All right! Ah'll admit it. It was me!'

Again and again Faither Broon's patience and perseverance paid off when interviewing suspects. A particularly long-drawn-out session lasted for ten hours without a break and Brown's colleagues were tired and hungry. One eventually plucked up the courage to suggest that it was time for a cup of tea. Brown stared at him and said nothing. Then he slowly took a bar of chocolate from his pocket, broke it into squares and passed them round. Nothing more was said about the tea break.

Perhaps the story is apocryphal. Even if it is, there can be no better proof of someone's status than the creation of urban myths about them.

★ ★ ★

One thing is certainly no myth: Brown's success in tracking down killers. Over his career it has been estimated that he played a key part in solving at least twenty murders.

Take the case known as the Jedburgh dance hall murder, for example. The market town in the Scottish Borders was not noted for violence but in June 1957 the body of twenty-three-year-old Patrick Honour, who lived at Hartrigge, about a mile from the town centre, was found slumped against the wall near the entrance to the Town Hall where a dance was taking place, barely fifty yards from the local police station.

Three girls who left the dance at about 11.20 p.m. discovered the body. One of them had earlier been dancing with Patrick, who liked to dress in 'Teddy Boy' fashion but, as a local priest confirmed, was in reality a quiet young man 'who would rather sidestep a fight than face up to it.' He had been stabbed several times and his mother told reporters: 'I would sacrifice my own life to find the killer of my son.'

Help was sought from Glasgow CID and Alex Brown was despatched to the Borders to investigate – no doubt because his boss Bob Colquhoun was already fully occupied leading the hunt for the murderer of seventy-two-year-old Nan Wilson in Garnethill.

During the night of the Jedburgh murder, statements had been taken from dancers attending the event and Brown spent much of the day sifting through these. This led him straight to a twenty-three-year-old local man, William Simpson, who bore a grudge against the victim as a result of a minor disagreement over money. Witnesses had seen Simpson turn up at the dance with a friend and challenge Honour to a fight outside, in the course of which Simpson produced a knife and Honour received a fatal stab wound in the heart. He was later found guilty of culpable homicide and sentenced to twelve years' imprisonment in Perth Prison. A few months into his sentence, he was allowed to visit a Perth dental surgery where he escaped from his escort, jumped over a wall and drove off in a lorry parked nearby. He lost control of the vehicle and just managed to open the driver's door and roll out seconds before it crashed.

Within two hours of making his desperate escape bid, he was back in custody.

On the very same day that Brown had first arrested Simpson in June 1957, another brutal killer was appearing in the High Court of Glasgow as a result of the detective's efforts earlier that year. That case, too, had been cleared up in a matter of hours. On the night of Saturday 23 March, the bodies of twenty-seven-year-old Elizabeth (Betty) O'Donnell and her two young children, Patrick aged two and a half and twenty-month-old Elizabeth, were found battered to death in their top floor flat at 72 Inglefield Street, Govanhill. The level of violence was appalling. The killer cut his victim with a knife, choked her and hit her with an electric iron. The infants lay huddled in a bed in the kitchen, having been struck repeatedly with an iron or bottle.

Mrs O'Donnell had been due to attend a party that night in the Gorbals area and when detectives arrived at the address at 4 a.m. her friends were still singing and dancing the night away. It's easy to imagine how Brown's tried and tested methods of silence and patience would soon elicit a name and, just seven hours after the bodies had been discovered, twenty-four-year-old Malcolm McNaughton was dragged from his bed in Hickman Street – only a few hundred yards away from the scene of the crime.

While all this was going on the husband, Cornelius ('Neilly'), was in Barlinnie serving a sentence for housebreaking – an irony not lost on reporters who pointed out that both husband and killer found themselves under the same roof. On 30 March Neilly, accompanied by two warders, was allowed out of prison to attend the funeral of his wife and children.

When the case reached the High Court in Glasgow that July it made legal history. McNaughton was to plead not guilty but there were no fewer than fifty-seven witnesses to call on if required. However, McNaughton's counsel, Mr. I.M. Robertson, indicated that his client wished to change his plea to guilty. As a consequence, proceedings lasted for less than three minutes. Passing a sentence of life imprisonment, Lord Carmont (famed for his severity on razor gangs) told the killer: 'You have pled guilty to this very grave charge, which in other times might have resulted in far more serious consequences.' He was referring to the fact that the case was the first time a plea of guilty had been accepted since the passing of the new Homicide Act earlier that year which placed limits on the categories of killers who could be executed. Capital murder was now defined as 'murder in the course of furtherance of theft', 'murder by shooting or causing an explosion' and 'murder of a police officer acting in the execution of his duty'. In other instances, life imprisonment rather than hanging was to be the mandatory sentence.

The Homicide Act had received Royal Assent on 21 March 1957 – just two days prior to the crime which in other circumstances might have led McNaughton to the gallows.

What possessed him to carry out such an act? McNaughton had met Cornelius O'Donnell in Barlinnie and became a friend of the family, often visiting and playing with the children. There was no suggestion at his trial of any kind of liaison with Mrs O'Donnell. McNaughton told his mother that he did not know what came over him and could not remember killing the children. 'It will always be a mystery,' concluded one CID man. 'Even McNaughton seems unable to solve it.'

★ ★ ★

In January 1958, Alex Brown came face to face with one of the most manipulative criminals of all time: Peter Manuel. It turned out to be the climax of his career.

The story of Manuel's multiple murders has been told in depth in various books, most recently in A. M. Nicol's *Manuel: Portrait of a Serial Killer* (2008) and *Peter Manuel: Serial Killer* by Hector MacLeod and Malcolm McLeod (2009). Understandably, these accounts concentrate primarily on the workings of Manuel's mind rather than on the manner in which the police outwitted him.

Briefly, the background is as follows. Peter Thomas Anthony Manuel was born in New York in 1927 where his father hoped to build a more prosperous life than in Scotland. However, the family returned to the UK where the young Manuel started on his life of crime, ending up in a succession of different schools and young offenders' institutions in both England and Scotland. By 1955, he had served a prison sentence for rape and had returned to live with his family in Fourth Street, Birkenshaw, Uddingston. He attacked twenty-nine-year-old Mary McLaughlin but defended himself in front of a jury in Airdrie Sheriff Court which returned a verdict of 'Not Proven'.

The first of the crimes that would lead to his final trial at Glasgow High Court occurred on 2 January 1956 when seventeen-year-old

Anne Kneilands was murdered and her body left near the East Kilbride golf course. On 24 March, Manuel was arrested for a break-in at Hamilton Colliery, the trial being set for October. Before that, on 17 September, he broke into the house of William Watt, the owner of a chain of bakery shops, who lived at 5 Fennsbank Avenue in Burnside. Watt was away on a fishing trip and the house was occupied by his wife, sister-in-law and sixteen-year-old daughter Vivienne. All three were shot by Manuel. However, suspicion fell on the homeowner himself, and there followed the bizarre interlude of Watt's arrest, with the police attempting to prove that he managed to leave the Cairnbaan Hotel near Lochgilphead, Argyll, drive back to Glasgow in his Vauxhall Velox and return to the hotel by morning. Watt accordingly found himself in a cell at Barlinnie Prison – at the same time as Manuel was beginning a sentence for his break-in at the colliery.

It was here that Manuel's compulsive desire to be the centre of attention led to his undoing. Manuel told Watt's solicitor, Laurence Dowdall, that he knew the identity of the real killer, in the process revealing that he also knew far too much detail about the inside of 5 Fennsbank Avenue.

Nearly a year passed until Manuel was released from Barlinnie in November 1957. He immediately arranged to meet up with Watt, possibly with the idea of extorting payment in exchange for information about the murder of his family. He then made his way to Newcastle by train for a job interview where he is believed to have murdered a taxi driver, Sydney Dunn, on 7 December.

Back in the West of Scotland, Manuel broke into the manse of the Rev. Alexander Houston in Mount Vernon early on Christmas Day where he stole a camera and gloves which he gave his family as presents. Three days later, on 28 December, he assaulted and murdered another seventeen-year-old girl, Isabelle Cooke, and buried her in a field.

Manuel's reign of terror reached its climax on New Year's Day 1958, when he shot Peter and Doris Smart and their eleven-year-old son Michael in their bungalow in Sheepburn Road, Uddingston. Over the next few days, he returned to the house to open and close curtains and feed the cat and drove away in Peter Smart's Austin A35. It was the discovery of this car lying in the Gorbals on 6 January that led the police to check up on the Smarts' house, where they discovered the bodies.

It's at this point that Alex Brown comes into the picture, along with his colleague Detective Inspector Tom Goodall, himself a future CID chief. For the next few weeks their activities would be reported in the newspapers on a daily basis.

In the early afternoon of Tuesday 7 January 1958, the Chief Constable of Lanarkshire, John Wilson, made an official request for assistance from Glasgow CID. The Lanarkshire detectives had already been drawing on Glasgow's forensic back up; now further help in the form of the expertise of senior detectives was sought. However, it is clear that this request was fully expected, as CID Chief Robert Colquhoun had already drawn up arrangements which he was waiting to put into operation when required, and Brown and Goodall, his two best officers, were standing by for this task. Goodall, who had been promoted to Detective Inspector the previous year, was selected both for his evident ability (he was to rise from the rank of sergeant to Chief Superintendent in seven years) and for his valuable links to informers in the Gorbals criminal underworld, many of whom had been involved with Manuel to a greater or lesser extent.

On the morning of 3 January, Superintendent Myles Duncan of the Lanarkshire force was asked if he had requested assistance from Glasgow CID but his reply was 'No, certainly not.' Yet, two days previously, while the rest of Scotland was sleeping off its New Year hangover, Brown had met with the Lanarkshire Chief Constable and spent the day touring various locations with Lanarkshire officers. He later said that 'after he had familiarised himself with the area, it was decided to await further developments and possibly the girl [Isabelle Cooke] being traced.'

In passing, it's interesting to note that, although Brown's official involvement in the Manuel enquiry was just beginning, it was not the first time that his path had crossed with one of the principal figures involved. After William Watt was cleared of any suspicion regarding the murder of his family, he undertook his own investigation by establishing contact with the criminal underworld. When interviewed after the Manuel trial, Watt said that 'Mixing with criminals was not entirely new to me . . . I did some plain clothes work during the war [when he served as a war reserve constable attached to the Eastern police Division]. Superintendent Alex Brown was my sergeant then. I used every ounce of police training I could remember and spent a lot of money on drink for my criminal contacts in my lone enquiries.'

Brown received the news of his secondment to the Lanarkshire enquiry on 7 January while he was at Sandyhills Golf Course with a search party looking for the body of Isabelle Cooke. Thereafter, he established his base at Bothwell police office and one of his first acts was to have a camp bed set up in the station so that he could be on call at any hour of the night. Over the next couple of weeks, there would be many occasions when he had no more than three hours' sleep. It was made clear that Glasgow was not 'taking over' the investigation; the city CID men were there to assist 'under the direction of the Chief Constable of the county'. Statements to the press over the ensuing days were made, not by Brown, the man of few words, but by his Lanarkshire colleagues. Superintendent Murdo McKenzie was in charge of the investigation into the Smart murders and Superintendent Myles Duncan directed the Isabelle Cooke enquiry. Chief Inspector Muncie and Detective Inspector Robert McNeill continued to play prominent roles in the investigations.

Another week was to pass before Brown set eyes on Peter Manuel for the first time and the pressure on the police for 'a result' during that period was intense. 'It is time the police did something about these murders,' one local man told a reporter from *The Bulletin*. 'If Glasgow CID could not help, they should go to Scotland Yard.' But Brown was the master of the waiting game. Evidence was patiently being accumulated which would ultimately lead to Manuel's conviction. Goodall's notebooks reveal that he spent much of this time investigating bank-notes found in Manuel's possession.

A key figure in this process was a man called Joe Brannan. While content to be associated with Manuel in matters of theft, he was shocked by the series of murders in Lanarkshire and Detective Inspector McNeill managed to recruit him to keep track of Manuel's activities and report back. It was Brannan who passed on the crucial information that Manuel had been so short of cash on the last day of December that he borrowed money from his mother yet the next day, he was freely spending money in the bar of the Woodend Hotel, Mossend. A check of the serial numbers revealed that the banknotes he had used came from the same batch that Peter Smart had withdrawn from the Commercial Bank of Scotland prior to the holiday period.

Brown further established that the gun used to kill the Smart household, a Beretta, had been acquired by Manuel with assistance from a criminal well known to the police, Sam 'Dandy' McKay – the man who, the following year, would be one of the gang that carried out the Shettleston bank raid. Through his network of informants, Brown also traced how Manuel had purchased a Webley revolver in September 1956, prior to the Watt murders.

During this time, detectives had Manuel under constant surveillance. By 12 January, Brannan indicated that Manuel was growing increasingly 'edgy' as he had expected the police to come for him and as a result he suggested that he and Brannan should travel to London.

Early in the morning of Tuesday 14 January, Brown and Goodall, accompanied by Muncie, McNeill and some other Lanarkshire officers, arrived at the Manuel home at 32 Fourth Street, Birkenshaw. Peter's father, Samuel, who had a track record of covering for his son, was just leaving for work when Brown showed him his warrant to search the premises. Brown told Peter Manuel that he should get dressed and accompany him to Bellshill police station for an identity parade and, after protests, he was taken away at 7.30 a.m. He would never see the inside of his house again.

The search revealed the camera and gloves stolen from the Rev Houston's manse and when Manuel Senior could not satisfactorily account for these he, too, was arrested. Throughout the visit Goodall meticulously noted down everything said by his boss and by members of the Manuel household, his first notebook entry on this momentous day being timed at 6.45 a.m. and the last at 11.40 p.m.

Brown astutely informed Peter Manuel that his father had been charged with theft, providing what Allan Nicol describes as 'a rare opportunity to exert emotional pressure on a spree-killing psychopath in the one area in which he was decidedly vulnerable' – his relationship with his parents.

And it worked. In the early hours of 16 January, Manuel asked to see Inspector McNeill who deliberately kept him waiting. The killer gave a written commitment to provide information on the 'unsolved crimes' in the area if he was allowed to see his parents. In one of the earlier books on the case, *The Hunting Down of Peter Manuel* (published in 1973 by John Bingham who wrote it with input from Muncie) the author describes Manuel's action at this point as 'the greatest and most inexplicable decision of his life'. It was presumably inevitable that he would sooner or later reach a stage when he had to accept that the game was up but it appears that the arrival of that moment was hastened by concern for his father's predicament.

A car was sent to collect Manuel Senior, in handcuffs, and to pick up Mrs Manuel. The couple were ushered into a room where, in the presence of Brown, Goodall and McNeill, their son made a full confession, at the end of which he said that he would show the officers the location of the body of Isabelle Cooke. The two Detective Inspectors set off with Manuel to Burntbroom Farm on the other side of the Glasgow to Hamilton railway line from Isabelle's home, with Brown following in a separate police car. It was here that Manuel uttered the chilling words: 'I think I'm standing on her.'

The body was found almost immediately, about three feet below the surface in an area of the field that had only been ploughed the day before. Nearby night-shift workers reported 'hearing the soft thud of spades biting into the wet ground' and Isabelle's remains were taken to the Glasgow police mortuary for a post-mortem.

Back at Hamilton Police Station, Manuel sat down and wrote out a detailed confession to the eight murders. According to Douglas Grant's account in *The Thin Blue Line*, 'It was then 6 a.m., and for Detective Superintendent Brown and his colleagues who had been on continuous duty for twenty-six hours it appeared time for some much needed sleep.'

But Manuel wasn't finished yet.

While being driven to Barlinnie Prison, he offered to point out where he had disposed of the murder weapons. He claimed to have thrown the Beretta that killed the Smarts into the River Clyde from the King's Bridge near Glasgow Green, and dropped the Webley which killed the Watts from the eleventh spar of the footbridge at South Portland Street. Grant adds the authentic detail that Brown marked the spot by scratching it with a penny.

After this night of intense activity – during which he never even managed to lie down on his camp bed – Brown returned to Glasgow to update Colquhoun and Assistant Chief Constable James Robertson. After a few hours' rest he was back in Lanarkshire to continue enquiries and the press announced that a man was likely to be charged with murder the following day. On 18 January, Manuel was duly named as being charged with killing Anne Kneilands and the Watt family and the following day police in Hamilton confirmed that he was also charged with the Cooke and Smart murders.

Brown now turned his attention to the guns. Additional senior Glasgow officers were drafted in to assist: the search for the weapons in the murky waters of the Clyde was overseen by Detective Superintendent Henry Crawford while Chief Inspector Robert Kerr, head of Govan CID, followed up lines of enquiry regarding the source of the guns in Glasgow. In addition, Brown was reported on 22 January to be assisting colleagues from Durham CID who had arrived in Hamilton in connection with Manuel's suspected involvement in the murder of Sydney Dunn, the Newcastle taxi driver, the previous December. A conference involving what the *Evening Times* called the 'murder triangle' teams of Lanarkshire, Glasgow and Durham detectives lasted until midnight.

Meanwhile, the River Clyde was refusing to give up its secrets.

A 5 cwt electro-magnet was borrowed from Colville's steelyard and operated from a barge with a crane. Conditions were so cold that water splashed on the protective clothing worn by the search team turned to ice within a few minutes. There were newspaper headlines like 'Fifth Day of Search for Gun' but the story gradually faded from the front pages. Then a different tactic was tried: Brown arranged for David Bell, a skilled diver from the Clyde Navigation Trust, to join the search. It took him less than half an hour to locate the Webley. The Beretta was found a few days later about fifty yards from the river bank in fourteen feet of water.

By 12 February, Brown told the *Evening Times* that his daily activities in Lanarkshire were 'virtually over now' and that he had returned to his Glasgow headquarters. Five days later, Chief Constable John Wilson wrote a glowing letter of thanks to his Glasgow counterpart, Malcolm McCulloch:

> When . . . I asked for the support of an experienced senior Detective Officer, you readily made available the services of your Detective Superintendent Alexander Brown and Detective Inspector Thomas Goodall. I was indeed fortunate to have these Officers for, knowing something of their qualities, I was confident of their ability in the trying times ahead. From the outset they fitted into the team selected for the enquiries, and it was ever gratifying to have such an efficient and harmonious unit. I kept in regular touch with them and know that these men worked for long hours without complaint and nothing was too hard for them to tackle.

Needless to say, the criminal fraternity had not put their activities on hold during these frenetic weeks just because the police were preoccupied with Manuel. In late January, Colquhoun had taken charge of yet another murder. Forty-one-year-old John Orr was found near Glasgow Green, stabbed in the neck, less than twenty-four hours after his release from Barlinnie. He had been seen arguing with a woman in a café in Howard Street on the Saturday night and the Chief

Superintendent put out an appeal for information about a female aged around twenty-five, with 'dyed blonde hair and a squint in one eye' but the case was inevitably overshadowed by the Lanarkshire drama and no arrest was made.

Another on-going case led to a remarkable tribute to the character of Alex Brown being paid during a trial at Glasgow Sheriff Court the following month. A man had been arrested abroad on fraud charges and he was being defended by a well-known solicitor of the era, Bill Dunlop. Dunlop noted that at the end of 1957 the accused had contacted Brown with 'certain information of great value'. At that time, he explained, Mr Brown was busily engaged in matters in Lanarkshire but 'it was typical of that man's greatness that he had come to court today to back him [the accused] up.'

Brown's role in the Manuel case would again receive considerable press attention during the trial in the High Court of Glasgow, which began on 12 May 1958. The drama of the proceedings intensified when Manuel decided to take over his own defence, allowing him to revel in the opportunity to question the detectives who had previously questioned him. Inevitably, Manuel put a very different spin on what had happened during the interviews in the Lanarkshire police offices in January. He now maintained he was forced to write the confessions to save his family. Among the numerous accusations he made were that Brown refused to allow him a lawyer, that he said he would 'crucify' the Manuel family if a full confession wasn't forthcoming and that he would implicate Manuel Senior in the Smart murders. 'I was seriously concerned about this man Brown's threats,' said Manuel. 'He was raging like a lunatic!'

If there was any truth in these claims, Brown must have been a very different man from the one described by everyone else as quietly spoken, reticent, reserved and patient. Another comment attributed to Manuel is perhaps nearer the mark: 'I could handle the others, but I couldn't handle Brown.'

Manuel's line that he was the victim of an elaborate conspiracy didn't convince the members of the jury. At 4.50 p.m. on Thursday 29 May, they unanimously found him guilty of the murders of the Watt and Smart families and Isabelle Cooke. The judge, Lord Cameron, raised the black cap above his head and pronounced the inevitable: 'death by hanging'. At the end of the proceedings his Lordship asked to see Brown, Goodall and McNeill in chambers, presumably to express his thanks for their work, though they never divulged what he had said to them.

And after that, as one journalist neatly put it, Manuel went to the gallows and Alex Brown returned to his desk at police headquarters.

# 10

## *Men or Monsters?*

*Male Killers – Female Victims, 1957–60*

Criminologists, psychiatrists and sociologists have long debated the factors that turn men or women into killers. Are the roots of their actions to be found in their personalities or are they shaped by environmental factors such as family background, housing conditions and education? In other words, does a person become a criminal as a result of nature or nurture?

The question seemed more than an academic one in 1958 when the west of Scotland had lived through Peter Manuel's killing spree. It may not have been a very scientific analysis, but few would have disagreed with the conclusion of the trial judge, Lord Cameron, when he said that 'every once in a while, someone like Peter Anthony Manuel comes along who is mad, bad and dangerous'.

During the years when Robert Colquhoun was in charge of the CID – years which overlapped with the period of Manuel's murders, trial and execution – several other brutal killings of vulnerable women took place, some of them involving an even greater degree of violence than those carried out by Manuel who, prior to his execution, had described himself as 'the foulest beast on earth'. In none of these cases was the killer acting in accordance with a plan; instead, they reveal how, in certain circumstances, an individual can suddenly lose control and end up perpetrating the most vicious of crimes.

And there were few crimes more vicious than the killing in May 1958 of twenty-eight-year-old Margaret Doyle who lived with a Polish former soldier called Franciszek (known as Franek or Frank) Gacek in Hill Street, Garnethill. One journalist dubbed the area 'Glasgow's death row' as less than a year earlier, seventy-two-year-old Nan Wilson had been murdered in her flat in the same street and, in 1952, the body of four-year-old Betty Alexander had been found close by.

As Garnethill was a conveniently placed central location with plenty of rooms to let, it housed a floating population of minor celebrities appearing at the Alhambra Theatre, the Empire and the many other places of live entertainment which Glasgow had in the 1950s. The area has thus always been notable for its cosmopolitan feel and it later became the centre of Glasgow's Chinese community. Hill Street has also been home to numerous prominent figures in the city's life, such as the writer and artist Alasdair Gray and Rev Dr Nevile Davidson, minister of Glasgow Cathedral between 1935 and 1967. Mrs Davidson used to say that it wasn't unusual to see bloodstains on the pavement after a violent Saturday night yet it was important to her husband that he should live there, in the heart of the city, amongst ordinary Glasgow citizens.

Only yards away from the minister's manse, yet inhabiting a totally different world, was Margaret Doyle, living in a single room at 46 Hill Street with her two children while Gacek was away working on hydro-electric schemes in the Highlands for which he sometimes earned £30 a week – more than double the average manual worker's wage at the time. When he came home for the weekends, the other tenants of the house were used to hearing noisy drinking sessions and fights on Saturday nights. Until about a year before her death Margaret had been living with a couple called Eva and Joe Kotarba. Eva was the mother of 'Glasgow's Godfather' Walter Norval who did not approve of her involvement with Kotarba, another Pole with a reputation for horrific violence against women. His friend Gacek had been conscripted into the German infantry during the Second World War and was later taken prisoner by American forces. He came to Scotland as a prisoner-of-war and was subsequently transferred to the Polish Resettlement Corps, which assisted soldiers who did not wish to return to Poland, now under a Communist regime. Over the next ten years, he appeared in court on at least twelve occasions, charged with offences such as assault, disorderly behaviour and living on immoral earnings and he served several short prison sentences.

On the night of her death, Margaret Doyle had been out dancing and arrived back at Hill Street around midnight in a drunken state. Other couples in the street saw her crying and they escorted her back to the door of her house where they left her saying she was afraid of getting a beating. Gacek, too, had been out drinking heavily and required to be helped home.

Fortunately, the two children were being looked after by a friend of their mother.

Five single rooms on the ground floor and basement of 46 Hill Street were sub-let and the tenants heard the banging and shouting that followed. 'It was terrible listening to it,' said one. 'I wanted to put my hands over my ears.' 'We didn't go across,' said another. 'We thought we might get a hammering too.' Eventually all went quiet.

Early next morning, Gacek turned up at the Northern police office, having brought along Walter Norval for support. He was interviewed by an officer well known to Norval: Joe Beattie, then a Detective Constable. Gacek's story was that he had come home late at night and found Margaret dead.

Beattie, Detective Inspector Sam Paton and Detective Inspector John Scott immediately set off to inspect the premises. The room was in darkness and when they switched on the light, it fused. Another bulb was borrowed and it lit up a scene that shocked even these hard-bitten investigators. A woman's body, almost naked and with severe head injuries, lay on the bed. The wall was covered in blood to a height of three feet above the bed and the room strewn with bloodstained clothing and linen. An attempt had been made to clean up and there was a bucket that appeared to have a mixture of water and blood in it. In a corner lay a child's tricycle, damaged and stained with blood.

Detective Chief Inspector Neil Beaton, head of the Northern CID, was called from home and Superintendent George Maclean and his team from the Identification Bureau were soon on the scene. The medical experts Professor Andrew Allison and Dr James Imrie arrived to the sound of church bells calling worshippers to morning services. Fingerprints from the tricycle, a palm print from a wardrobe and a footprint from a child's cot were taken, all of them later confirmed to be Gacek's.

In spite of the evidence, Gacek pled not guilty at the trial in the High Court in July. He said he woke from a drunken sleep in a chair to see Margaret Doyle lying dead on the bed. He ran to Kotarba's house in Ashley Street and he in turn fetched Norval who accompanied him to the police office. Gacek said he had spent the evening at the Locarno dance hall where he had smuggled in a half bottle of whisky. There he met Margaret who struck him on the back of his head with her handbag. He later became so drunk that a member of the dance hall staff had to see him home; Margaret arrived back later but by that stage 'the drink had knocked him out'. 'I cannot remember hitting Margaret with anything', he told the police.

Counsel for the defence, D.C. Anderson, QC, said that if the jury were satisfied that Gacek was so much under the influence of drink as to be incapable of forming an intent to kill, it was open to them to find him guilty of culpable homicide. This was the unanimous verdict of the ten women and five men on the jury and Gacek received a sentence of fifteen years in prison. He was sentenced on the same day that Peter Manuel was executed.

Gacek may seem to have got off lightly. Ten years later, he was released and later took up with a prostitute. He treated her no better than Margaret and, in 1973, there was another murder.

But this time, Gacek was not the killer: he was the victim.

★ ★ ★

In February 1959 the journalist and novelist Bill Knox, who later assisted Colquhoun in compiling his memoirs, was pleased to see his latest crime story being serialised in the *Evening Times*. Entitled 'Death Department', it was set in an imaginary city centre store in Sauchiehall Street where police were investigating a series of thefts and two murders. They traced some of the stolen fashion stock to a smaller retail outlet in Dennistoun and, to illustrate that instalment of the story, the newspaper sent out a photographer to take a photo of a typical clothes shop which was then retouched, the real name being replaced by a fictional one. The photographer happened to pick premises in Cathcart Road near Hampden Park stadium. The owner, a Mrs McGhee, was amused to see her shop being used as an illustration to a murder story and called in at the newspaper office to ask why it had been selected. The staff explained that it had been a purely random choice and, curiosity satisfied, she went on her way.

There was nothing particularly remarkable about all this – except that, two months later, fact replaced fiction when Mrs McGhee was found brutally murdered behind her own shop counter.

Helen McGhee was a fifty-eight-year-old widow whose husband, a doctor who worked in a mental hospital in Larbert, had died six years earlier. She continued to live in their Pollokshields flat but decided she needed to get involved in something new and, about a year after her husband's death, took over a baby linen shop. She was a quiet woman with a kindly manner, which is perhaps why she let in a young man one evening after closing time. He probably spun her a tale about needing a last-minute present and she prepared a parcel of baby clothes for him. A young woman who lived in a tenement a few yards away stopped to look at a garment in the window display and noticed a tall man at the counter. It did occur to her at the time that it was strange to see a customer there well after business hours. The same man had also been seen on other evenings, loitering in a nearby close watching the shop.

Mrs McGhee was due to visit her brother-in-law for a family birthday celebration that evening, 12 April, but by 9.30 p.m. there was still no sign of her, so he went to the shop with a spare key. He noticed her Austin Cambridge was not parked in its usual place and, on entering the shop, found her body lying on the floor with multiple stab wounds. The till had been rifled and on the shop counter lay a selection of boxes of clothing items, some wrapped parcels and a milk bottle. He picked up the phone – having the presence of mind to lift the receiver with a handkerchief in case there were any fingerprints – and called the police.

Southern Division CID alerted Colquhoun who soon took command. He made tracing the car his first priority. Details were flashed to every police force in Scotland and it was found at 3.30 a.m. abandoned five miles away on the outskirts of Cambuslang. First, the fingerprint team went over the interior of the car and then Colquhoun opened the boot, where he found the murder weapon, a special type of butcher's knife with a narrow point designed for removing bones from meat. There was also a milk bottle top and a copy of a newspaper, which, it was assumed, was the one the killer had been pretending to read as he hung about outside the shop waiting for closing time.

Teams of detectives went round butchers' shops to check whether any knives were missing. Two senior officers from Headquarters, Superintendents Bob Kerr and Henry Crawford, were seconded to Southern Division to help, while the search around Cambuslang was led by Detective Superintendent William Muncie of the Lanarkshire force who had played a prominent role in the investigations into the murders carried out in his area by Peter Manuel.

Then, on 15 April, Colquhoun made a surprise announcement: 'We know the identity of a man we wish to interview'. He was stated to be seventeen years old, but his name was not made public. In his autobiography, the Chief Superintendent explained how a couple came to tell him that their son, a butcher's apprentice, had returned home on the Saturday night in a distressed state and had left home the next day. The parents went to the shop where he worked, to learn that he had been sacked a fortnight earlier, though since then he had followed the same routine each morning, leaving the house as if going to work. As he had already been in trouble with the police, his fingerprints were on file; they matched the prints found in the shop and in the car, on the milk bottle top and on the newspaper.

A more accurate description of the suspect could now be issued to every policeman on the beat and reports of possible sightings started to come in. The focus briefly moved to Dunbartonshire where a youth fitting the description was seen near the Forth and Clyde Canal and police dogs carried out a nighttime search. 'Every police officer in Britain is now looking for this youth,' said Colquhoun. Next, he was allegedly seen eighty miles from Glasgow by a businessman in Newton Stewart, Galloway, leading to another fruitless search. A description was circulated of the type of suitcase the youth had taken from home and, because he had been to London before, the possibility that he would return there provided a further line of enquiry.

But the search ended just two miles from where it had started. On 19 April another seventeen-year-old butcher's apprentice spotted his former workmate in a close in Lawmoor Street, Gorbals, and alerted a policeman on duty. The youth, now named as John McGilvray of Cambuslang, gave himself up and was taken to the local police office. When Colquhoun arrived to charge him, he immediately said, 'It was all me. I did everything'. It seems that his motive was to steal money so that he could pretend he still had earnings, thus concealing the fact that he had been sacked.

If so, he had committed 'murder in the course or furtherance of theft' – and that was a capital offence.

However, when the case came up for trial at the High Court of Glasgow in July the judge, Lord Sorn, made it clear that the death penalty would not apply as the accused was under eighteen. The psychiatrists were called upon to suggest an explanation of the accused's behaviour. Dr William Blyth considered that McGilvray had the emotional maturity of a child of only twelve or thirteen, while Dr Hunter Gillies thought 'his responsibility was diminished by virtue of his psychopathic personality'. In his view, McGilvray was 'not insane but approaching the borderline. In the passage of time, he might mature and become more normal.' He was found guilty and ordered to be 'detained during Her Majesty's Pleasure'.

By coincidence, the newspaper on which McGilvray's prints were found was a copy of the *Evening Times* – the second occasion on which that title had been connected to a story of murder in a clothes shop.

★ ★ ★

One Monday morning in October 1959, Mrs Minnie Wilson, a teacher at Abbotsford Primary School on the south side of Glasgow, did not turn up for work. This was most unlike her, and the headmaster phoned home but received no reply. When she did not appear on the Tuesday, it was clear that something was wrong and the Head arranged for a friend to go to her flat in Albert Road, Pollokshields. Again, there was no answer, and the police were called. When they forced an entry, Mrs Wilson was found lying on the bedroom floor with her throat cut and with severe injuries to her head. Nearby lay a poker and a bread knife.

The word Colquhoun used to describe the violence of the attack was 'maniacal' – to such an extent that one early line of enquiry involved checking with mental institutions to see if any patient had escaped. There were more specific clues to follow up as well: a bloodstained man had been spotted near the scene and detectives were sent round laundries to check whether any heavily stained clothing had been handed in. In addition, fingerprints were found on the toilet cistern and a diamond-patterned shoeprint on the bedspread. Initially, though, neither of these leads produced any results. The fingerprints did not match any on file and, said Colquhoun, 'when we traced [the bloodstained man] he quickly proved that he had been involved in a simple brawl, and was out of our reckoning.'

The breakthrough came when police traced a couple who had lodged with Mrs Wilson for a few weeks in 1957. Thirty-three-year-old prison warder Robert Menzies and his wife now lived in Duke Street and Colquhoun sent some of his men to take fingerprints, using the well-known police line that they were needed purely for elimination purposes. The prints turned out to match those found on the cistern but this was not necessarily conclusive, as it was not impossible that they could have remained there since Menzies' brief tenancy. However, when questioned, Mrs Wilson's cleaner was adamant that this could not be the case, as she carefully cleaned the cistern area each week.

Any remaining doubt in Colquhoun's mind disappeared when he went round to see Menzies and noticed he was wearing shoes with rubber soles in a diamond pattern.

Menzies confessed and, just before the High Court of Edinburgh closed for the New Year holiday in December, pled guilty to non-capital murder for which he was sentenced to life imprisonment. Because of his plea, his court appearance lasted only sixty seconds and as a result the full details of what happened were not stated in court or reported in the newspapers. However, his Criminal Case File reveals the sequence of events that led up to the crime and give a glimpse into the perpetrator's state of mind.

Menzies was well educated and widely travelled. He worked for a time in the jewellery business before joining the Cameronians, and later transferred to the Military Police where he served in India and Malaya. He held the rank of Lieutenant in the Malayan police until he took up a job as manager of a rubber plantation in 1956. Then, because of his wife's health, he returned to Britain where he was employed as a prison officer at Barlinnie in 1957. By nature he was quiet and kept to himself but he had a vicious temper and was fond of boasting that he had guarded Peter Manuel at Barlinnie at the time that Manuel was awaiting execution, though there is no evidence that he did.

Mrs Menzies taught at Abbotford Primary School alongside Minnie Wilson, and for a few weeks in 1957, the couple and their three children took up Mrs Wilson's offer of accommodation in her spacious seven-room flat until they found a place of their own.

Two years later, Menzies chanced to run into his old benefactor while he was on sick leave as a result of being assaulted by a prisoner who had broken his nose. In his statement to the police, he described what happened next:

> I was going to the pictures that night and met her in the bus queue at the Coliseum. She spoke to me, told me that she had bought a cooker and a

second hand wireless for either £12 or £13 and that the man was going to deliver them to her house in his van. She knew I tinkered about with things and asked me to go home with her and see if they were worth the money. I went with her and we sat and smoked. She had a drink of whisky. Nobody came to the house except the cleaner. After the cleaner had gone she made advances to me. I don't do these things and I got up and put on my coat in the hall. As I was making to go out she asked me to stay the night. I said, 'if I was going to do that it would not be with you', or something like that. She then struck me across the nose with the back of her hand. You know my nose had been broken. I lost my head and struck her. What happened after that I don't know but when I came to I was standing in the kitchen with a knife in my hand.

Colquhoun had certainly been on the right lines when he sent his men to check laundries for bloodstained clothing, for Menzies continued:

I was in an awful mess. I tried to clean up as best as I could. I got sort of squared up but my coat was in a terrible mess. I rolled it up, left the house and got a taxi at the Registrar's Office. When I got home about 11 p.m. my wife was in bed. She had an injection from the doctor and was sleeping. I wrapped the coat in paper and put it under the floor boards in the empty room. I washed my shirt and it has been washed six times since. It is a drip dry. My wife gave me some anxious moments afterwards asking about my coat. I think she thought it was in the cleaners. I want you to believe that I never stole anything in my life.[4]

That last point was crucial; had there been stronger evidence that theft was the motive, Menzies could have been charged with capital murder.

But there was a third possibility under law. In September 1960, Menzies petitioned the Secretary of State to the effect that 'Mrs Wilson suggested sexual intercourse, she struck him on the nose and then,

---

4. Criminal Case file, Robert Murray Menzies, Crown copyright, National
   Records of Scotland (HH16/448).

because of a previous injury to his nose, this caused him such pain as to result in a blackout during which he killed her.' Menzies' purpose in petitioning was to ask for these circumstances to be taken into account when his case came up for review. The legal opinion expressed at the time was that, had this account been put forward at the trial as the basis of a plea of not guilty to murder but guilty of culpable homicide on the grounds of diminished responsibility, it might – if successful – have resulted in a fixed term of imprisonment rather than a life sentence.

It was no doubt something that Menzies reflected upon many times before his death in 1990 at the age of sixty-four.

★  ★  ★

In retrospect, the violent end to the stormy relationship between Gacek and Margaret Doyle might seem to have a certain tragic inevitability about it. But the teenage apprentice butcher John McGilvray had parents who cared for him, even though they knew they had to do the right thing and report him to Colquhoun. Robert Menzies, too, came from a good home and was himself a family man with a varied career in law enforcement.

Yet in all three cases, something triggered a sudden loss of self-control and they not only killed but did so with an exceptional degree of violence. Maybe the American novelist Alice Sebold, author of *The Lovely Bones* (2002), was on to something when she wrote, 'Murderers are not monsters, they're men. And that's the most frightening thing about them.'

# 11

## *The Patient and Perceptive Golfer*

### Detective Chief Superintendent Bob Kerr, CID Chief 1960–63

If there was one television programme that Chief Superintendent Bob Kerr could not bear to watch, it was *Z Cars*. He had no time, he said, for 'their way of speaking and interviewing, the attitudes to each other inside the force – that's all quite foreign to any real-life police office'.

This was a man who knew what he was talking about, for he spent thirty-seven years at the sharp end in Glasgow's police force during which he not only took part in 100 different murder enquiries but played a key role in tracking down the bank robbers who carried out the two largest and most daring raids of the era, in Ibrox in 1955 and Shettleston in 1959. No wonder they called him 'the man the crooks love to hate'.

One of a family of nine children, Robert Hannah Kerr was born in 1903 at New Luce, a remote village in Dumfries and Galloway. His father was a shepherd and both Robert and his brother William initially followed in his footsteps. However, after serving in the First World War, William took up a job as a railway signalman and this brought him into frequent contact with the local police constable who persuaded him that joining the police would be a worthwhile career.

William took his advice and eventually ended up as Chief Constable of Kirkcudbrightshire.

Influenced by his older brother's example, young Robert decided to pursue a similar calling; he, too, was fascinated by police work and his mother used to say that he was always reading crime reports in the newspapers. Rather than joining the local Wigtownshire Constabulary he moved to Glasgow in 1926, where his married sisters were now living. Behind this decision lay a personal tragedy: in 1923 Robert had married May McDowall who died of tuberculosis two years later at the age of only twenty-two. Ten years later, he remarried, but he regularly returned on holiday visits to his mother, who later moved into the Old School house in New Luce, and to his former in-laws.

Robert enrolled at the Oxford Street Training School at the same time as Alex Brown, and the two remained close friends on and off duty throughout their careers. Both men had that dogged sense of determination and painstaking attention to detail that are the hallmarks of the successful investigator. In fact, there is one classic story that has been said to involve Brown when the detective concerned was actually Kerr. During an enquiry into a safe breaking, he was searching a suspect's house when he noticed a selection of old fountain pens lying on the mantelpiece. Picking one of them up, he observed that it had no nib and he looked more closely inside the cap where he found a piece of rolled-up paper. He dug this out with a pin and discovered that it was a left luggage ticket for an attaché case containing £4,000 and further tickets, which in turn led to the recovery of even more of the cash.

Bob Kerr started off his duties in the Southern Division and quickly revealed a talent for finding out information, which led to him being given the opportunity to carry out plain clothes work in 1929. Two years later, he joined the CID in Govan (G Division), an area near the River Clyde which in these days was lined with shipyards. Promotions came regularly: he made Detective Sergeant in 1938, Detective Inspector in 1946 and Detective Chief Inspector in 1953. Kerr gives the impression of being a solid, reliable officer prepared to devote long hours to the vital but unexciting work of evidence gathering, a process which at times meant extensive travelling through the country as he did in the mid-fifties when, as head of the Govan CID, he brought the raiders of the Ibrox branch of the British Linen Bank to justice. Sheriff Irvine Smith, QC, who acted for the defence in the trial, summed him up as 'a quietly spoken, patient and immensely perceptive man'.

Kerr expected from his men the same level of commitment he showed himself. 'We had to work round the clock,' said one, 'and sometimes Bob Kerr could be ruthless in keeping his men at work, but he never put a man on a job when it wasn't vital. As a result, his success rate was outstanding.' Similarly, he once stressed to his nephew, who joined the Metropolitan Police, the importance of devoting time to keeping in touch with the wives of criminals who had been sent to prison as this allowed access to informal sources of information; the occasional reward of a few pounds would often prove money well spent.

In 1959, Kerr took up the role of Superintendent at Headquarters (H Division) and succeeded Robert Colquhoun as CID Chief in September 1960, holding that post until retirement three years later allowed him more time to pursue his passion for golf. He died in 1973 at the age of seventy at his home in Rowan Road, Dumbreck – just minutes away from the scene of the Ibrox raid with which his name was always associated.

It might originally have been Robert's older brother who inspired him to join the police, but there's no doubt that the Chief Constable of Kirkcudbrightshire was greatly impressed by his younger brother's achievements. In his autobiography *Into the Unknown* (1984), William affectionately summed up Robert's career as follows:

> In a couple of years in the big city, he would probably have dealt with as many criminal cases as I had done in the whole of my service in quiet Galloway. I was to see a lot of him as the years went by, and never ceased to thrill on listening to his accounts and experiences of one big case after another. His was the labour of love of a man who had joined the police because he 'wanted to be a policeman' and possessed an ambition that was in due course to take him to the top of the Department he so much

enjoyed giving his thirty years of service to . . . When Bob Kerr died, half the population of Glasgow lined the route to his funeral.

★　★　★

'He looks like a proper detective,' said a *Glasgow Herald* columnist who interviewed Robert Kerr in 1960. 'He adds a lean and sallow appearance to his policeman's height and, perhaps, more important, his unruffled calm has always proved crisis-proof.' That quality had been amply demonstrated by Kerr during the previous five years when he played a leading role in two of the longest and most complex criminal investigations in 1950s Glasgow: the 1955 Ibrox raid (examined in chapter seven) and the Peter Manuel murders of 1956–59.

Manuel's criminal career had, of course, started long before 1956. By then he had already carried out a string of housebreakings and three attacks on women, one of which put him in Peterhead Prison for a long stretch. He was also constantly attempting to boost his sense of self-importance by approaching the authorities with the offer of supposedly 'confidential' information. He told the American Consulate in Glasgow that he had access to intelligence crucial to national security and was interviewed by Special Branch because he claimed to have knowledge about Burgess and Maclean, the two British agents who had systematically passed on secrets to the Russians before dramatically defecting to the Soviet Union in 1951.

It was Manuel's alleged access to inside information that brought Detective Chief Inspector Kerr of Govan CID (as he then was) into contact with him for the first time during the investigation into the Ibrox bank raid. In an undated letter written after the Manuel trial, the detective gave an account of his initial conversation with the Lanarkshire criminal:

> I consider [Manuel] a man of very low mentality but possessed of the most vivid imagination I have ever known. During the inquiries into the Ibrox bank robbery he telephoned me and without telling me who

was speaking gave me the names of three men who had committed the robbery – one of the names he gave was his own. When later interviewed, he admitted he had made the phone call and needless to say any information he gave was false. One thing he strongly maintained was that no Englishmen were involved and that rumours about such were all made up to put me off the scent.

Naturally, the truth turned out to be quite the opposite: as the investigation proceeded, Kerr would make extensive enquiries in England resulting in several arrests. It only took a quick phone call to Lanarkshire CID for Kerr to confirm that the man named Manuel was a dangerous fantasist.

The following year, Manuel was again claiming to be in possession of vital information, this time concerning the triple murder of William Watt's family. In what A. M. Nicol describes as 'one of the most stunning investigative own goals ever scored in recent British criminology', Lanarkshire police had arrested Watt who thus ended up in a cell in Barlinnie Prison at the same time as Manuel was serving a sentence for an earlier break-in. Like many who found themselves in a tight spot in this period, both Watt and Manuel felt the solution was, in the catchphrase of the time, 'Get me Dowdall!' – a reference to the leading defence lawyer, Laurence Dowdall. Dowdall was already representing Watt when Manuel wrote to the lawyer asking him to take up his cause too – and offering him some information 'to our mutual advantage'.

Dowdall knew Kerr well, describing him in his memoirs as 'a wonderful man and a very close friend with profound knowledge of malefactors all over the country'. At this stage, Dowdall had not encountered Manuel and he asked the detective for his opinion. Kerr replied that Manuel was 'an inveterate liar and he's also got a paranoid hatred of the police'.

This time, however, the information Manuel had to offer was of great value: it helped to put the noose around his own neck.

Manuel maintained that Watt must be innocent of killing his family because he, Manuel, knew who the real culprit was. In the course of several conversations, he revealed to Dowdall so much detail about the interior of the Watt house and about the manner in which the killings were carried out that it became clear that only the murderer himself could be so well informed. Dowdall passed this on to Kerr who, he said, 'unofficially gave me all the help and encouragement he could'. Glasgow police were not at this stage officially involved in the enquiry being carried out by the Lanarkshire force. However, while both lawyer and detective believed Manuel was the perpetrator, they needed proof. Kerr suggested to Dowdall that they should bide their time; Manuel's incessant desire to feed his own ego was such that, sooner or later, he would make a mistake.

Watt spent sixty-seven days in Barlinnie before he was released as a result of Dowdall's efforts on his behalf – though there were some within Lanarkshire police who still harboured their suspicions, as did many members of the public.

As the police had failed to find the killer of his family, Watt was now determined to act as his own detective. According to an interview he gave to the *Daily Record* in June 1958, he had been recommended (presumably by Dowdall) to speak to Bob Kerr who might be able to help him. Before he met with Watt, Kerr had to seek permission from the procurator fiscal as the investigation into the Watt murders was not a Glasgow CID case. Their first meeting, which lasted three hours, was a fruitful one for them both. Watt was a broken man and he convinced Kerr that 'his tears were real'. Kerr and Watt were both sure that Manuel was the killer and Watt was profoundly grateful for the detective's response. 'He was the one officer who would listen to me,' he said. 'For the first time, I had found a policeman who believed in me . . . Kerr was the man who made me believe there was still justice in the world.'

However, Manuel was still in prison serving his sentence and Kerr told Watt that 'you can't do anything until he comes out. All you can do is try and find out what you can'. This Watt proceeded to do, hanging around disreputable pubs, making underworld contacts, buying drinks and picking up whatever clues he could. Things began to look promising when he tracked down a man who claimed to have supplied Manuel with a gun. The information was passed to Lanarkshire CID but they did not consider it a strong enough lead.

Then, at the beginning of November 1957, Manuel was released from Barlinnie and he asked Dowdall to arrange for him to meet with Watt – which was exactly what Watt wanted. The idea of that meeting had been run past Bob Kerr, as well as Alex Brown and Tom Goodall, all of whom agreed that it should go ahead.

The killer and the bereaved bakery owner met face to face in the Whitehall Restaurant in Renfield Street, Glasgow at the start of December, with Dowdall present at the start. The story is retold in various books about Manuel and the episode has been imaginatively recreated by Denise Mina in her 2017 novel *The Long Drop*. According to Dowdall, Watt began by threatening to 'tear Manuel to pieces' but he managed to regain his self-control; as he later said, 'I had to bring him to justice. One false move by me might have ruined everything.' After a long drinking session with Manuel, Watt knew he had found the murderer.

From this point on, events moved quickly to a conclusion. In less than a month, Manuel went on to murder seventeen-year-old Isabelle Cooke and the three members of the Smart family and (as discussed in chapter nine) Brown and Goodall were called in to assist Lanarkshire police. By 16 January 1958, sufficient evidence to charge Manuel had been gathered and he had confessed to eight murders. The process of collecting further detailed evidence continued for some time afterwards and, while not formally seconded to Lanarkshire, Bob Kerr played a major role in the investigations at the Glasgow end, being responsible for tracing the property stolen by Manuel in Lanarkshire and sold on in Glasgow, thereby helping to track his movements and confirm his presence at various crime scenes. Kerr was often present at the top-level conferences held in Lanarkshire police headquarters in Hamilton to review the progress of the various lines of enquiry.

On the occasion of Bob Kerr's elevation to Chief Superintendent, the *Glasgow Herald* columnist 'Pursuivant' summed up what the new

CID Chief saw as his twin achievements in the Manuel investigation:

> He finds considerable satisfaction in the fact that William Watt was cleared of complicity after he had interviewed him, and he claims that, as soon as Manuel cropped up in the enquiries, he had no doubt who was guilty.

Kerr may not have been 'the man who caught Manuel' – the journalists bestowed that title on Alex Brown – but that doesn't make his contribution any less important.

★ ★ ★

As far as policing in the West of Scotland was concerned, the consequences of the Manuel case continued long after the mass murderer went to the gallows on 11 July 1958. All kinds of obvious questions were being asked: why did the police take so long to catch him? Why was an innocent man locked up? Why was the Glasgow force, with its greater resources, not called in sooner? Was there too much petty rivalry between the Lanarkshire and Glasgow police?

Labour MP for Maryhill William Hannan raised all these issues and more in Parliament. While he made it clear that he wasn't blaming individual officers, he felt that some reorganisation of Scottish policing was necessary. In particular, the time taken by local police chiefs to make up their minds to call for outside assistance seemed to him an area that needed urgent examination. He put forward a solution:

> What is the objection to the formation of a central investigation department in Scotland? It would be mobile and furnished with the most up-to-date equipment, wireless, and so on, and could move at speed into an area in which it was required . . . while the trail is hot.

This drew a rather complacent response from Niall Macpherson, the Joint Under-Secretary of State for Scotland who argued that it was not realised how often other police forces made frequent use of the Glasgow CID and added, 'I would not like it to be assumed from the Manuel case that there is anything radically wrong with crime detection in Scotland.'

Nevertheless, in 1960, Scottish police forces did start to combine their resources. April saw the formation of the Scottish Criminal Record Office, based in Glasgow, acting as a central resource for all Scottish forces with an index of 230,000 criminals, 53,000 photographs and 176,000 sets of fingerprints. Then, in November, a new unit known as the Regional Crime Squad came into operation as a result of an agreement between the Chief Constables of Glasgow, Lanarkshire, Renfrewshire and Dunbartonshire. Previously, said Glasgow's recently appointed Chief Constable James Robertson, a great deal of inconvenience had been experienced when detectives from other forces made daily visits to Glasgow to investigate crimes committed in their areas by criminals from the city and a Glasgow CID detective had to be detached to accompany the outside officer in his enquiries. The Regional Crime Squad was made up of thirteen detectives from four adjacent police forces, who were able to operate across a much wider area, thereby 'denying to criminals any kind of protection from a geographical boundary.'

When this development occurred, Bob Kerr had only been in charge of Glasgow CID for a matter of weeks and one of his achievements over the next three years was to ensure the new system operated effectively. It was the first step in a process of wider co-operation, which, fifteen years later, resulted in the amalgamation of eight different West of Scotland forces to form Strathclyde Police.

★ ★ ★

On 1 October 1960, the day Bob Kerr officially took over from Bob Colquhoun as CID Chief, the BBC screened the first episode in a new series of the long-running police drama *Dixon of Dock Green*. The creator of the series, Ted Willis, told viewers that 'the mixture this winter will be much the same as before'. The same could be said of the cases Kerr would face in his new role.

Just three days into the job, he was confronted with a type of murder that he would have witnessed more than once in his three decades as a detective. Shortly after 7 a.m., a man on his way to work was passing a children's playpark at Glasgow Green, barely 200 yards from the Central police station in Turnbull Street, when he spotted the body of a woman in her fifties, dressed in a pale blue plastic coat and hanging from the railings. He ran to the police station and within minutes detectives were on the scene under the direction of Kerr and Superintendent Henry Crawford. The woman, a known prostitute with no fixed abode, had been throttled with her headscarf and her head violently forced between the railings.

The crime was rapidly solved as the culprit, a twenty-five-year-old barman, walked into the Southern police station and gave himself up. At his trial in December, he told the court that he saw a headline in a newspaper stating that a woman had been murdered at Glasgow Green and said to himself, 'That must have been me.' The killer had a history of depression and epilepsy and often took 'turns', after which he failed to remember what had occurred. On the day of the incident he saw a man and a woman having a heated argument. Then the woman approached him and asked him to go with her. He remembered putting his hands round her throat but awoke the next morning with no further recollections and went about his usual routine, taking his younger sister to school and going to the public house where he was employed.

Medical experts considered that the killer 'had an abnormal personality accompanied by outbursts of pathological rage sometimes without provocation' and that 'he must have been temporarily insane and unable to form the intent to murder'. He was found guilty of culpable homicide and sentenced to fifteen years' imprisonment.

Almost a year later, Kerr oversaw the inquiry into another death which could only have happened in Glasgow. The press dubbed it 'the follow, follow murder' – a reference to the anthem sung by fans of Rangers F.C. Sixteen-year-old Tommy Gillies from Govan was singing it as he made his way along Copland Road with a friend when he was subjected to a vicious assault. Detectives kept vigil at his bedside but he died twenty-four hours later. Again, the matter was swiftly cleared up with the arrest of two youths aged seventeen and nineteen.

The circumstances surrounding the murder of taxi driver John Walkinshaw were more unusual. In the early hours of Monday 24 July 1961, Ronald Finlayson ordered a taxi to pick him up at an address in Tormusk Road, Castlemilk. Concerned at its non-arrival, Finlayson went downstairs where he heard the distinctive throb of a diesel-engined cab and found the driver inside, dying from three gunshot wounds. He used the taxi's radio to call for assistance.

Taxi drivers are bound by a strong sense of camaraderie and the CID could rely on their full co-operation. The fare displayed on the meter on Walkinshaw's cab read 10 shillings and four pence [approximately 52p], and another driver made test runs from Tormusk Road to various city centre locations in an attempt to narrow down where the cabbie had picked up his last customer. The Taxi Cab Association also held a meeting to raise money for a reward for information leading to the arrest of whoever committed what Kerr described as 'this stupid, senseless crime'. 500 drivers turned up to show their solidarity and also to voice their complaints about the frequency of assaults on taxi men. The Chief Superintendent told a press conference that 'many, many people have come forward in response to our appeal in the newspapers'.

A massive door-to-door enquiry in the Castlemilk area involving 1,430 calls led to an arrest on the morning of John Walkinshaw's funeral on Thursday 27 July. At 6 a.m. Kerr, accompanied by a team that included Detective Chief Inspectors Tom Joyce and Tom Goodall, took twenty-nine-year-old Walter Scott Ellis from his bed to a cell in the Southern police station.

Six hours later, Kerr and Joyce mingled with mourners at Riddrie Park Cemetery. A crowd of 1,000 lined the streets as a cortege of black cabs left the murdered driver's house in Easterhouse and wound its way to the graveyard, where it appeared that half of Glasgow's taxi drivers had turned up to honour their colleague whose coffin was carried to his grave to the strains of a piper playing 'The Skye Boat Song'.

The case seemed to be progressing towards a conviction, but the evidence presented at the trial at the end of October was not as clear-cut as the police had hoped. A fellow taxi driver identified Ellis as the fare he had picked up in Castlemilk around 2 a.m. 'somewhere between Tormusk Road and his [Ellis's] home at Stravanan Road'. The Advocate Depute suggested to the jury that it was rather strange that someone would require two taxis to take him home unless the explanation was that Ellis changed taxis because he shot the driver of the first one. Ellis, however, maintained, 'I was never in a taxi at the weekend.' A man had been seen running away from the scene of the shooting, but two witnesses had picked out the same individual in an identity parade, and it was not Ellis. Moreover, the forensic evidence was inconclusive: a palm print found in the taxi was likely that of the murderer, but it did not fit Ellis; despite the most meticulous search, no gun was found, nor was there any evidence that Ellis ever had one; bullets were found in his possession, but they were solid ones and not of the soft-nosed type which killed Walkinshaw. R. A. Bennett, QC, summing up for the defence, also referred to the Manuel case which was still in many people's minds, recalling how William Watt had been wrongfully imprisoned and stressing that Ellis was charged with capital murder; 'he did not need to remind the jury of the terrible consequences which would follow a decision against the accused'.

The jury's verdict was 'not proven'. Tom Goodall later expressed his own view in an unpublished manuscript giving an account of the case:

> It is certain that very little more evidence would have secured a conviction and that this was not forthcoming is no reflection on the work of those concerned in the investigation. I feel sure that Ellis was guilty. He may have had words with the taxi driver over the cost of the journey, but it is quite possible that there was no reason for the crime other than sheer wickedness. He had a gun which he wanted to use and he used it.

A grinning Ellis was pictured in the newspapers celebrating his release with wine and a cigar, promising that 'this murder charge has frightened me onto the straight and narrow', but he would go on to make many more court appearances.

Less than a month after the taxi driver trial, he was arrested and charged with serious assault and contravention of the Explosives Substances Act. Again, the first charge was found not proven but he was sent to prison for eighteen months for having four detonators hidden in his house, having unsuccessfully claimed that the police had planted them there. Detective Chief Inspector Donald Campbell of the Eastern Division left Ellis handcuffed to his sergeant in the bedroom and began to search the kitchen. There he found the detonators, hidden behind a skirting board. When he confronted Ellis with these, he had his response prepared: 'you planked them behind the skirting board'. The astute Campbell, however, pointed out, firstly, that he had not mentioned anything about finding them behind a skirting board and, secondly, that Ellis had not been in the room when the discovery was made. In June 1963 he was charged with housebreaking in a trial during which even his solicitor, Joe Beltrami, admitted that his client was 'a fairly experienced housebreaker with a criminal record'. That didn't stop Beltrami castigating the police for again allegedly framing Ellis, 'the pet hate of the Eastern Division'.

But Ellis's luck ran out eventually and he was sentenced to twenty-one years for armed robbery and attempted murder during a later raid on a Pollokshaws bank, for which he served fourteen years.

★ ★ ★

By the time Ellis was safely locked up, Bob Kerr had handed over the reins to his colleague Tom Goodall and was enjoying a retirement which allowed him to take motoring holidays in Europe and, above all, play more golf at Ralston golf club near Paisley. Throughout his career he had made a point of arranging his annual leave to coincide with the British Open and only missed the event once in twenty-five years. While attending the Swallow-Penfold Tournament at the Belleisle course in South Ayrshire some weeks before he retired in July 1963, he was informed that he was to be made an honorary patron of the PGA (Professional Golders' Association) – an indication of the esteem in which he was held in the golfing world. 'I'm very, very proud of that,' he said.

A delightful story in Sheriff Irvine Smith's autobiography *Law, Life and Laughter* shows how Bob Kerr was equally well-respected by his erstwhile adversaries, the defence lawyers. Writing in his eighties, the Sheriff could still vividly recollect an evening gathering which took place well over half a century earlier, at the end of the trial of the Ibrox bank raiders:

> [Bob Kerr] had been head of the whole investigation and, when it was over, all the defence solicitors and counsel involved wanted to know how he had gone about it and what the details were that did not come out in the trial. It was decided unanimously that we ask Bob Kerr to meet us over a dinner. He accepted the invitation and I arranged a comfortable and private room in the old Literary Club in Bath Street, Glasgow, for a Saturday night. The food was unambitious but good. The wine was ambitious, good and plentiful. Bob Kerr did not drink — the rest of us did. Come the end of the meal, Bob Kerr gave us his inside account. The lawyers listened, the interruptions were few, it was a sign of our fascination — we were entranced. Our guest held the floor for the rest of the evening. Neither I nor any of the others kept notes of what Bob Kerr said that night. . . It was an unforgettable night; an example of mutual respect, confidence and trust, which in my experience was and is unique.

These skills of communication continued to be demonstrated in retirement when Bob Kerr retained a high profile, giving lectures on crime and making television appearances. In the late sixties, the retired CID Chief watched with dismay as the crime rate continued to escalate, culminating in the Allison Street shooting of two officers in 1969, an event which prompted police wives to form a Public Protection Action Group to press for the reintroduction of capital punishment. Kerr was strongly in favour:

If Peter Manuel who killed goodness knows how many people were convicted now, do you realise that he would merely serve a prison sentence? That one day he might be allowed out again?

One of his most memorable addresses was delivered in March 1970 to a public meeting in the Couper Institute, Cathcart. In front of an audience of 500, he delivered a robust message, perhaps feeling a greater freedom to speak his mind now that he was retired from his official role. Crime, vandalism and hooliganism had reached an appalling height, he said, and together they now constituted the greatest menace to the well-being and happiness of the British people since civilisation began. Then he really got into his stride:

> We must take steps to silence for a long trial period the useless, sentimental voices of do-gooders who shout for reduced sentences and the like for criminal scum who take all and give nothing to society . . . In my thirty-five years' experience in Glasgow the abolition of measures from the birch to capital punishment went hand in hand with increases in vicious crimes.

It was just what the members of the audience wanted to hear and they rewarded him with a standing ovation.

The speech certainly revealed the steely side of the man famed for his 'unruffled calm'. Yet, in spite of all the frustrations, the former Chief Superintendent, who retained his youthful appearance in his sixties, was still able to look back on thirty-seven years of policing and say, 'If I could do it again, I'd do it gladly.'

# 12

## *The Almost Perfect Crime*

### *The Shettleston Bank Raid of 1959*

Detective Chief Superintendent Robert Kerr had a talent for tracking down bank robbers – which is just as well, as he had to deal with the two most daring raids carried out in 1950s Scotland: one in Ibrox in 1955 and the other in Shettleston in 1959.

As Chief Inspector in charge of Govan CID, Kerr led the first enquiry under CID boss Gilbert McIlwrick and, no doubt because of his earlier success, took responsibility for the second in his later role as a Superintendent at CID headquarters.

The Ibrox raid contained many of the elements typically associated with bank robberies – such as knocking out and tying up a delivery man and escaping in a getaway car – but the Shettleston one was carried out in a remarkably low-key manner with no violence. The first raid was dramatic and public; the second passed virtually unnoticed. In 1955, it took months of travelling across Britain to round up the culprits whereas in 1959 the police knew very quickly who the culprits were – the real challenge lay in proving their guilt.

Preserved amongst Bob Kerr's personal papers are detailed notes describing exactly how each stage of the Shettleston investigation was carried out over a two-month period and the affair is therefore worth a closer look as it provides a uniquely well-documented case study of his methods, clearly showing how his patience and perceptiveness led to two successful convictions. In fact, the episode was so remarkable for its outstanding detective work that Kerr gave talks on it as part of police training courses. He went as far as claiming that 'There was probably more effort and planning put into solving it than ever before done by any CID.'

On the morning of 30 April 1959, staff arrived at the Shettleston Road branch of the Clydesdale and North of Scotland bank to find that £35,050 had been stolen. Just after closing time the previous evening, a black car had parked nearby with two men inside disguised as bankers in bowler hats, false moustaches and glasses. One waited in the car while the other opened the bank door with a key and came out fifteen minutes later with a briefcase and bag containing the contents of the safe. He put the bags into the car and, speaking in a loud voice so that people on the pavement could hear, said to the driver, 'Sorry to have delayed you. Will you deliver these bags?'

The bank manager reported the crime to the police and very soon a top CID team was on the scene: Donald Campbell of the Eastern Division, Bob Kerr from HQ and the boss himself, Bob Colquhoun. 'It's a mystery. There are no suspects', was all they told the journalists; in reality, the detectives soon knew much more than they were giving away.

It was hardly necessary to be a brilliant sleuth to work out that this must have been an inside job. The first step was to interview the five members of the bank staff and the cleaner, who started work at 6.30 p.m. on the night of the robbery. The cleaner, described by Kerr as a 'likeable and obviously honest person', chronicled a series of unusual circumstances, none of which had aroused her suspicions. When she arrived, she found that only one of the two door locks had been engaged. Inside, she saw the tray from the safe with some money in it lying on the floor. She then noticed two bundles of notes amounting to £2,000 lying on a table. She also observed that the handle of the safe was at an unusual angle. In spite of all this, she simply tidied everything up and proceeded to do her usual cleaning and polishing of the office – thus wiping away any possible fingerprints. 'Surely a most remarkably unsuspecting woman if ever there was one,' concluded Kerr. Her evidence was, however, useful in establishing that the raid must have taken place in the hour after the staff had departed at 5.30 p.m.

Another helpful piece of information came from Edinburgh police who contacted their Glasgow counterparts to say that some months earlier an expert safe blower had been arrested for possessing a selection of moulds and false keys. These were brought to Glasgow and they fitted the bank safe.

When the staff members were interviewed, two casually mentioned that they had negotiated with Alexander Gray, a bank customer and Shettleston bookmaker, to secure some extra evening work keeping his betting office books. To the quick-thinking Superintendent this was a vital clue as he recognised Gray's way of operating. He was also aware that the Edinburgh safe blower had links to Samuel McKay, a notorious member of Glasgow's criminal fraternity, commonly known as 'Dandy'. The nickname is invariably attributed to his taste for smart clothes but, according to Detective Inspector Tom Goodall who worked on the case, that was a myth – he was called 'Dandy' because he loved reading the comic of that name. It was soon established that the black car spotted outside the bank had been loaned to McKay.

All in all, Kerr felt very satisfied with the progress made in the first twenty-four hours: 'Within the course of only one day [I] was satisfied in my own mind beyond all doubt that Gray and McKay were the culprits and that in some way or other they had found a way to take impressions of the safe keys.'

Now all he had to do was find the evidence that would convince a jury of their guilt…

It would not have been possible to arrest the two suspects at this stage anyway, as both had cleverly removed themselves from the scene in the hope that suspicion would be diverted from them. Immediately after the robbery, McKay took a plane to London where he was to have an operation on his nose; Gray, meanwhile, withdrew an appeal he had been pursing against a motoring conviction and reported to the police to serve a thirty day sentence in Barlinnie.

So Kerr decided to try a new technique: he would start what he called 'a cold war or war of nerves' as soon as the pair returned to Glasgow. He arranged for Gray and McKay to be shadowed twenty-four hours a day – and, without making it too obvious, the detectives let their targets know they were being watched. The idea was to see whether they tried to contact their informant within the bank branch and whether they would start to distribute the stolen money.

The relentless surveillance continued for some weeks and started having its effect. The robbers' wives talked about their sleepless nights and their anxiety about what was going on. McKay eventually approached Kerr and offered to phone him morning, noon and night to account for his activities in exchange for calling off the watchers at his home. When Kerr rejected the offer, 'Dandy' told him he was 'the most stupid detective in the Glasgow police' and threatened 'if you don't stop coming to the house then one night some of you will not come back!'

The surveillance continued.

This phase of the enquiry not only reveals much about Kerr's understanding of the criminal mind; it also sheds light on the way he managed his men. One detective constable who worked on the case remembers that each member of the team was allocated to a small group with its own defined task:

> It says something for Kerr's secrecy that to this day I still don't know how many officers were involved in the hunt for the robbers. My job was to watch just one man. I would report back daily to Bob Kerr who told me nothing of what was going on elsewhere. Eventually each of the teams made their own arrest and the gang was rounded up. It wasn't until the trial that the officers who had cracked the case began to learn the full details.

While all this was going on, the youngest bank teller, eighteen-year-old William Rae, suspected of being the insider who helped the robbers, had started to crack, thanks to an elaborate trap that had been set for him. An unknown man walked up to him as he was leaving the bank and handed him a note, supposedly from Gray. It stated that Gray was anxious about him and wanted to know if the police were following him. Rae was asked to phone a certain call box number at 6.30 p.m. that day in case his own home telephone was being tapped. When he made the call, it was answered by a waiting detective who told him that Gray had been unable to come to the phone in person and had asked Rae to write to him instead, care of the General Post Office in Glasgow.

When the detective told his boss that Rae had suspected nothing, Kerr was so overjoyed that he almost hugged him.

The young bank employee carried out the instructions and wrote a letter saying that he was all right; the police had stopped following him but he wanted his share of the money for his holidays and would like Gray to get in touch. This letter was intercepted when it arrived at the post office and handed over to the police.

Kerr now brought Rae to the Eastern police office and told him that things had changed since previous interviews. The young man continued to deny involvement until he was shown his own letter, at which point he started to cry and said, 'Oh Mr. Kerr, I'm glad this moment has come. I am the one involved. I want to clear it up for the sake of my parents and the others in the bank who are under suspicion.'

'Now was my biggest ever decision,' Kerr told an audience of detectives who must by now have been hanging on his every word. 'If I locked him up I would have a "mug" and the real culprits would go free. I couldn't reconcile myself to that – I must take a chance and the lad himself made my decision much easier when at a point I said I would have to inform his parents right away about his position, he said, "please do not tell them, Mr Kerr, till I do something to redeem myself in their eyes." That plea made up my mind – I would take the risk, though by that time I was conscious of something inside me saying, "He is a good boy and won't let you down." And that he proved to be, to my everlasting enjoyment.' Rae now supplied full details of how the keys were copied: the young teller slipped out of the bank with the keys from which Gray made hasty impressions in plasticine moulds in a phone box outside. Rae was to receive £100 for his trouble.

By these means, Kerr had implicated Gray. Now he turned his attention to McKay. Rae had only been taken to speak to him once, and was seated behind a screen so that he could talk to McKay but not see him – a trick 'Dandy' often used when a third party had to be accepted as an accomplice. Kerr's next move was to arrange for Rae to contact McKay at the Gordon Club in central Glasgow where he was the manager. Rae was taken to a telephone kiosk along with Detective Inspector Goodall who listened in to the conversation and later wrote a report containing a transcript of what was said. Introducing himself as Bill, the bank clerk asked to speak to Mr McKay and requested his share of the takings 'for his holidays'. McKay came across as perfectly amenable, and gave Rae instructions to take the subway to St George's Cross station that evening at 8 o'clock and walk along the left hand side of Great Western Road, taking care that he was not being followed. McKay would be there in person and told Rae on the phone that 'I'll point you out to a woman who will give you the money. It will be in Bank of England fivers. She's about thirty years of age but looks about twenty-five. She has black hair and is a good looker. She will put her hand up to her hair so you will know her.'

An hour before the appointed time, Kerr had two policewomen and two detective constables in position near the St George's Cross area and, just in case the targets came by car, he had a number of vehicles stationed at various points. Everything happened in accordance with the phone call. The black-haired woman met McKay in Great Western Road where he handed her a package in a large white envelope and pointed out Rae. She then walked past Rae who took the package, gave a nod of recognition and walked on without stopping. The woman, and her husband who was also present, were picked up by waiting officers, but the real prize was that McKay himself was standing in a close which provided him with a good vantage point. Yorkshireman Detective Constable George 'Yorkie' Lloyd had the satisfaction of going up to him and making the arrest, while another colleague approached from behind.

It had all gone according to plan – except for what happened next. The instructions given to young Rae were to return to the subway and travel to St Enoch Station in the city centre where he should meet up with Kerr and Goodall at 8.30 p.m. But they were slightly delayed and when they had not turned up by 8.35 p.m. Rae went to the cinema and later returned home.

Kerr said that had been the worst moment of the case for him. When he and Goodall arrived at St Enoch and Rae was not there, they not only thought that he had 'done a bunk' but that the strain of the whole situation might have caused him to commit suicide. They kept phoning Rae's home and eventually went there in person. It was Rae himself who opened the door for them. He immediately said, 'Ah, Mr Kerr, here it is' and handed over the package. By this stage his parents were in such a nervous state that his mother fainted and fell down the stairs.

The plan had worked, but in the closing moments Kerr had been left agonising whether he had pushed the young man too far. He was also amazed at his lucky break: why had someone as careful as McKay turned up at the fateful meeting place himself? Why did he not just send someone else? Bob Kerr never found out.

Early the following morning, Gray was arrested and a key capable of opening the bank door was found in his house. Then, in August, McKay's brother John was found in possession of a suitcase containing £5,175 in notes traceable to the bank. All the loose ends seemed to be neatly tied up: the perpetrators were charged and the trial set for the start of October.

Then, on the night of 27 July, the whole thing started to unravel. Dandy McKay escaped from Barlinnie Prison.

He had been in the hospital block for treatment for his nasal complaint and, just after midnight, managed to saw through the bars on a first floor window and lower himself to the ground using a sheet. He tied one end of a rope to a gate and threw the other end over the wall to accomplices who secured it as he climbed over to a waiting car. It later emerged that the bars of the prison window may have been sawn through in advance by helpers inside the prison, which would explain why no one heard anything on the night of the escape.

So began another investigation led by Robert Kerr. Roadblocks were set up and train stations, airports and ferry ports alerted. By 4 August McKay had been free for nine days and the hunt was taken over by Detective Chief Inspector Donald Campbell to allow Kerr to go on his summer golfing holiday.

No doubt the CID was less than amused to find the *Evening Times* had chosen that week to run a series of articles entitled 'My Amazing Escapes' by Johnny Ramensky.

Despite this setback, the trial went ahead at the High Court of Glasgow. William Rae, who had turned Queen's evidence, explained in detail how he had asked Gray the bookmaker for some part-time work to make extra money and said, 'he told me that if I helped him to rob a bank he would see me all right'. He explained the process of how the keys were copied, involving much trial and error, and made the dramatic revelation that there had in fact been two Shettleston bank raids; on the first occasion the thieves had not found enough money in the safe and decided to wait for a better opportunity. As the trial went on, much was made of the fear of Sam McKay that was widespread in Glasgow and Kerr himself mentioned that threats against his children had been issued by McKay. Gray contended he was the victim of 'a monstrous frame-up' by the police: Rae, Gray believed, had placed the blame on him because of his fear of McKay. Another witness agreed that 'a number of people in Glasgow were terrified [of McKay] and still are'.

As the trial reached its closing stages, the man who made the keys and the couple arrested in Great Western Road were cleared of any direct involvement in the crime. That left Alexander Gray and McKay's brother John to face the music. The latter was sentenced to three years imprisonment for reset and Gray received a ten-year sentence for the robbery. The judge, Lord Wheatley, told him that 'as a gambler you must realise that when the stakes are high the losses are also likely to be high'. During the week of the trial, the Gordon Club voluntarily closed its doors 'because of bad publicity'. When it reopened the police raided it and arrested fifty men who were charged with gaming.

But what had happened to McKay? Police had thought he would head to London where he had many contacts. He did, but only after lying low in Glasgow for a week. By mid-September he had reached to New York – in a first class cabin on the 'Queen Elizabeth', of course – and thence to Miami. 'All paid for by the bank,' mused a frustrated Kerr. After four months in the USA he came back to London, hired a car to pay a visit to Glasgow to see his family and even managed to get an accomplice to mail Kerr a photo of him taken in New York to make it look as if he was still on the other side of the Atlantic. Eventually he moved to a house in Killiney near Dublin where he lived comfortably with his Irish-born wife and two children under a false name until police arrested him on 27 June 1960 – exactly eleven months after his escape.

McKay initially appeared in the High Court in September and this time the police were taking no chances. The van transporting him from Barlinnie was escorted by four police cars, each containing four detectives. Observation vehicles were placed around the court buildings and extra police were on duty inside and at every entrance. When the trial got under way in November, McKay gave full details of his recent travels and was quizzed on his earnings as manager and part-owner of the so-called Gordon Bridge Club, in reality a gambling club which the judge, Lord Wheatley, described as 'that notorious place where every game of cards seems to be played except bridge'. In a good week he could take home £300–£400 and was able to buy a bungalow in Netherlee and a new car every year, graduating from a Ford Zodiac in 1956 to a Jaguar in 1959. Over the past five or six years he reckoned he had made about £14,000 but he gave the money to his wife to manage and was not sure where it all was. As for the Shettleston job, he denied being present on that occasion. He admitted that Gray had asked him to help pass on the package of money to Rae in Great Western Road and also that he had agreed to help change the proceeds of the robbery via his various gambling enterprises, in exchange for a fee of £5,000.

Lord Wheatley reminded the jury that 'if two or more people joined in the commission of a crime and it was proved that each contributed in some way, then each was held to be guilty of the whole crime. It is perfectly true', he went on, 'that no one purports to have seen McKay in the bank at that time. Therefore the Crown can only hope to find his participation either by inference beyond reasonable doubt, or by proving beyond reasonable doubt that he was guilty of this offence by accession [i.e. as an accessory].' On the other hand, if McKay was deemed to have become directly involved only after the event had taken place, he could not be found guilty of playing a part in the robbery but might instead be found guilty of 'knowingly receiving articles taken by theft and feloniously retained [i.e. reset].'

In spite of having Laurence Dowdall to defend him, McKay was found guilty of taking part in the theft and sent to prison for ten years. One of a family of seven children brought up in the Gorbals, he had served the usual criminal apprenticeship of approved school and borstal, and made his mark as a safe blower in the late forties. McKay could be ruthless – on one occasion he had an establishment that he saw as a rival to his club set on fire. But he also had a taste for comfortable living, hardly ever took alcohol and handled money in an astute and business-like fashion – all of which set him apart from the common villain.

Even though McKay was finally behind bars, the Shettleston bank raid probably set him up financially for the rest of his life. Tom Goodall did some calculations and reckoned the bungalow in Ireland and the latest car must have cost him in the region of £10,000, and he had £4,000 in an Irish bank account. Strangely, Goodall added that 'we asked the Bank in Glasgow to take proceedings against McKay with a view to recovering the house, car and money, etc. in Ireland. For some reason, they would not do this and all this was left in McKay's possession ... Mrs McKay will probably have the proceeds hidden away somewhere against her husband's return from prison.'

All the same, the career of the man known as 'the careful crook' was over. He faded into obscurity after his release from prison and died in 1984.

If Bob Kerr was not 'the man who caught Manuel', he certainly earned his place in the annals of crime as 'the man who caught McKay'.

# 13

## *Glasgow's Maigret*

*Detective Chief Superintendent Tom Goodall,*
*CID Chief 1963–69*

The former mining village of Cardenden in Fife is not a very big place but it happens to be where two figures concerned with the investigation of crime were born: Tom Goodall, Glasgow's CID boss in the sixties, and novelist Ian Rankin, creator of Inspector Rebus.

If Tom Goodall has an equivalent in the world of detective fiction, it is not so much DI Rebus of Lothian and Borders police, but Commissaire Maigret of the Police Judiciaire, Paris, the famous creation of the prolific Belgian writer Georges Simenon – who was, of course, very familiar in the UK, thanks to the BBC TV series starring Rupert Davies which ran from 1960 until 1963. Both the fictional sleuth and his real-life counterpart approached an inquiry in the same way, smoking their pipes and taking time to think through the problem; both would be the first to attend a crime scene in person and conducted investigations in a 'hands on' manner even though they were in the top jobs in their respective organisations and could easily have delegated. On call day and night, Goodall insisted on being informed whenever a major crime occurred. Such dedication took a heavy toll on his health and his early death in 1969 at the age of fifty-eight deprived the police service of a man once described as perhaps the best detective officer in the whole of Britain.

Thomas Millar Goodall was born on 28 November 1911 at Cardenbarns farm where his father James was employed. In the late 1920s, the family moved to the outskirts of Glasgow where Goodall Senior took over as farm manager at Garscube Home Farm, some of whose remaining buildings can still be seen near Canniesburn, Bearsden. This was the period of the Great Depression and young Thomas felt that joining the police offered the chance of a steady job. In August 1932, he was appointed as a probationary constable in the Glasgow force on a salary of 55 shillings per week [£2.75], which, after a year's service, increased to 65 shillings [£3.25]. The rest of his life would be spent in the city, though his lifelong support of Kirkcaldy-based Raith Rovers Football Club could be seen as a way of maintaining a link to his Fife roots.

Unlike some of his predecessors as Glasgow CID chief, Goodall was not initially a 'high flyer'. He started out on the beat in Partick and did not join the Southern Division CID until 1943 where he remained a Detective Constable until his promotion to Sergeant in 1956, thirteen years later. It was then that his career started to take off. The following year he was appointed Detective Inspector in the Gorbals, where he began to build up an impressive list of underworld contacts. The name Goodall was soon making frequent appearances in the newspapers and it is clear that his superiors regarded him as someone who had an ability to grasp opportunities and perform at a high level. When Lanarkshire approached Glasgow police for assistance during the Manuel investigations, Goodall was the one selected to carry out the crucial role of assisting Superintendent Alex Brown and his contribution was later rewarded with promotion to Chief Inspector.

Those who worked with both men were struck by the similarity between their methods: 'When you see Brown at work, you see Tom Goodall' was a typical comment. Like his mentor, Goodall was a man of few words; his press statements were brief and to the point and his characteristic method was to say little when conducting an interview.

He would listen attentively, using body language that would invite people to open up to him. Carefully filling his pipe and rolling a match between his fingers, he would let the suspect do the talking while giving himself plenty of time for reflection.

Again, while both these detectives could be implacable in pursuit of their quarry, they were also noted for their humanity. 'A good detective must have a heart' was one of Brown's favourite sayings. Goodall's daughter Alison remembers that, every Christmas, the family would make up a 'Christmas box' of food and toys for the wife and three children of a petty criminal who regularly found himself 'inside' over the festive season.

Soon after the Manuel trial Goodall further proved his worth during the enquiry into the 1959 Shettleston bank raid when, as described in Chapter Twelve, he accompanied the young bank clerk William Rae to a telephone box to make arrangements to collect his share of the proceeds, thus using a small fish to catch a much larger one – the notorious bank robber and gambling club manager Sam 'Dandy' McKay.

A rather unorthodox tribute to Goodall's skills as a detective came from one Archibald McLellan Cochrane, the self-styled 'Tontine poet' who resided at the Tontine Hotel, a model lodging house opposite the old Police HQ in St Andrew's Street. The paths of the poet and the detective must have crossed at some point and thereafter Cochrane regularly mailed Goodall handwritten copies of his verses written in Scots, one of which read as follows:

> Nae smarter chiel, you will agree,
> Than Goodall o' the C.I.D.
> Once our Tam gets on your trail
> You'll damn'd soon find yourself in jail.
> Indeed, it disna pay ataw,
> When Tam's aboot, tae break the law.

One figure from the criminal underworld who would have understood these sentiments was Jimmy Boyle, who ended up as a successful author and sculptor living in the south of France – a far cry from his former life which began with petty thieving in the Gorbals as a boy and finished with a life sentence in the seventies. His spell in the Special Unit at Barlinnie proved his redemption, giving him an opportunity to develop his creative talents and write an autobiography entitled *A Sense of Freedom*. Even as a child, he says, the name of Goodall was well known to him and, though he had never seen him in person, 'Goodall was spoken of with fear'. While he was still a schoolboy, Boyle and his pals used to cover their faces with balaclavas and make desperate attempts to raid local shops, in spite of being recognised by everyone in the area. They decided to give up this particular activity after Goodall arrested them and held an identity parade. Then, in 1964 Boyle, now aged twenty, was hauled from his bed in the early hours of the morning by a posse of detectives. They threw a blanket round him and took him to Central Police HQ where 'standing behind the bar of the station was a line of top cops, the head of whom was Goodall, who stood there, pipe in mouth, staring at me.' A uniformed inspector then read out a charge of capital murder, of which Boyle was later acquitted.

By that stage Goodall had assumed overall control of the CID on the retirement of Bob Kerr in 1963, whose deputy he had been for the previous two years. This 'quiet, slightly stooping man who seldom smiled' (as the veteran crime and court reporter Arnot McWhinnie once described him) had originally taken twenty-four years to go from constable to sergeant yet it now took him only seven years to rise to the rank of Chief Superintendent – making him, at the age of fifty-two, the city's youngest CID boss since William Ewing.

As his one-time colleague Metropolitan Police Commissioner David McNee said about his own career, 'It's not how you start but how you finish that counts.'

On departing, Kerr told Goodall: 'you have truly earned the job'. He received a host of congratulatory letters and telegrams on his appointment, not only from officers in other police forces but from people in all different levels of society. One, from his bank manager at the

Clydesdale Bank, expressed the 'hope that you will have a very happy and successful – albeit quiet! – tenure of office.'

There was little chance of that. During the six gruelling years that followed, Tom Goodall would confront a greater series of challenges than any of his predecessors.

★ ★ ★

They called him 'the man who was always there'.

Again and again, the new CID chief would be at the scene of a murder and more often than not he and his men had the whole enquiry wrapped up in a matter of hours. In an era before forensics had assumed their current importance, he had an uncanny skill for reconstructing a crime scene.

In July 1963 a forty-two-year-old woman was found battered to death in her home in the top flat of a tenement in Garscube Road. On the floor below, her mother lay seriously ill, having been given the last rites by a priest, unaware that her daughter was dead. Goodall, along with Detective Chief Inspector Elphinstone Dalglish of CID headquarters and Detective Chief Inspector Robert McFarlane of Maryhill, arrived at the flat and within three hours the husband of the woman had been arrested. In February 1964, a forty-nine-year-old bus driver was found lying in Nithsdale Street, Strathbungo by a man out walking his dog. Under Goodall's direction, investigations took place throughout the night and a twenty-eight-year-old made an appearance at Govan Police Court charged with murder the following day. The following April, police were called to a house in Blackhill where the body of a mother of four children lay in her kitchen. At one o'clock police brought out the husband from the house, his head covered with a curtain. While the children's clothing on the washing line fluttered in the breeze, detectives took away a garden fork and lawn edge cutter.

And so the litany of violent crime went on . . .

Incidents of this kind were occurring in 1960s Glasgow on a weekly, and sometimes daily, basis. Very often, more than one enquiry into a serious assault or murder would be going on simultaneously and Tom Goodall would either be leading these personally or closely monitoring the progress of a divisional CID team. Invariably, it would be the Chief Superintendent himself who would issue the press announcements. In February 1965, for example, the front page of the *Evening Times* reported that, as a result of enquiries led by Goodall the previous day, a youth of seventeen appeared in court for assaulting a butcher in his shop at Kinning Park and stealing £40; at the same time, the Chief Superintendent issued an appeal for information on four youths seen crossing Victoria Bridge in the early hours of the morning after a twenty-one-year-old man had been found dying of a stab wound in Clyde Street. No sooner was one case closed than another opened.

The investigation into the murder of Mrs Emma Dufour in January 1962 provides an outstanding example of Goodall's methods. The seventy-three-year-old of Belgian origin lived alone in a flat with two rooms and a kitchen in Maryhill, which had already been struck by tragedy: her husband, a shoemaker, committed suicide there a few years earlier.

Mrs Dufour's grandson David worked nearby and was in the habit of calling round each day for his lunch. Arriving at the usual time on Wednesday 24 January, he let himself in using his own key, to find his grandmother lying on the floor in a pool of blood. He called for the police and an ambulance but it was clear that she was already dead.

Initial impressions suggested suicide. A blood-stained knife with a serrated edge lay beside her within reach, and it was possible that she had cut her own throat. But the more Goodall and his men examined the scene, the more suspicious they became. The old lady's handbag lay on the table in the centre of the room and a spot of blood was found on this and on the tablecloth. Among the contents were a diary, a rosary, a travel concession ticket and a number of safety pins. Once the body had been photographed and then removed, a comb and two safety pins were discovered underneath. 'This', deduced Goodall, 'indicated that there had been some interference with the handbag before the woman's death, as safety pins were lying in the bottom of this handbag.'

Furthermore, forensic examination of a hair found on the comb showed that it did not come from the victim.

A pan of peeled potatoes lay on the sink draining board and the gas cooker was turned on low – actions which did not indicate suicidal intentions. A thorough search for fingerprints revealed nothing and the lack of evidence of any forced entry suggested Mrs Dufour may have opened the door to the person who killed her.

Years of experience suggested to Goodall that this was the type of crime that might have been committed by teenagers in the course of an attempted robbery and he had a list compiled of young persons between fourteen and twenty-one years living in the area who had previously been in trouble of any description. Witnesses from Mrs Dufour's close mentioned seeing two boys on the stairs; one of them lived next door to the old lady and the other, when traced, proved to be one of the names on the list. While being driven to Maryhill Police Station, this seventeen-year-old youth confessed that he had hit Mrs Dufour over the head with a metal bar and had cut her throat. He said he then threw away the metal bar and dumped his blood-stained jeans in the canal.

The total haul from the robbery amounted to one shilling and four pence [about 7p].

Reflecting on the sequence of events later, Goodall said, 'this case shows the tremendous need of great care being taken in the examination of the locus of any serious crime. This case could well have been written off as a suicide and it makes me wonder how many cases of suicide are, in fact, murders. One has only to think of how easy it would be to murder someone, for example, by gassing them and making the circumstances appear to conform to suicide.'

Tom Goodall's track record in clearing up these murders is indeed impressive, but the CID was not only dealing with the consequences of domestic abuse, hooliganism and violence; it was also battling against a rise in organised crime in the city.

In January 1964, four masked bandits rammed a van taking payroll cash to a factory in Polmadie, escaping in another car with £4,300. In

June, Glasgow's biggest-ever jewellery raid took place at the premises of Edwards and Sons in St Vincent Street where safe blowers took their cutting equipment in under cover of a golf bag and worked over the weekend, isolating the alarm system and opening two safes and a strong room to steal £70,000 worth of jewellery. Just fifty yards away from the jewellers was a branch of the British Linen Bank and, in March 1965, another similar raid occurred there, with oxyacetylene equipment being used over the course of a weekend to break into a strong room. This time the thieves made off with a haul of £25,000. Goodall stated that police forces throughout Britain had been alerted and noted that he was searching 'for skilled operators who had planned the raid with great care'.

In 1966, Glasgow CID scored a notable victory when the investigation into another bank raid led to one of the city's most notorious criminals being locked away for a very long stretch. In April, three masked men burst into the Pollokshaws branch of the National Commercial Bank, ordered the staff to lie on the floor and began stuffing cash into a holdall. Two staff members were injured with a shotgun before the raiders made off in a stolen Ford Consul with an estimated £20,000 in cash. A quick-thinking neighbour who witnessed the raid wrote down the car's registration number and notified the police. Goodall once again took charge and appealed for anyone who had seen the car being abandoned a short time after the robbery.

The Easter holidays were coming up – but not for the CID. They were already busy looking for a gang who had made off with £8,000 by hijacking a payroll car in Springburn and when the Pollokshaws raid occurred scores of detectives had their leave cancelled. At least their sacrifice wasn't in vain: at the end of April Elphinstone Dalglish travelled down to London to recover some of the money from the left luggage office at Euston Station and three men – Alexander McIntyre, John Neeson and Walter Scott Ellis – appeared for trial in July. Though witnesses from the bank confirmed their identities, Neeson maintained he had an alibi and was with another man arranging to move furniture to a new flat in Maryhill. Ellis offered an even less convincing story, claiming that the money found in his possession had not come from the bank but from someone he knew called Dougie who – for reasons best known to himself – had paid for Ellis to take a trip to England. Ellis' Counsel, J. R. Fiddes, QC, also tried to cast doubt on the identification by the bank staff: 'To what extent can you believe a man who was in a highly emotional state at the time?'

The judge, however, took a different view. He highlighted the violence used in the raid: an assistant manager received as many as 100 shotgun pellets in his body. 'That a decent and law-abiding citizen should be shot down in this way is sufficient to revolt anyone with the slightest feeling for humanity.' Former Chief Superintendent Bob Kerr and others had often been outspoken about what they perceived as 'soft' sentences, but they would undoubtedly have approved of Lord Hunter's concluding remarks:

> I have reached the conclusion that it is essential to make an example of the accused in this case if there is to be a chance of preventing others following a similar course. The accused, particularly McIntyre and Ellis, have had ample opportunity to reform in the past which has not been taken. [Ellis had nineteen previous convictions, and both McIntyre and Neeson had eight.] The prospects of reform being about as remote as they could be, particularly in the case of those two, I think the matter which should be given by far the most weight is the protection of the public.

Ellis was sent to prison for twenty-one years, McIntyre for twenty and Neeson for eighteen – said at the time to be the heaviest sentences ever imposed by a Scottish court for a crime of this kind.

The annual salary of a Chief Superintendent in 1967 was £2,325, and Tom Goodall had earned every penny of it.

★ ★ ★

It's well known that, a decade after Peter Manuel's killing spree, Glasgow was terrorised by another killer who committed three murders. But it wasn't the man the press called 'Bible John' – it was a twenty-year-old called Sammy McCloy. Over the last forty years a steady stream of books and theories about the three killings attributed to Bible John has appeared, but the story of McCloy has been largely forgotten.

From September 1967 onwards, a number of violent attacks took place in streets easily reached from Paisley Road West on the south side of the city. In September 1967 Mrs Elizabeth Lang was assaulted in Levernside Road but she managed to pull a ring with a red stone from her attacker's finger. The following month fifty-seven-year-old Mrs Josephine McAllister was brutally attacked in Craigton Road, Govan when returning home late on a Saturday night after visiting her elderly mother. She was punched, kicked, raped and murdered, and her partially clothed body left on a railway embankment. Then, in March 1968, a neighbour of eighty-year-old James Brand and his seventy-five-year-old wife Janet who lived in Montrave Path noticed their front door lying open and called the police who found the elderly couple had been murdered.

This time, a young man had been seen running away from the scene around 12.30 a.m. by residents of the Moss Heights flats which over-looked the Brands' house. Police had a good description of the route taken by the fugitive.

Tom Goodall directed operations from a mobile caravan set up near the scene, from which he issued his press announcements. The caravan was one of a number of innovations introduced during his tenure of office; it could not only be used as a convenient base for local enquiries but served as a reassuringly visible sign to the community that the police were at work. Inevitably, CID men soon gave the caravan a nickname: 'Uncle Tom's Cabin'.

Routine strategies were immediately deployed: a team of 100 detectives began door-to-door enquiries, the area was searched with tracker dogs and checks made with local mental hospitals. Goodall reminded the public that 'In addition to probably being blood-stained, the assailant must have arrived home after 12.30 a.m. on Tuesday.'

It took just over a week to track down the killer, thanks to two palm prints found in the house in Montrave Path. Having studied the locations of the various attacks, Goodall was convinced the culprit was a local man and – in an ambitious move reminiscent of the operation to fingerprint every male in the Garnethill area after the murder of four-year-old Betty Alexander in 1952 – he instructed his men to collect the palm prints of every male in the square mile around the locations where both Mrs McAllister and the Brands had been killed.

When detectives arrived at the door of a house in Paisley Road West where twenty-year-old Samuel McCloy lived with his older sister, they found a match. Known as 'Simple Sammy' as a boy, McCloy had no track record of violence. He even had a steady girlfriend, shorthand typist Margaret Watkins of Paisley, who confirmed that 'he never made improper advances towards me'. His sister was equally shocked to find out what he had done, though she was well aware that since the death of their mother in 1967 his behaviour had changed – he used to be quiet but became noisy, unruly and started drinking.

After his arrest, he sent Margaret a series of letters from prison and she read extracts to the court during his trial in June. 'I pray to God for forgiveness every day and night,' he wrote. 'I don't know what came over me to do it . . . I am glad I have been stopped. I keep thinking I might have done it again. I can't control myself sometimes.'

Later on, Margaret Watkins reflected on her lucky escape: 'I went hand in hand with a monster.'

Psychiatrist Dr Wolfgang Kiernan said that in his opinion McCloy had been insane at the time of the offences. He believed the chances of him being improved by remedial treatment to be 'so slim as to be non-existent'. It would be a most sanguine man who could say that he might improve during his lifetime', he added. According to Dr George Swinney, physician superintendent of Woodilee Mental Hospital, 'McCloy's reason and judgement were overwhelmed by his abnormal sexual drive' and he recommended that he be placed in the care of expert psychiatrists. The judge, Lord Cameron, said that there was only one punishment that the law allowed him to impose – life imprisonment.

Ironically, the trial took place during Mental Health Week, which was designed to make the public more aware of the problems of mental illness.

Just over two weeks before McCloy killed the elderly couple in their own home, the body of a twenty-five-year-old nurse, Pat Docker, had been found in a lane yards away from where she lived in Langside. No one knew it at the time, but this was the first in another series of murders of women, all of whom had been picked up at the Barrowland dance hall – the start of what came to be known as the Bible John saga which, to this day, continues to grip the imagination of the public.

By contrast, the crimes of McCloy live on only in the faded pages of old newspapers – simply because he was caught, tried and locked away, whereas the Bible John cases remain unsolved.

★ ★ ★

In spite of Tom Goodall's many notable successes in putting killers behind bars, lawlessness in the city continued its upward trend throughout the 1960s. In the ten years from 1957 to 1967, recorded crimes of violence rose from 1,116 to 3,536 – an increase of 200%. In the same period, the murder toll in the city trebled from eleven cases in 1957 to thirty-nine in 1967. 'Scotland 1968 – a nation on the verge of being conquered by crime,' screamed one headline in the *Scottish Daily Express*.

The various concerns of police and public were brought sharply into focus after the 'Bloody Easter' weekend of 1968 when as many as fifty different fights and assaults, mostly stabbings, were reported over the holiday. Over the weekend, the Royal and Western Infirmaries were under intense pressure and one surgical team worked almost non-stop for a sixteen-hour stretch. The incident that received most publicity was the death of eighteen-year-old Philip Comerford, an apprentice printer found lying in a pool of blood in Springboig just a few minutes after attending a Good Friday service at St Paul's R.C. Church in Shettleston. By 2 a.m, the sixteen-year-old culprit had been arrested. On Easter Monday, the violence continued with what was described as a 'running battle' in Tynecastle Street involving forty youths and several girls.

In almost all these instances 'offensive weapons' were involved, leading Chief Constable James Robertson and others to call for 'stop and search' powers for police officers. However, the government resisted such demands: Willie Ross, Secretary of State for Scotland, thought that 'what happened in Glasgow at the weekend is not a condemnation of the police or the powers of the police but the social failure of education: we must provide uplift.' The *Scottish Daily Express* dismissed that as 'claptrap': 'The uplift that citizens want most are fast vans to wheel the neds off to Barlinnie.'

Nearly fifty years on, the issue of stop-and-search is still being debated with just as much passion.

Predictably, the violence on the streets also led to renewed calls for the restoration of capital punishment, which had been abolished three years earlier. The *Express* stated that in a single week it had received 21,961 letters in favour with only 126 against. However, Tom Goodall was never one of those in favour of the death penalty. His daughter vividly remembers the family having breakfast on the morning Peter Manuel went to the gallows. Shortly after eight o'clock, she said, 'Manuel will be dead now.' Her father plainly looked upset and told her not to talk about it; he did not think it right that a man should know the time and place of his death.

The arguments over the causes of crime and the most appropriate punishments would continue but in the short term the police had to take some urgent steps to contain the situation in April 1968 as another weekend approached. Robertson called a meeting of his CID chiefs to arrange for each division to supply men for a special 'anti-violence squad' to spend the weekend on patrol in selected streets where trouble was most likely. 'We're certainly not going to have another weekend like last,' said Goodall. 'Steps have been taken that I think will go a long way to controlling violence in this city.'

By 1 a.m. on the Saturday night there had been three assaults, and twenty-three people charged with breach of the peace. On the Monday it was reported that the operation had cut Glasgow's weekend toll of stabbings by more than a half, with twenty-nine injuries, six of whom remained in hospital. Hardly something for the city to be proud of, but it was seen as a step in the right direction.

Simply repressing outbreaks of violence was not, of course, going to solve the problem permanently. An increasing amount of crime was committed by young people under seventeen and one of the more imaginative attempts to tackle this trend was the famous Easterhouse project of pop singer Frankie Vaughan. Having grown up in a tough Liverpool setting, he knew something about gangs and violence and came to Glasgow to see if he could help. He proposed a weapons amnesty and, putting his money where his mouth was, donated £3,500 for a youth centre, which was eventually provided. The gesture, and Vaughan's continued interest in the area, was generally appreciated in the city though, by itself, the initiative could hardly eradicate deep-seated territorialism and violence. But it was credited with establishing, for the first time, some degree of communication between officialdom and the gang members.

\* \* \*

The image of Tom Goodall portrayed in the press and confirmed by those who worked with him was of a quiet man who sat smoking his pipe, deep in thought as he wrestled with the complex strands of an enquiry. 'I've seen him . . . pipe-smoking his way through murder investigations with the skill and wisdom of a man dedicated to his job forty-eight hours of the day,' was how 'Pat Roller' of the *Daily Record* put it. Yet three of his most dramatic cases showed that he could also assume the role of a man of action when faced with armed and dangerous criminals.

In November 1958, the *Glasgow Herald* reported an incident in the Gorbals under the heading 'Officer in Manuel Case Hurt' – a sure sign that Goodall's high-profile role in that inquiry had cemented his reputation. CID had received information that a car had been spotted in Camden Street which had been used in a burglary in West Kilbride, Ayrshire in the course of which £1,000 worth of jewellery had been stolen. The thieves were looking for buyers and Goodall came up with a typically astute move. At the time two Indian police officers, one a Sikh who wore a turban and the other a Hindu, were attending a training course in the Identification Bureau at HQ. Goodall asked them if they would go to the Camden Street house and find out if the jewellery was there by acting as prospective buyers. They were instructed to say they were prepared to buy it but would have to leave in order to get the necessary money for the transaction. They duly reported back to Goodall at an agreed rendezvous and he took the decision to raid the premises, accompanied by Detective Sergeants Farmer and Sloan and Detective Constable Watson.

They arrived at exactly the right moment. A man called Jack Marsden and two associates were sorting out the loot, which they hastily tried to cover up with a newspaper. Thirty-eight-year-old Marsden, also known as John Edmiston, was no stranger to the CID: he had progressed through the system of approved school, borstal and prison since the age of ten and had eighteen previous convictions. Sloan and Watson approached Marsden to search him, while Goodall and Farmer did the same with the other two men. Marsden shouted, 'Don't come any further; you're not searching me.' The officers grabbed him but he managed to put his hand inside his jacket pocket and pull out a pistol and, as Goodall and Farmer advanced towards him, he fired, grazing Goodall in the right thigh. 'I felt some pain in my leg,' he said, 'and I rolled up my trouser leg and found that I had a small abrasion high up on the inside of my right leg. The abrasion had black blood coming from it, but the bleeding was very slight.' The others managed to force their assailant to the ground, but not before he had fired a second shot. Fortunately this one only penetrated the floor.

Marsden's advocate, A. A. MacDonald, later argued that the gun had gone off accidentally when the officers jumped at him. 'He is a fool, but he is not a violent criminal,' said MacDonald. Marsden pled guilty to a charge of 'assault on the police in the execution of their duty' and was sent to prison for ten years. Released early, he was then stabbed to death in an Edinburgh flat in 1965.

After the shooting incident Goodall was taken by car to the Royal Infirmary where doctors told him that if the bullet had been a fraction of an inch closer to his leg, it could have severed a vital artery and killed him.

It was typical of the man that, after treatment, he went straight back to his office and resumed duty.

In August 1966, Goodall successfully hunted down an even more dangerous gunman wanted by Scotland Yard for his involvement in the murder of three policeman in London. Plain-clothes officers in an unmarked car were suspicious of three men in an old Standard Vanguard estate car in Braybrook Street, East Acton, near Wormwood Scrubs Prison. Three shots were fired, two at the officers who approached the men and the third at the driver of the police car. As a result of a tip-off from an underworld source, the estate car was located in a Lambeth garage and one of the men arrested. The two others, described by Scotland Yard as 'dangerous and both known to be armed', were named as Harry Roberts and John Duddy. The latter was a Glasgow man who had gone to London about ten years previously and it was reasonable to assume that he would head back home. Officially, Glasgow CID's comment was that 'There is no indication of any kind that Duddy is in Glasgow but the possibility exists that he could be. In that event fairly extensive enquiries were going on'. In fact, forty specially selected detectives were visiting his known haunts in the city and rounding up his relatives for questioning. It was his brother Vincent, shocked by the details of the London murders which had provoked nationwide outrage, who agreed to take police to where he was hiding, a tenement in Stevenson Street in the Calton district – only 100 yards away from the Eastern Division police headquarters. Armed officers with protective shields made their way to a first floor flat at 1.30 p.m. where Duddy was found, unarmed and offering no resistance. The arrest was carried out by Goodall himself, and amongst the detectives with him were James

Binnie, a future CID Chief, and David McNee, later Metropolitan Police Commissioner.

Duddy was then quickly despatched to Scotland Yard. Two of their officers had flown up to Glasgow and spent an hour at the Central Police Station before returning to London on a BEA (British European Airways) flight the same evening. A twenty-seat section at the back of the aircraft was sealed off and occupied only by Duddy and the two detectives.

The third wanted man, Harry Roberts, employed his military training to survive by hiding in a wooded area in Hertfordshire before being caught in November. All three were sentenced to life imprisonment.

Duddy's arrest was one of the highest points of Tom Goodall's career but, as ever, his statements to the press were brief, factual and to the point. Whatever the potential danger, he considered he was doing no more than carrying out his duty. 'Seniority matters in these things,' he said afterwards. 'We cannot send a younger man out to do something we should do ourselves.'

Goodall's final encounter with a gunman, just weeks before his own death, was by far the most dramatic. The sequence of events began with a break-in at the bungalow of a Mr and Mrs Ross in Ayr in July 1969. The elderly couple were left tied up and although Mr Ross recovered, his wife died three days after the ordeal. Police suspected two men well-known to them, Paddy Meehan and James Griffiths, the first of whom was to feature in a long-running saga during which he was found guilty of murdering Mrs Ross and imprisoned, though he was cleared and given a royal pardon seven years later.

Meehan's alleged accomplice, Griffiths, came from Rochdale, Lancashire and police received a tip-off that he was currently posing as an antiques dealer and staying in an attic flat in Holyrood Crescent in the West End, just behind St Mary's Episcopal Cathedral in Great Western Road. When five detectives arrived at the address on the morning of 15 July, Griffiths panicked and opened fire, not only on the officers but on passers-by, wounding several people.

Armed officers then arrived and Goodall took command, sealing off the area. However, the culprit had managed to escape from the rear of the building, making his way towards North Woodside Road. From there he ran to Henderson Street where he shot a driver and hijacked his car. Two senior officers, Chief Superintendent Malcolm Finlayson and Detective Superintendent James Binnie, were in hot pursuit and they recognised Griffiths as he drove past. Heading north towards Possilpark, he abandoned the car and entered the Round Toll Bar where he demanded brandy. He then stole a lorry and drove to Kay Street, Springburn and took refuge in an empty top-floor flat where he continued to fire at random at pedestrians on the pavement below while police frantically tried to shepherd people to safety, including children from a nearby play park.

Finlayson crept up the stairs, pointed his revolver through the letterbox of the flat and shot Griffiths. He had aimed for the shoulder but the bullet pierced his aorta and the gunman died a few minutes later.

From beginning to end Griffiths' rampage had lasted eighty-five minutes, in the course of which he had fired more than 100 shots, wounding a total of thirteen people, one of whom died. One witness described it as being 'like a movie about Chicago'. That afternoon, Goodall addressed a packed press conference, with several revolver holsters and a handful of cartridges lying on the desk in front of him. He summarised the sequence of events and said that the manhunt had been the biggest in the city for twenty years, but withheld the culprit's name until his relatives had been informed. Griffiths had committed a string of offences in England, and had recently been in prison for robbery with violence, but when he was named in the press the day after the shooting incident, his landlady in Holyrood Crescent described him as 'a real gentleman – well-spoken and well-mannered'.

The police were praised for their response. 'I would like to say that the city is proud of her police force who, without thought for self, went after this man,' said the Lord Provost, Donald Liddle, an opinion endorsed by the *Evening Times*: 'Glasgow police have done well . . .

They have shown a realism and balanced judgement which increases public confidence in them.'

It was another feather in Tom Goodall's cap.

The siege of Holyrood Crescent was the third time the Chief Superintendent had directed an operation involving a gunman. Sadly, 1969 would end with an even worse multiple shooting when, the day before Hogmanay, Howard Wilson, a disgruntled former policeman carried out a bank robbery in Linwood with two accomplices – one of whom was another ex-cop. Inspector Andrew Hyslop, a former colleague of Wilson, spotted him taking the loot into his flat in Allison Street on the south side, and when he and two other officers went to the flat to investigate, Wilson opened fire. The two constables were killed outright and Hyslop was paralysed for life.

But Tom Goodall did not live to witness that incident. The previous year he had moved from a police house in Jordanhill to a bungalow in Hutchison Drive, Bearsden where, after a rare afternoon of relaxation weeding the garden, he collapsed with a heart attack on 12 October 1969. Attempts were made to resuscitate him in the ambulance on the way to the Western Infirmary, without success.

Bailie James Anderson, Glasgow Corporation's police convener, reckoned that 'he may have killed himself with overwork by insisting on being called out to any major crime no matter when it happened.' At the time of his death he was on the verge of being appointed to a newly created Assistant Chief Constable post with special responsibility for the CID. An insight into the way things worked in these days was given when the deadline for the post was extended until the end of October in order to provide 'an opportunity to other officers who have not submitted an application because they thought Chief Superintendent Goodall was the best man for the job'. In the meantime, his deputy Elphinstone Dalglish took over as acting head of CID.

Four hundred mourners flocked to Linn Crematorium for the funeral, including representatives from every police force in Scotland. For a time the switchboard at CID headquarters was jammed as people from all walks of life phoned in to pay their respects.

The phone rang in the Hutchison Drive bungalow and Alison Goodall answered. A gruff voice enquired, 'Dae ye mind if ah come tae the funeral? Ah knew yer faither. He put me away for murder.'

The Rev Alan Boyd Robson of Kelvinside Parish Church, where Tom Goodall had been an elder, captured the mood of the whole of Glasgow in a moving tribute:

> We have today a city in which the tide has turned and law and order are beginning to get on top of crime and lawlessness, and this is in no small measure due to the influence of Chief Detective Superintendent Tom Goodall. He has become identified in the minds of countless thousands of simple people as the man who, in their name, opposed and tackled wickedness and crime and violence and everything they hated and feared.

It was a legacy of which any detective would have been proud.

# 14

## *The Student of Human Nature*

*Detective Superintendent Joe Beattie,*
*In Charge of the Northern, Maryhill and Marine Divisions*
*1969–73*

Whenever the name of Joe Beattie is mentioned, it's invariably prefaced by the adjective 'legendary'. And with good reason. Few police officers have been held in such high esteem by colleagues, criminals, lawyers and public alike.

Beattie became a household name in Glasgow in the early seventies because of his adept use of the media in the search for 'Bible John', the name coined by a reporter for the man thought to have been responsible for the murders of three women between February 1968 and October 1969. But Bible John was never caught and that was something that weighed on Joe Beattie's mind right up until his death in February 2000 at the age of eighty-two.

In retirement, he was always keen to share his fund of anecdotes about life as a detective and I spent many fascinating hours listening to his recollections while researching a series of articles on crime in Glasgow. The culmination of that series was to be a piece on Beattie himself, but he would read over each draft and always want it altered in some way. 'Don't mention that story – his family's still around.'

'Don't mention me by name – use a made-up one instead.' Eventually I asked him, 'Why the reticence, Joe?' His reply was typically direct and brutally honest: 'Anybody who reads that will say: "If Joe Beattie was so bloody clever, then why did he no' catch Bible John?"'

Those who knew him and worked with him know there are far better reasons why Joe Beattie should be remembered – not only for the cases he *did* solve but for what he was. Beattie often described himself as 'a student of human nature' and it was above all his interest in people that accounted for his success in solving crimes and for the esteem in which he was held on both sides of the law. He was a consummate actor, able to adopt a demeanour appropriate to whoever he happened to be dealing with. Len Murray, the highly respected lawyer and after-dinner speaker, wrote in his autobiography *The Pleader* (2002) that Joe 'always gave the impression of being a rather slow and cumbersome thinker but that was a role which he cultivated and developed, playing it to perfection. Joe deceived many a cross-examiner into thinking that they would have no difficulty with him.'

The well-known Glasgow defence lawyer, Joe Beltrami, could certainly vouch for that. He never forgot a courtroom encounter with Beattie near the start of his legal career, when the future Superintendent was a detective constable in the Northern Division. The case concerned an alleged burglar that Beattie claimed he had seen running away from the scene of the crime. As outlined in Beltrami's book *The Defender* (1980), Beltrami asked Beattie how he was able to identify his client, given that it was dark and the man was so far away that the officers could not catch him:

> Beattie, wily as ever, hesitated – and I pounced, with a bored glance at the jury for effect: 'Come on, answer the question – you surely under-stand it.' Gaining in confidence, I added, in my euphoric state, 'What sort of eyesight do you have anyway?' I didn't know he was leading me on to the punch. In his own time he looked at me with what I thought might be pity, perhaps it was disdain, and said: 'Sir, (thus giving me my place and about to put me in it) my eyesight is perfect. I was a night pilot

in Bomber Command during the last war' . . . At that point the prospect of success for my client evaporated – nay, disintegrated.

Likewise, in the interview room Joe Beattie was a master of the 'good cop, bad cop' routine. He would let someone else question an unco-operative suspect for a time. Then, when no progress had been made, he would barge into the room, fumbling with a packet of cigarettes and box of matches, clumsily spilling them over the table and giving a general impression of ineptitude. Once his colleague had left the room, he would ask in a conspiratorial voice, 'What was that guy on about?' Invariably, the recalcitrant interviewee would find himself saying a lot more than he'd intended.

This innate understanding of human nature was allied to powers of observation as sharp as any Glasgow ned's razor. One murder case was solved because Beattie noticed that the kitchen knives in a suspect's house were just too clean and shiny. In another, the only clue was a Swan Vesta match found near the body of an elderly woman. From his intimate observation of the habits of tenement dwellers, Beattie knew that the men of that particular street never used Swan Vestas. He conducted door-to-door enquiries and found himself confronting an individual whom he felt intuitively was the culprit. Ordering the man to empty his pockets, he found . . . a box of Swan Vestas.

In William McIlvanney's Glasgow detective novel *The Papers of Tony Veitch* (1983), there's a character who says, 'Ah know people. See that Sigmund Freud? Ah coulda learned him about people.'

It could have been Joe Beattie's epitaph.

Joe Beattie was one of the class of '46: the men who joined the police after wartime service. He had a distinguished record as a fighter and bomber pilot and used to tell the story of how he got into the Royal Air Force. During an interview he was asked, 'What school did you go to?'

'Oakbank Public School,' he replied, referring to his elementary schooling in the Maryhill area of Glasgow.

'Public School?' The officers on the panel nodded to each other in approval.

Joe Beattie was immediately accepted.

His RAF service took him from Glasgow to the United States via several UK bases, the one at Middle Wallop near Salisbury being the most significant as he met his wife Joan when stationed there. He once joked that he nearly became famous as 'the only RAF pilot to bomb his own country'. He had just taken off in a Boeing Flying Fortress from Wick with a full bomb load when one of the engines blew up and he coaxed the crippled plane out over the sea and jettisoned the bombs in Sinclair's Bay.

After a spell at the Oxford Street training school, Joe Beattie would set out each morning from his tenement home in Grafton Square in Townhead to the Northern Division headquarters in Maitland Street which took in the Cowcaddens and Garscube areas, at that time full of overcrowded and unwholesome closes, none more so than those of Lyon Street. Today, not only the buildings but the street itself has disappeared; a primary school playground now occupies the site. Lyon Street, it is said, was a hard street that bred hard men. More than 200 emerged from its closes to serve in the First World War, giving it the reputation of being the most decorated street in Britain. Much local speculation exists about the whereabouts of a roll of honour which used to hang in a long-since demolished pub in the area.

It was in this part of Glasgow that Walter Norval was born in 1928, not far from Cowcaddens subway station. Quickly learning to fend for himself, he formed a gang known as 'the Wee Mob', breaking into shops and getting involved in gambling and fights. Norval would later acquire a fearsome reputation as 'Glasgow's Godfather', and he and Beattie crossed paths on many occasions over the next few decades – see Robert Jeffrey's *Glasgow Godfather* (2003).

In these days – and right up until 1962 – Glasgow's streets were criss-crossed by tramlines. To this day where tenement buildings survive in Maryhill Road and elsewhere, you can still see the metal hooks high up on the walls to which the wires that provide the motive power were once attached. Norval's biographer Robert Jeffrey tells of one of his early tricks: timing a break-in to coincide with the passing of a tramcar as its thundering noise could mask the sound of a shop window being smashed. Money or any saleable goods would then be quickly grabbed; the youths would disappear up a dark close and easily dispose of the loot to black market traders.

A broken shop window and a tramcar also featured in two of Joe Beattie's early experiences as a beat cop, albeit on separate occasions. In these days, newsagents used to place the headlines of the latest editions outside their shops, posted on much larger and heavier billboards than are used today. A favourite prank would be for unruly children to pull these over and run away before the resulting crash brought the shopkeeper charging onto the street. One particular boy delighted in tormenting a Garscube Road newsagent in this way on a daily basis.

Joe was escorting school pupils at a crossing when the hot-tempered shop owner came running up to demand that he should arrest the young delinquent.

'Come and see this, Joe! That wee McKinnon's put a brick through ma windae!'

'Did you see him do it?'

'Naw, but ah seen him knocking over ma boards last night. He must have put a brick in ma pail this morning while ah wis daeing the windaes an ah had tae go in tae serve somebody.'

The custom at the time was to rub the window with a bar of soap and rinse it by throwing a pail of water over it. Joe was secretly amused at young McKinnon's ingenuity.

'So, what you're saying is that you threw a brick through your own window! I can't arrest the lad for that.'

The shopkeeper stormed off in disgust.

On another occasion, Constable Beattie was patrolling in Garscube Road when he saw a figure dash across the street into the path of an oncoming tram, which was shaking and clanking its way towards

Shieldhall on the other side of the city. Frantically the driver banged on his bell to sound a warning and applied the brakes but the man paid no attention and was swept under the wheels as the tram screeched to a halt.

The passengers descended and a crowd of curious pedestrians gathered round while the constable got down on his hands and knees and peered underneath to see what he could do. The extent of the man's physical injuries could not be determined but it was only too obvious that he was paralysed by fear. Beattie received no answer to his questions except heart-rending shrieks.

The tramcars of that era had a protective barrier at the front and rear known as the 'cow-catcher' – or 'coo-catcher' in Glasgow vernacular – and, jammed as he was between this and the front bogie wheels, there was no possibility of pulling the man free. The only solution was to contact the depot for lifting gear to be sent out to raise the tram.

Tension mounted as more onlookers gathered, drawn by the incoherent screams of the hapless victim. Eventually the giant tram was slowly raised. Removing his police helmet and tunic, the young officer crawled carefully beneath, as twelve and a half tons of metal hovered precariously above him. Now he could see the problem: the man's clothes were caught in the wheels. He called to a bystander to fetch a knife from a nearby butcher's shop and eventually cut the terrified victim loose and laid him tenderly on a stretcher ready for the waiting ambulance to take him to hospital.

But the drama was far from over. To the astonishment of the watching crowd, the man leapt to his feet and ran away. Still brandishing the butcher's knife, Beattie ran after him, calling to him to stop, that the ambulance was waiting for him, that they just wanted to check he was all right . . . The chase led to a close in nearby Edington Street and Beattie charged up the stairs just in time to see the figure disappear into a house. He hammered at the door, which was opened by a wee Glasgow 'wifie' in apron and curlers. Confronted with this panting figure in shirtsleeves wielding a carving knife, she could be forgiven for failing to recognise she was in the presence of a police officer!

'Oh mister, mister, leave him alane!' she pleaded. 'The puir man's deaf and dumb!'

Only then did Joe fully understand the terror felt by the pathetic figure, now cowering behind a chair.

Joe Beattie joined the CID in 1952 and was transferred to the Eastern Division. When promoted to Detective Sergeant in September 1960, he found himself back where he started, in the Northern. Yet, whether in uniform or plain clothes, he continued to have equally unpredictable encounters in the course of his daily duties.

One of his most unlikely roles was to deliver a baby, but this is what happened when, passing through the Roystonhill area in a patrol car at 5 a.m. with a CID colleague, he spotted a barefoot man running down the street, hotly pursued by a uniformed constable. Assistance was obviously required. The car screeched to a halt, the two plain-clothes men jumped out and grabbed hold of the fugitive. But when the out-of-breath uniformed man eventually caught up, he yelled, 'Let him go – his wife is having a baby!' At that point the panicking father-to-be broke free and started running back home. All three cops jumped back into the car and followed him to his home in James Nisbet Street – and not a moment too soon, for his wife was just about to give birth. It turned out that the husband had dashed out of the house to seek help but could not wake any neighbours and starting running down the street where he ran into the constable doing his rounds. Joe received many accolades in his career, but the relieved father's must have been one of the most heartfelt: 'The cops were great. I can't thank them enough!'

Joe Beattie does seem to have had a knack of turning up at the right place at the right time. One prominent legal figure certainly had reason to be grateful when he defused a tricky situation in the Sheriff Court.

Business was just getting under way again after the New Year holiday at Glasgow Sheriff Court where a meeting of creditors was taking place to discuss the affairs of a Cypriot restaurant owner called Nicholas Perdikou whose business had fallen into financial difficulties. Clearly this was the straw that broke the camel's back, for the desperate restaurateur decided to take matters into his own hands and made his way to the court armed with a dismantled shotgun in a leather case and a bandolier of cartridges. Whether he would have used it is a matter for conjecture, but Beattie, who by this time was a Superintendent and second in command of the CID, received a phone call with an urgent tip-off: 'Mr Beattie! Perdikou's going to shoot the Sheriff!'

Joe set off immediately with some of his men and arrived in time to see the Cypriot ascending the stairs, wearing a long raincoat under which he was clearly trying to conceal something bulky. Beattie undid the buttons of Perdikou's coat, removed the shotgun and hauled him off to the cells, while the prisoner exclaimed, 'I'll show them. They're worse than the Mafia!' When the case came to court, Joe – who was famous for his use of humour in the witness box – was asked about that comment by the procurator fiscal depute.

'The Mafia is a criminal organisation?'

'Yes, in America mostly – we hope,' replied the Superintendent.

By then, however, Perdikou had changed his story. The previous night he had been out shooting hares, he said. He left the gun and ammunition in his car and when he reached the court, where he was going to see his solicitor, he decided it was better not to leave the firearms outside and brought them in with him. An expert witness told the court that the weapon, if used at close range, would have 'a devastating effect'. Sheriff Frank Middleton sentenced him to nine months in jail, telling him that 'the court has a duty to protect the ordinary members of the public from the kind of dangers created by your acts.'

It goes without saying that the Sheriff also cancelled Perdikou's firearms certificate and confiscated the gun.

★ ★ ★

That court appearance, which took place on 6 January 1971, must almost have seemed a welcome distraction to Joe Beattie compared to the harrowing task he had been engaged on since the New Year.

On Saturday 2 January 1971, the Superintendent enjoyed a rare day off at Ibrox stadium where – along with 80,000 other spectators – he watched Rangers play Celtic. The weather was dull and foggy and the game uneventful – until, in the last few moments, Celtic scored. It was all over as far as Rangers' fans were concerned, and some began to make an early departure to avoid the crowds.

Then, just before the final whistle, there was a huge roar. Colin Stein had equalised for Rangers.

Joe had hardly arrived home when the phone rang. It was the Chief Constable, Sir James Robertson. 'Were you at the match, Joe? Well, can you get back here right away? There's been a terrible accident and I want you to take charge.'

Somehow, a huge number of people leaving the stadium on Stairway 13 fell on top of each other, leading to the tragic loss of 66 lives. Chief Superintendent Angus McDonald directed his men to form two lines, above and below where the incident occurred, ensuring that other spectators were channelled away from the stairway – an action thought to have prevented even more casualties. 'Operation Emergency' kicked in, involving 200 police officers and a fleet of twenty ambulances.

Joe Beattie's role over the weeks that followed was to coordinate a police enquiry from Govan police office. Teams of officers were drafted in to conduct interviews with as many eyewitnesses as possible. A Fatal Accident Enquiry, held in Pollokshaws Burgh Hall in February, followed the police investigation. By that time Beattie was able to provide the enquiry with more than 1,000 statements.

In such situations, myths quickly take hold. Some said that the human pile-up was caused when departing Rangers supporters, hearing the roar when their team scored, turned back on the stairway and ploughed into others who were leaving. The patient gathering of evidence by Beattie and his team was crucial in establishing the truth. The enquiry concluded that 'the downward pressure of the crowd above forced other persons to fall or collapse on those who had fallen first and as the downward pressure continued, more and more persons were heaped upon those who had fallen or were pressed hard against them.'

The passage of almost half a century has not erased the horror of that black day in Glasgow's history.

★  ★  ★

Joe Beattie once ruefully commented that his twenty-five-year career in the CID began with the unsolved murder of Betty Alexander, the four-year-old girl found dead in Garnethill in 1952, and ended with the Bible John case which similarly remains open. Much has been written about these cases over the years and they continue to exercise a fascination for those interested in crime but many other murder enquiries in which Joe Beattie played a part have long since faded from public memory.

Some of these followed a familiar Glasgow pattern: a night of excessive drinking leading to unprovoked violence. One case of this type from 1953 stayed in Joe Beattie's mind as it took place on Christmas Day and seemed all the more senseless as those involved were related to each other.

Twenty-two-year-old James Heaney and his thirty-year-old brother-in-law had spent an evening drinking in pubs in the Roystonhill area, later adjourning to a friend's house for chips and a cup of tea. At about 10.30 p.m. they set off home through a lane leading to Tharsis Street and met three men coming towards them. One of them, twenty-nine-year-old John McGinlay, made some remark to Heaney who replied with the poignant words, 'This is Christmas. You ought to forget about these things.' McGinlay then drew a knife and started making stabbing gestures for some minutes until Heaney's friend said, 'Come on, let's go home.' Heaney walked towards him and then fell to the ground. McGinlay and his companions, meanwhile, had walked away, though one returned and helped to carry Heaney home. At the end of the lane they were laughed at by a group of teenagers who assumed Heaney was drunk and incapable. Two police constables appeared but they came to a similar conclusion and did not investigate further, though they did assist the group in carrying him back to the close where his brother lived. It was only as Heaney staggered up the stairs that they saw blood pouring from the left side of his stomach.

McGinlay, however, denied he was responsible. The knife – which, according to a witness, he put in one of his companion's pockets with the instruction to dispose of it – was produced in court but he claimed not to recognise it. All he could say was that he had drunk so much that night that he had only the vaguest recollection of what happened to Heaney, whom 'he had known since he was a kid' and who was a cousin of his brother-in-law. McGinlay's wife also appeared in court and explained that he had arrived at her mother's house around 1 a.m. 'hopelessly drunk' and collapsed into a chair. About 3 a.m. she dragged him back home and put him to bed until the detectives arrived soon afterwards to arrest him.

The judge in this sorry tale of knife crime (whose name, appropriately enough, happened to be Lord Blades) told the members of the jury that they had to decide whether or not 'these men were so befuddled that they just did not know what had happened'. The jury gave McGinlay the benefit of the doubt: found guilty of culpable homicide rather than murder, he was sent to prison for five years.

This was not the first time Joe Beattie had encountered John McGinlay, a man with a colourful past. In retirement decades later, the detective could still recall the details of his story:

> I always had a soft spot for McGinlay. He had been drafted into the army during World War II and ended up in the Middle East. He deserted and managed to make his way to Cairo where he caught a ship that took him home to Glasgow. Then he was arrested for burgling a public house. He and his accomplices completely cleared the pub of its stock – they only left the barrels because they couldn't get them through the doors. We tracked them down to a top floor tenement where about fifty people were busy consuming the supplies from the pub as quickly as they could, mixing Glayva with Guinness! It was a dangerous situation: fifty drunken men against two cops. If it hadn't been for McGinlay, they'd have thrown me out of the window. I was able to flash my torch

to signal to the beat constable below and he sent for reinforcements and a van. Sometimes the police had to come and go with the criminals, so we made an agreement: we'd only arrest four of them if they pled guilty.

Handling situations of that kind depended on brawn as much as brains, but on many other occasions it was Joe's mental agility that led to an arrest. A particularly violent double murder in a flat in the Kinning Park area was solved through his eagle-eyed scrutiny of the scene. A man and his seventeen-year-old deaf-mute daughter had been horrifically mutilated with a knife, suffering a total of thirty-four stab wounds between them. The discovery was made by a friend of the girl who had come to collect her for a night out at the cinema and when she reported the crime, detectives were there in minutes sealing off the area. The manic killer had left behind the murder weapon, a kitchen knife covered in blood, though he had the presence of mind to wipe the handle clean to ensure there were no fingerprints on it. He had also made some attempt to clean up the appalling amount of blood he had shed but while the identification bureau was examining the premises Joe noticed a mark on the patterned linoleum covering of the hallway which turned out to be a toe print. It seemed the killer had removed his shoes and socks to avoid leaving a blood-stained shoe print but had not noticed he'd stepped on blood with his bare feet. In the 1960s the specialist discipline known as forensic podiatry had hardly developed but it had been established that a toe print could be as distinctive as a fingerprint.

The detectives now had a useful clue – but they needed a suspect. It was here that Joe Beattie's famous sixth sense kicked in. The usual routine of going up and down stairs knocking on doors had started, including those of other members of the family living nearby. When Joe questioned one of them, a sixteen-year-old youth, he had a strong feeling that he was looking at the culprit. An impression of his foot was taken and found to be identical with the one found on the floor. Beattie took the suspect back to Plantation Street police office where at first he denied being the killer but later that evening the detective was with him in his cell noting down particulars of his previous history when, sitting with his head in his hands, he suddenly exclaimed, 'Oh my God, why did ah dae it?'

As a touching postscript to this story, the newspapers reported that the deaf girl had been in the habit of meeting with her friends at Govan Cross. The day after the killing only a few turned up. They talked to each other in sign language and one girl started crying. Then they all went their separate ways.

Another murder inquiry that illustrates Joe Beattie's investigative skills occurred in August 1966 when he was working alongside Tom Goodall, then in charge of the CID. The incident did not attract the usual press attention as it was pushed off the front pages by the story of gangland boss Arthur Thompson's car being blown up by a booby trap bomb, resulting in the death of his mother-in-law who was in the passenger seat.

One afternoon neighbours saw smoke coming from a window on the second floor of a tenement in Golspie Street, Govan. When firemen broke down the door of the burning flat they found the naked body of forty-two-year-old Laurence Allen whose clothes had been piled on top of him and set alight. The victim's head had been battered beyond all recognition.

Following his usual practice, Goodall was soon on the scene with Beattie and other colleagues from the so-called 'murder squad' though the detailed investigation was officially the responsibility of the head of the Divisional CID, Detective Chief Inspector Alex Hume of Govan. Goodall was soon able to announce: 'This is murder. The person or persons responsible had also attempted to set fire to the house.'

As Govan detectives started door-to-door enquiries, the tenant of the flat arrived home from his work at one of the local shipyards. He was able to tell police that Allen had been lodging with him for the past ten days. The victim had been separated from his wife for six years and was said to be a quiet man who had been out of work for a year because of illness. He was seen entering the close with a younger man at about 3 p.m. on the day of the fire and information from his sister allowed detectives to piece together how he had spent the previous few hours in various pubs on the opposite side of the river.

Goodall indicated to the press that an early arrest was not expected but by 30 August newspapers were reporting that a seventeen-year-old male had been charged with the murder. However, press accounts rarely reveal the step-by-step enquiries that ultimately produce an arrest.

According to Beattie, the first important lead came from a taxi driver who confirmed that he had picked up two men from the Kelvin Hall area and taken them through the Clyde Tunnel to Govan. It was known that the pair had been drinking in pubs in the area. It was also known, though not stated in press reports, that Allen had been an inveterate gambler. Joe therefore thought it was worth making enquiries in nearby betting shops to see whether he had placed a bet on the day of the crime. By this time the illegal street gambling that was rife in an earlier era had been replaced by legalised betting shops, which rapidly appeared in high streets from 1961 onwards.

The hunch proved correct. He had indeed placed a bet that afternoon. Detectives then started following up the gamblers who had placed bets on either side of the victim's, on the assumption that one would have been his companion – and his killer.

It was the custom to write a number beside a bet – a carryover from the old days when the punter would identify himself using a 'nom de plume'. The most obvious choice was a date of birth or house number. 'One number that came up was 1248 – the number of a close in Argyle Street,' said Joe. 'I remember it because it was just across the road from the only tree in that stretch of Argyle Street.' Detectives called at these premises and took a seventeen-year-old male into custody.

The sordid details of the events in Govan in August came out during the trial in the High Court in November. The youth had been drinking with the victim in various pubs and went back with him to the Golspie Street flat. Allen asked him to go out for a message; when he returned the older man was naked and started making advances towards the frightened youth by trying to kiss him on the neck. Then he drew a knife and stood in front of the door, blocking the exit. 'The man was jumping about like a madman,' said the youth's mother in court. 'My son said he tried very hard but just could not get out of his road, so he lifted a hammer and struck him on the head.'

The jury accepted that the accused had acted in self-defence; he was found guilty of culpable homicide and sent to a young offenders' institution for two years.

Less than three years later, the same man – now described as an 'unemployed labourer' – was back in court again, charged with a bizarre attempted murder. On Christmas Day 1968 it was alleged that he induced a thirteen-year-old boy to enter his house in Argyle Street by promising to give him a bicycle. Once inside, he threatened to hit the youngster with a hammer if he did not lie down on the floor and allow him to tie up his hands and feet. Next, he put the terrified boy on a chair, placed his head inside the loop of a tie he had fastened onto a door frame and proceeded to push the chair away. The boy remembered nothing else about the incident until he was found lying outside the flat on the landing making moaning sounds, which were overheard by a passing police constable.

The teenager was later subjected to yet another ordeal – this time by counsel for the defence during the trial in April 1969. The tie was placed round his neck again and the whole scene re-enacted in front of the court. Then he was accused of lying.

'Why did you say the man hanged you?'

'Because he did.'

'That is a pack of lies, is it not?'

'No sir.'

'Were you experimenting on yourself in his house?'

'No sir.'

'Have you ever experimented by putting a tie round your neck?'

'No sir.'

'You know boys do that sort of thing?'

'Yes.'

'Have you known boys who have done this?'

'No.'

The boy wasn't the only person to receive a grilling during that trial. Detective Inspector George 'Yorkie' Lloyd, a 'neighbour' of Joe Beattie on many enquiries, told how he had made thirty or forty calls at the accused's house in an attempt to retrieve the chair for evidence purposes but had to admit that when he eventually gained entry by forcing the door he had removed the wrong one.

Fortunately, the court endorsed the expert medical opinion that the accused was 'suffering from a personality disorder which is a form of mental illness' and was therefore 'a dangerous person in need of treatment under conditions of special security'. He was sentenced to be detained in the State Hospital, Carstairs, without limit of time.

This time, the story did make the front pages.

★ ★ ★

Of all the high-ranking detectives covered by this book, Joe Beattie is unique in one significant respect: his name is inextricably linked with a single enquiry, the hunt for 'Bible John'. Beattie immersed himself in the case to such an extent that at least one fellow detective is on record as saying it became an obsession with him. He famously made the claim: 'I know more about this man than I do some members of my own family. If he walked into the most crowded of rooms I would pick him out immediately.'

The CID team working on the case was so familiar with the man they were after that they referred to him as 'BJ'.

The Bible John saga is not the story of a murderer caught but of a myth created. It began in February 1968 with the discovery of the body of twenty-five-year-old auxiliary nurse Pat Docker in a lane near her home in Langside on the south side of the city. Eighteen months later, thirty-two-year-old Jemima McDonald was strangled in a disused tenement in Bridgeton. The third crime followed after an interval of only two months when, at the end of October 1969, an early morning dog walker came across the body of twenty-nine-year-old Helen Puttock just a few hundred yards from where she lived in Earl Street,

Scotstoun. The night before they died, each of these young women had been at the Barrowland dance hall near Glasgow Cross and similarities were evident between the way they had been killed and the positions in which their bodies were found.

In spite of exhaustive investigations led by Tom Goodall, the enquiries into the first two murders led nowhere but in the case of Helen Puttock detectives had much more to go on, as she had been accompanied by her sister and both women had shared a taxi home with the man suspected of killing her. Jeannie, the sister, was therefore able to give a very precise description of his appearance and remembered many details of their conversation. The press seized on one point in particular: the man, who introduced himself simply as John, was said to have quoted from the Bible. An early headline in the *Evening Times* read 'Bible Man Sought in Murder Hunt'; from there, it was but a small step for one creative journalist to come up with 'Bible John'.

The story of the massive investigation that followed – the 50,000 statements taken, the nights spent by detectives mingling with Barrowland dancers, the checks of dental records for a man with crooked front teeth, the famous artist's impression which appeared all over the city and still haunts the imagination of anyone alive at the time – was first told in depth by Charles Stoddart in his 1980 book *Bible John: Search for a Sadist*. Since then, plenty of other writers have put forward theories, some more credible than others, variously identifying Bible John as a serving police officer, as the Yorkshire Ripper, Peter Sutcliffe and, more recently, as the serial killer Peter Tobin.

Press reports of the early stages of the manhunt were based on statements issued by Chief Superintendent Elphinstone Dalglish, who had hastily been drafted in as CID boss after the sudden death of Tom Goodall barely three weeks before the discovery of Helen Puttock's body. Earlier in the year Beattie had been promoted to the rank of Superintendent in the Marine Division where the murder took place, and Dalglish put him in charge of the investigation. His name became increasingly prominent in the newspapers from mid-November onwards, particularly in connection with the artist's impression, and a photo survives of him holding the painting. 'We think it's a very good painting of the man,' he said, 'and we plan to reproduce it for posters which will be circulating widely.' But the hoped-for breakthrough never came.

In a book published in 2013 called *Dancing with the Devil* author Paul Harrison claimed that both Goodall and Beattie felt that they were hunting for an individual whose profession placed him beyond suspicion. The writer further states that Beattie had started to investigate the possibility of someone within the police service being responsible but was instructed by his superiors not to pursue this line of enquiry.

One retired senior officer confirms that he was called in for an interview of this kind by Beattie; as if that wasn't enough, his mother-in-law then told his wife that she thought he resembled the picture of Bible John in all the posters!

The enquiry gradually wound down but was never officially closed, and in the 1990s the case hit the headlines once again. In 1994, the forensic lab of Strathclyde police circulated a memo to all divisions holding material (known as 'productions') relating to unsolved murders, requesting them to submit these for examination in the light of new DNA techniques. The productions from the Helen Puttock murder case had been stored in the old Partick Marine Division office and a semen stain on her tights enabled a DNA profile to be obtained. This led in due course to the exhumation of an earlier suspect called John Irvine McInnes, who had committed suicide in 1980. In addition, an expert in forensic odontology carried out a comparison between the remains of McInnes' teeth and photographs of a bite mark on the dead woman's wrist.

But the optimism that the case would be cleared up once and for all proved unfounded. The official report from the Department of Biological Anthropology at the University of Cambridge, which had special expertise in extracting DNA material from corpses, concluded that 'there is not sufficient evidence from the current DNA information to link John McInnes to the scene of the murder of Helen Puttock' while Professor Donald MacDonald, Professor of Oral Pathology at the University of Glasgow, stated that 'it is not possible to make a valid judgement about the probability that the mark on Helen Puttock's wrist was a bite made by John MacInnes.'

The exhumation of McInnes was part of a wider review of the case which Strathclyde police set up in September 1995 and this found various anomalies in the original investigation. Documentation relating to a total of 5,031 actions taken at the time remained in the files, but no paperwork existed for action no. 14, an enquiry carried out in Lanarkshire on 2 November 1969 presumed to involve McInnes; there were conflicting opinions expressed by surviving officers as to who appeared in an identity parade around that time; the statement of a woman who regularly attended the Barrowland ballroom and claimed to know the identity of the killer was missing; the bite mark on Helen's arm had not been intimated to members of the original enquiry team. In addition, while much emphasis had been placed on the description of the possible killer by Helen's sister, who shared the cab journey with him, others who saw the man, such as the taxi driver and Barrowland stewards, do not seem to have been asked to view suspects in an identification parade or by photographs.

Hindsight, of course, is a great thing. Policing methods have evolved over the previous thirty-five years and the reasons why certain lines of enquiry were prioritised over others at the time can now only be a matter of guesswork.

Just to add yet another dimension to the many mysteries surrounding Bible John, completely different opinions have been attributed to Joe Beattie himself. In January 1996, the *Glasgow Herald* quoted him as saying, 'No one ever really thought there was one man who killed three times. The cases were never really linked.' By contrast, Harrison includes the following quotation from Beattie in his book: 'Do I think it was one person who committed this series of crimes? Looking back, yes, I honestly do.'

★ ★ ★

Dealing with death on a daily basis can take its toll on those who have to carry out such a duty. Joe Beattie's way of switching off from the strain of the job was to come home after a long shift and throw himself into his DIY projects. One of his favourite sayings was, 'The polis was such a destructive job that when I came home I wanted to do something creative.' For much of his life he lived in a bungalow in Bearsden and continually made alterations to the property with his own hands, building an extension and devising his own form of central heating and double glazing in an era when his neighbours would have been huddled up in front of a coal fire with ice forming on the inside of the windows. When Tom Goodall moved into a house nearby, he experienced some difficulties with the heating system. He didn't send for a plumber – he called up Joe Beattie.

In 1973, the Superintendent took on a new role as Deputy Commandant of the Scottish Police Training College in Perthshire. After three years in that post, technically a secondment from the Glasgow (and subsequently Strathclyde) force, he retired in October 1976 and carried out security work with the Caledonian Crane Hire Company for a time.

In retirement Joe fought a long battle against ill health but never lost his sense of humour or interest in people. On one of the last occasions I visited him, workmen were resurfacing the road outside his house. 'See that guy standing there?' he said. 'He's been in Barlinnie. Look how slowly he's rolling that cigarette. They learn to do that inside because they've got so much time on their hands.'

And with that, he went back indoors after his customary send-off: 'The blessing of Joseph go with you.'

# 15

## *Young John and the Toeprint Man*

### *Forensic Pioneers*

Nowadays, the chances of solving a crime without a forensic team are about as likely as meeting a teenager without a smartphone.

In the early post-war years, however, not everyone in the police was convinced of the importance of the forensic approach. Period photos invariably show the locus of a murder being searched by detectives in their usual garb of raincoat and hat with scant attention being paid to possible contamination of the crime scene.

In the mid-fifties, only about 1% of investigations undertaken by Glasgow CID required the services of the Scientific Bureau. Some older officers even drew a distinction between 'the scientific method' and 'common sense' policing. 'Detectives, especially the younger ones', opined an anonymous contributor to *The Police Journal* during the 1940s, 'are apt to spend too much time in considering details which they think may be of use to a scientific expert, instead of realising that the crime can be elucidated by means of their own common sense and that ample ordinary evidence is available.'

But two Glasgow men, one from the University and the other from the CID, played a key role in changing that way of thinking: John Glaister and George Maclean.

For over thirty years, Glaister (1892–1971) was Professor of Forensic Medicine at the University of Glasgow, a post he took over from his father, also called John – hence the epithet 'young John'. He had started giving lectures to Glasgow police soon after graduating in the 1920s and then went abroad for a three-year stint at the University of Cairo. While in Egypt he solved a murder case through the examination of a sun helmet known as a topee, worn in tropical countries. On it he discovered a hair that did not belong to the dead man and when police supplied him with specimens of hair from twelve different suspects, the killer was identified. Glaister's *Medical Jurisprudence and Toxicology* was for long the standard textbook on the subject. Graphically illustrated with photos of the mutilated bodies of victims of murders, suicides, fires and accidents, it is hardly bedside reading.

Also involved in working with Glasgow police alongside the professor were two of his colleagues, Dr Andrew Allison who retired in 1953 and Police Surgeon Dr James Imrie. Virtually every murder investigation in post-war Glasgow involved at least one of these men.

As with so many other innovations in policing, it was Sir Percy Sillitoe who saw the need for developing forensic resources inside the Glasgow force. When he moved from Sheffield to take over as Chief Constable, he brought Sergeant Bertie Hammond to run a fingerprint and photographic branch, later known as the Identification Bureau.

Medical expertise plus forensic technology plus skilful detective work: it was a winning formula that could achieve spectacular results, most famously demonstrated in 1935 when the teamwork of Glaister, Hammond and Detective Lieutenant William Ewing secured the conviction of Dr Buck Ruxton for the murder of his wife and maid.

Glaister's ground-breaking efforts enabled Mrs Ruxton's remains to be identified by X-raying her skull at the same angle as an existing portrait photograph and superimposing one over the other. Hammond, for his part, pioneered new fingerprinting techniques. The fingertips from one dismembered body had been cut off to make identification more difficult while another hand, discovered later, was in an advanced state of decomposition. But Hammond had a theory that even if the outer skin (epidermis) was not present, the layer underneath would show the same fingerprint characteristics. 'To prove it,' said Glaister, 'he deliberately burned his own fingertip with a cigarette, and, after the skin blistered, cut off the surface layer, then fingerprinted the dermal skin underneath. The result matched his original prints.' Ewing's role in the enquiry combined patient police work – such as methodically checking lists of missing persons and vehicles seen in the area where the body parts were found – with flashes of insight: he was the one credited with the suggestion that the various body parts might have come from two females, rather than a man and a woman as originally thought.

It was a classic example of the old saying about genius being 1% inspiration and 99% perspiration.

When Bertie Hammond retired in 1942 with the rank of Superintendent, the running of the Identification Bureau was taken over by George Maclean who had joined the police force in 1923. His interest in nature led him to study botany and bacteriology at Glasgow's Royal Technical College, which later became the University of Strathclyde. He played a key role in many murder investigations, such as the 1942 Gertrude Canning case, which involved an attempt to fire test bullets from thousands of revolvers at a military base, and the 1950 Pollokshields Station murders when he established that the gun belonging to Charles Templeman Brown had fired the fatal bullets. His efforts were rewarded by promotion to Superintendent in 1951 and Chief Superintendent in 1956 and when he retired in January 1967 he had reached the rank of Deputy Chief Constable.

Maclean's big break came in 1952 when his help in securing the conviction of a thief from a toe print left at the scene of the crime gained him the nickname that stuck for the rest of his career: the Toeprint Man.

Early one morning in June, a baker arrived at the Bellshill and Mossend Co-operative Society's bakery in Lanarkshire to find that there had been a break in. He called the local police who immediately noticed a strong smell of explosives and found a safe lying on the floor. Clearly the attempt to blow it open had failed; the door had jammed, the safe was lying on its side as the thief had made another effort to

219

force open the door. The intruder had moved about the premises in his bare feet and as there was a faint covering of flour on many surfaces, he left a clear print of his big toe.

About a month later, a man with a record of safe-blowing was caught in a railway goods yard acting suspiciously and he was questioned about the robbery at the bakery. Copies of his toe prints were sent by Lanarkshire police to the Glasgow Identification Bureau who found a clear match and he was charged with the crime. At the trial in November, the accused's counsel grilled Maclean for nearly two hours, arguing that there were insufficient precedents for identifying people in this way. But Maclean countered with examples from a hospital in Chicago where toe prints had been used to identify babies since 1915. He added that 'the make-up of the skin on fingers and toes is substantially the same, containing similar arches, loops and whorls.' The chances of two people having the same toe print were estimated to be 10,000 billion to one. The man was found guilty and sentenced to three years in prison, a conviction secured entirely because of the toe print – there was no other supporting evidence.

In his summing up, the judge, Lord Birnam, said: 'I think this is the first time that a toe print has been brought before the Court. Perhaps you and I are making history.'

They were indeed. Suddenly the quiet, studious detective, who liked to study plants and served as a lay preacher in his spare time, became famous. 'That print is going right round the world,' he said. Police chiefs in San Diego requested a copy of the photos and enquiries flooded in from places like Ceylon, South Africa and Rhodesia – countries where it was more common to go barefoot and where police had shown more interest in this form of identification than their European counterparts. Someone even wrote a poem about it, which began:

> Eeny, meeny, miny, mo,
> Catch a burglar by his toe

and ended:

Fingers, toes and noses blue,
Elbows, knees and earholes too,
What's an honest crook to do?

The discovery of toe prints wasn't the only pioneering work going on in the Identification Bureau. A separate department called the Scientific Branch was set up in 1945, specialising in areas such as ballistics, chemistry, handwriting, hairs and fibres. The police experts worked closely with the University of Glasgow's Forensic Medicine department and gave talks to students there, and in 1946 Professor Glaister transferred to the police laboratories his collection of specimens of animal hairs, all mounted and catalogued.

The man in charge of the Scientific Branch was James McLellan who, unusually for a policeman in that era, had a degree in Chemistry. Like all his colleagues, he started off pounding the beat, in his case in the Eastern Division, ending up as an Assistant Chief Constable in the newly formed Strathclyde Police force in 1975.

McLellan frequently published technical articles on advances being made in scientific methods of detection. One technique he worked on in the mid-fifties involved the use of ultra-violet light to catch thieves, ideal for use in shops or offices where an employee was suspected of stealing regularly. A trap would be set by sprinkling a fluorescent powder called anthracene which, though invisible without a UV lamp, was insoluble and could remain on hands or clothing for a long time, unaffected by washing. In one case, money was being taken almost every weekend from a safe in an office with a staff of three: manager, male clerk and typist. Detectives placed powder in strategic positions in order to catch the culprit; traces of it were found only on the manager's hands, because he was the one responsible for locking and unlocking the safe. McLellan takes up the story:

Neither of the two remaining staff members had the slightest vestige of powder on them and matters might have rested there but for a chance remark of the typist [who was leaving to get married]. She said that she would not be sorry to leave the office as the atmosphere was unpleasant and so changed from the time when they used to share the premises with a firm now in the adjoining office. A visit to this office and a slight bit of persuasion led to their staff being examined and a male clerk detected. In his possession were four keys – safe, strongroom, manager's office and outside door. His office closed at 1.00 p.m. on Saturday and his victim's at 12.30 p.m. and during this half hour he was committing the thefts.

The UV method had paid off – but the ever inventive McLellan was already thinking of more efficient methods. He speculated that if it were possible to obtain a 'safe radioactive powder' then it could be detected on the suspect through the use of a 'contamination meter' without the need for darkness or special lights. And he had a still more radical idea for the future: 'Sooner or later someone will use a television camera for the job.'

But even McLellan couldn't foresee that a time would come when city streets would be under CCTV surveillance . . .

In another intriguing mystery cleared up by the Scientific Branch, the solution was found, literally, hanging by a thread. On 1 January 1953, just minutes after the bells had ushered in the New Year, a taxi driver left his Austin seven-seater outside a tenement close near Bridgeton Cross and went up to collect his passengers. When he came down a few moments later the car had disappeared. Soon afterwards, eyewitnesses saw it being driven at speed in the direction of King's Bridge over the Clyde but before crossing it failed to negotiate a bend and struck two lamp standards, colliding head-on with a third. Police arrived to find an unconscious man, Stewart Mulligan, lying about a yard from the driver's door and another, Gordon Agolini, spread across the front passenger seat with his foot jammed between the clutch pedal and floorboard. Each had a bottle of liquor in his pocket, which had smashed in the course of the accident. Mulligan died without regaining consciousness. Agolini said he did not know him and could remember nothing about the incident.

This raised all kinds of questions. Had Mulligan been thrown out of the car on impact or had he been a pedestrian in the wrong place at the wrong time? Had Agolini been the driver or was he a passenger in the front seat whose foot became jammed under the pedal because he was thrown sideways during the collision?

Investigations began to fill in the two men's backgrounds. Agolini worked in a pub which he left at 11.30 p.m., having had several drinks in the course of the evening. The post-mortem on Mulligan showed he had not consumed any alcohol and relatives confirmed he had no driving licence.

Minute examination of a variety of marks and tears on the dead man's clothing revealed several useful clues which suggested that Mulligan had not been run over by the vehicle. In the rear compartment, McLellan found a blue-coloured fibre identical to the material of Mulligan's suit; his sleeve had a tear and blue paint mark on it matching the paint on an inside pillar where there was a door lock catch that could have accounted for the rip. His injuries strongly suggested that he had been thrown from the rear of the taxi. One of the investigating officers, Inspector Colin MacCallum of the Traffic Department, concluded that 'he was probably in the act of leaving the vehicle when it struck the pole and the fact that it swung in a clockwise direction threw him from it.'

The steering wheel and gear lever of the car were both buckled and impact with these was the most likely cause of the injuries to Agolini's upper body, confirming that he was the driver. On the basis of this evidence, Agolini was convicted of stealing a car and of dangerous driving, though the initial charge of culpable homicide was dropped. He was sentenced to eighteen months' imprisonment.

But there remained one aspect of the mystery that neither the Traffic Department nor the Scientific Branch could clear up. How did two apparent strangers end up in a stolen taxi?

In addition to Maclean and McLellan there was a third 'Mac' who rose to prominence within the Identification Bureau: Superintendent Charles McNeill, who took over from Maclean in 1960. Tragically, his tenure was only brief: in June 1962 he was travelling back from a police conference in Dumfries along with Tom Goodall and two officers from Lanarkshire when their car was involved in a road accident. His three colleagues were injured but McNeill lost his life. Bob Kerr, CID boss at the time, broke down and wept when he heard the news.

★ ★ ★

'Was it murder or was it suicide?'

It sounds like the start of a typical crime novel, but that was exactly the question faced by Constable Angus McAllister when he was on night duty in Duke Street in March 1968. A man ran up in a greatly distressed state and told him, 'It's my wife; she's thrown herself out of the window.' In nearby Craigmore Street a naked woman with serious head injuries lay on the pavement and the man, whose name was John Swan, pointed up to an open window in the top flat directly above her body. He told the constable that they had had an argument in the kitchen because he had been drinking, after which she then locked herself into the room and threw herself out the window. When asked why she was naked, Swan replied, 'She always goes to bed like that.'

Detective Chief Inspector Robert Brown of the Eastern Division took charge and the Identification Bureau carried out a meticulous examination inside the flat, where they discovered a series of clues, which led them to doubt Swan's version of events.

The woman's clothing was scattered over the floor. On the mattress lay broken glass from a shattered electric light bulb above the bed recess. There was a noticeable mark on the plaster of the wall above the bed and plaster dust had fallen onto the bedclothes, indicating that the damage was recent. On a chair outside the room lay a meat cleaver, one edge of which corresponded to the indentations on the wall. There was some water on the floor of the room and a mop lying in the hallway. Significantly, the door had no lock and nothing in the sparsely furnished room could be pushed against it to prevent it being opened.

From their observations of the scene, detectives reached the conclusion that a row must have taken place between Swan and the victim, twenty-four-year-old Ellen McGregor, to whom he was not actually married. It seemed likely that in the course of their argument Swan assaulted her, caused her to lose consciousness and then tried to revive her by throwing water on her. Given that the bed was covered with broken glass and plaster, it was unlikely that McGregor would have been lying in it naked. Detective Chief Inspector Brown therefore surmised that Swan had stripped her and pushed her out the window. On the basis of this, he was charged with murder.

Further discrepancies emerged when the body was examined. The post-mortem showed that death resulted from a fractured skull caused by the fall but there were also facial bruises, which the pathologists attributed to the victim having been punched at least three times. Drawing on their years of experience, the medical experts knew that anyone committing suicide would have jumped out of the window rather than passing through it backwards head first and facing up. Here, the investigation was assisted by the fact that after years of pollution caused by coal fires, many sandstone tenement buildings in Glasgow were covered in grime. An intended suicide would have first sat on the windowsill; in that case, marks from the soot would have been found on Ellen McGregor's buttocks. However, the nature of her injuries suggested that she had not come out of the window feet first and samples of debris taken from her back corresponded with material from the window sill, further confirming that she had been pushed out of the window while unconscious.

Detectives decided to test their theory using a novel method. Very early the next morning, a Sunday, they arrived at the flat with a dummy of roughly the same size and weight as the dead woman. They proceeded to push this out of the window five times in different ways. Each time it was pushed head first on its back, the dummy landed in exactly the same way as the body had been found.

There isn't generally much scope for humour in murder investigations, other than for those of a macabre turn of mind. But there was some light relief during the trial of Swan in the High Court in June when Nicholas Fairbairn for the defence quizzed Chief Inspector Brown about this episode:

> FAIRBAIRN: 'The dummy bore very little relation to the physical characteristics of a human body?'
> BROWN: 'It was the best we could do, I'm afraid.'
> FAIRBAIRN: 'I am not suggesting you should have thrown a real body out of the window.'
> BROWN: 'Well, we couldn't get any volunteers.'

Fairbairn failed to convince the jury that Ellen McGregor had committed suicide and Swan was found guilty of culpable homicide and sent to the State Institution at Carstairs 'without limit of time'. He died in 2004 at the age of sixty-six.

Advances like DNA profiling might have been a long way off in the fifties and sixties but by using technology, whether in the form of toe prints and ultra-violet lamps, or by minutely examining fibres and pushing dummies out of windows, the Scientific Branch of Glasgow police demonstrated on countless occasions that painstaking scrutiny of a crime scene could lead to a conviction.

In his lectures to students, Professor Glaister was fond of quoting some words of the nineteenth-century American writer Ralph Waldo Emerson: 'There is no den in the whole world to hide a rogue. Commit a crime and the earth is made of glass.'

The eminent professor and his colleagues in the police certainly played their part in making that statement come true.

# 16

## *End of an Era*

### *Strathclyde and Beyond*

In May 1945, crowds lined George Square as servicemen and women marched past the City Chambers and Cenotaph in a ceremony marking Victory in Europe.

Thirty years later, almost to the day, another march past was held in the same place. This time the personnel involved were from the city's police force. It was described as a 'stand down' parade for, at midnight on 15 May 1975, the City of Glasgow police force ceased to exist.

That didn't mean crime in the city had been completely eliminated. It meant that, as a result of a massive reorganisation of local government, Glasgow became part of Strathclyde Region, an area covering the whole of southwest Scotland, taking in both the industrial central belt and remote islands. Henceforth, Glasgow police became No. 1 Area of Strathclyde police, which, with nearly 7,000 officers, was the second largest force in the UK.

Long-serving officers at the 1975 parade who remembered being on duty at the VE Day party in George Square thirty years earlier could hardly fail to reflect on how things had changed.

They had policed the city through the years of post-war austerity, the 'never had it so good' era of the fifties and the 'permissive society' of the sixties. They had seen the crumbling tenements of the old slum areas swept away and the population dispersed to vast new housing estates on the outskirts of the city. They had seen a host of social changes and they had their own theories about how these affected criminal behaviour – fathers opting out of their responsibilities in the home, mothers going out to work and spending less time with the children, a decline in religious and moral standards, the loss of a sense of community and the rise of television which, some said, contributed to social breakdown as it led to a drop in attendance at churches, cinemas, clubs, dances and other social gatherings. They had seen a new generation of teenagers grow up who got their own way at home and seemed to think they could do what they liked outside. They had seen an increase in the level of violence on the streets. Fights used to be settled with fists – the 'square go' as it was called; now the young thugs were carrying knives on the basis that 'to defend yourself against a knife, you needed a knife'.

And, most of all, they had seen their job become more and more difficult. One officer spoke for many when he said:

> In the old days the sight of a policeman meant something. The youths who hung about street corners had some respect for the cop . . . because they knew they might get a boot on the backside if they were cheeky to him. Now teenagers laugh at the cops and threaten to exercise their rights as citizens if the cop dares to suggest such a remedy.

Comedian Billy Connolly expressed the same point in his own inimitable way. Growing up in the Partick and Anderston areas in the fifties, he had already detected signs of the changing attitude of the police towards youngsters on the streets: it was, he said, 'the end of the kick-in-the-arse era, just before "If I catch you, I'm going to tell yer faither".'

During the sixties, the organisation of the police force had also changed beyond recognition.

The old-fashioned police stations dating from the nineteenth or early twentieth century were gradually being replaced. The Northern Division headquarters in Maitland Street were so cramped that it was not uncommon for interviews of suspects to take place in the toilets. In 1968, Glasgow Corporation set aside £1.5 million for the purpose of modernising police offices.

The ban on married women serving as police officers was lifted, and the requirement for five years' service before promotion from constable to sergeant was also scrapped. More controversial was the introduction of an accelerated promotion scheme to attract university graduates into policing. The Scottish Police Federation said that the priority ought to be putting more officers on the beat to combat violence. With that in mind, the recruitment of civilian back-up staff was favoured, the aim being to take over more of the paperwork in order to free up officers for front line policing.

A new system called 'unit beat policing' was developed in an attempt to find ways of monitoring the big housing estates where the old-fashioned beat system had proved impossible to operate through lack of manpower. Joe Jackson, who later belonged to the Serious Crime Squad, remembered being on the beat in Easterhouse in the early sixties when he and two colleagues were expected to patrol an area with a population of 50,000. In due course, Panda cars were provided and these could be summoned by radio to assist the few available foot patrols.

It was all a long way from how things were done in the years after the Second World War, when beat cops patrolled the streets with only a whistle to call for help if needed.

Nevertheless, the number one resource remained the men and women on the beat and, in 1975 as in 1945, pay and conditions still lagged behind other occupations. At one point in the mid-sixties policemen were leaving in droves for jobs in Canada where the starting salary in Toronto police was £1,874 compared to £700 in Scotland. It was not until the late 1970s that remuneration improved significantly.

At the time of the inauguration of the new Strathclyde force, Glasgow still required 600 more officers to bring it up to strength, and even some of the official literature about the launch of the new Region didn't exactly sound enthusiastic about the challenges that lay ahead:

No one pretends that the change will be easy. Different forces and brigades have proud and separate traditions. Demarcation disputes are bound to occur . . . But, fortunately, the men at the top seem aware of the administrative hazards.

The man at the very top was David McNee, a tough Glasgow detective who, since 1971, had been Chief Constable of Dunbartonshire. McNee saw his number one priority as being to keep up morale and he and his assistants took time to travel across their vast domain to meet with the different local constabularies. Inevitably, rivalries and resentments carried over into the new force; there were accusations of favouritism when it came to promotions, and it was common to hear expressions such as 'the Lanarkshire Mafia', 'the Ayrshire Mafia' or 'the Glasgow Mafia', depending on where your loyalties lay.

Within Glasgow, there was a certain amount of continuity with those who filled senior positions in the Strathclyde force. After Tom Goodall's sudden death, his second in command Elphinstone ('Elphie') Dalglish replaced him as CID Chief for a few months before his own appointment to an additional Chief Constable post in early 1970 with special responsibility for major crime. Meanwhile, Detective Superintendent James Binnie was appointed head of the CID in February 1970, becoming an Assistant Chief Constable in Glasgow in 1973 and Strathclyde in 1975. In charge of the CID from April 1973 onwards was Detective Chief Superintendent Hugh McKenzie, the last to hold that post as part of the City of Glasgow Police.

The old system of steadily working your way up within the same force from constable to Deputy CID Chief and eventually CID Chief – the career path of previous post-war CID bosses in Glasgow – was gone.

If the structure of policing was changing, so was the nature of crime. The activities of figures like Walter Norval and Arthur Thompson signalled a move away from street fighting for its own sake into more organised crime. A new problem – drugs – would soon be added to all the old ones. Other powerful figures like Tam McGraw would come onto the scene. Then there were the so-called Ice Cream Wars of the 1980s, a territorial battle between criminals selling drugs from ice cream vans that led to an arson attack resulting in the deaths of six people.

Yet more positive developments also lay ahead, like the work of the Violence Reduction Unit of 2005 and related measures involving social work and public health agencies in an attempt to break the cycle of violence in communities. In the twenty-first century crime would drop significantly, notably the murder rate, and by 2016 there were claims that Glasgow had shed its image as the most violent city in Britain.

And the trend towards centralisation of policing that saw Glasgow incorporated into Strathclyde would reach its logical conclusion in April 2013 with the formation of Police Scotland, a single force covering the whole country.

Tracing all these trends in detail would be a story for another time. But it's safe to say that, whatever form crime and policing may take in the city in the future, there will always be a need for detectives of the calibre of Ewing, McIlwrick, Colquhoun, Kerr, Goodall, Brown, Beattie, McNee and many others like them.

For the words of the late journalist John Quinn – the man who coined the term 'Bible John' – remain as true today as they were when he wrote them more than fifty years ago: a quiet Saturday night in Glasgow is as rare as an Irish stew on a Mexican menu.

## _Glasgow Police Museum_

The Glasgow Police Museum offers a unique opportunity for visitors to step into the compelling and dramatic history of the United Kingdom's oldest police force.

Painstaking research has uncovered interesting, little-known facts concerning the lives, careers and personalities of the characters who policed the city during 200 years of its history.

Also on display is Europe's largest collection of police uniforms, headgear, badges and insignia from police forces all over the world, comprising over 5,000 colourful items.

Opening hours:
1 April – 31 October:
Monday – Saturday 10.00 – 16.30;
Sunday 12.00 – 16.30

1 November – 31 March:
Tuesday 10.00 – 16.30;
Sunday 12.00 – 16.30

Group visits welcome throughout the year.

Glasgow Police Museum
First Floor
30 Bell Street
Merchant City
Glasgow
G1 1LG
Scotland

Website: www.policemuseum.org.uk
E-mail: curator@policemuseum.org.uk
Telephone: 0141 552 1818

# Sources and Further Reading

**Books:**

Beltrami, Joseph, *The Defender* (W & R Chambers, Edinburgh, 1980)

Bingham, John, *The Hunting Down of Peter Manuel* (Macmillan, London, 1973)

Bloom, Clive, *Bestsellers: Popular Fiction since 1900* (Palgrave Macmillan, London, 2002)

Blundell, R.H. and Wilson, G. H., *The Trial of Buck Ruxton* (William Hodge & Company, London, 1937)

Boyle, Jimmy, *A Sense of Freedom* (Pan Books, London, 1977)

Brown, Les, and Jeffrey, Robert, *Glasgow Crimefighter: The Les Brown Story* (Black & White, Edinburgh, 2005)

Collier, Paul and Taylor, Donald S, *Stairway 13: The Story of the 1971 Ibrox Disaster* (Bluecoat Press, Liverpool, 2007)

Colquhoun, Robert V., *Life Begins at Midnight* (John Long, London, 1962)

Dowdall, Laurence and Marshall, Alasdair, *Get Me Dowdall!* (Paul Harris Publishers, Edinburgh, 1979)

Fraser, Donald M., *The Book of Glasgow Murders* (Neil Wilson Publishing, Glasgow, 2009)

Glaister, John, *Final Diagnosis* (Hutchison, London, 1964)

235

Grant, Douglas, *The Thin Blue Line: The Story of the City of Glasgow Police* (John Long, London, 1973)

Harrison, Paul, *Dancing with the Devil: The Bible John Murders* (Vertical Editions, 2013)

Jackson, Joe, *Chasing Killers* (Mainstream, Edinburgh, 2008)

Jeffrey, Robert, *Blood on the Streets: A – Z of Glasgow Crime* (Black & White, Edinburgh, 2004)

Jeffrey, Robert, *Gentle Johnny Ramensky* (Black & White, Edinburgh, 2010)

Jeffrey, Robert, *Glasgow's Godfather: The Astonishing Inside Story of Walter Norval* (Black & White, Edinburgh, 2003)

Jeffrey, Robert, *Glasgow's Hard Men* (Black & White, Edinburgh, 2002)

Kenna, Rudolph and Sutherland, Ian, *In Custody: A Companion to Strathclyde Police Museum* (Clutha Books, Glasgow, 1998)

Kerr, William, *Into the Unknown* (Vantage, New York, 1984)

Knox, Bill, *Court of Murder: Famous Trials at Glasgow High Court* (John Long, London, 1968)

MacLeod, Hector and McLeod, Malcolm, *Peter Manuel, Serial Killer* (Mainstream, Edinburgh, 2009)

McNee, Sir David, *McNee's Law* (Collins, London, 1983)

Mina, Denise, *The Long Drop* (Harvill Secker, London, 2017)

Murray, Len, *The Pleader: An Autobiography* (Mainstream Publishing, Edinburgh and London, 2002)

Nicol, A.M., *Manuel: Scotland's First Serial Killer* (Black & White, Edinburgh, 2008)

Patrick, James, *A Glasgow Gang Observed* (Third Edition, Neil Wilson Publishing, Glasgow, 2013)

Pieri, Joe, *The Big Men: Personal Memories of Glasgow Police* (Neil Wilson Publishing, Glasgow, 2001)

Sillitoe, Sir Percy, *Cloak Without Dagger* (Pan Books, London, 1955)

Skelton, Douglas, *Bloody Valentine: Scotland's Crimes of Passion* (Black & White, Edinburgh, 2004)

Skelton, Douglas, *Glasgow's Black Heart: A City's Life of Crime* (Mainstream Publishing, Edinburgh and London, 2009)

Smith, J. Irvine, *Law, Life and Laughter: A Personal Verdict* (Black & White, Edinburgh, 2011)

Smith, Paul, *Heist: The Inside Story of Scotland's Most Notorious Raids* (Birlinn, Edinburgh, 2014)

Stoddart, Charles, *Bible John: Search for a Sadist* (Paul Harris Publishing, Edinburgh, 1980)

**Criminal Case Files (all Crown copyright, held in the National Records of Scotland, Edinburgh):**
John Caldwell (HH16/642/1)
James Ronald Robertson (HH16/642/17 and HH16/643)
John Reid (HH16/409)
Robert Murray Menzies (HH16/448)

**Newspapers and journals:**
*Glasgow Herald*
*Daily Record*
*Evening Times*
*Evening Citizen*
*The Bulletin*
*Scottish Daily Express*
*Sunday Post*
*The Police Journal*
*The Wire* [Strathclyde police magazine]